Technology Meets Fl

CW00664537

Eric van Heck

Technology Meets Flowers

Unlocking the Circular and Digital Economy

 Springer

Eric van Heck
Erasmus University Rotterdam
Rotterdam, The Netherlands

ISBN 978-3-030-69302-2   ISBN 978-3-030-69303-9   (eBook)
https://doi.org/10.1007/978-3-030-69303-9

This Springer imprint is published by the registered company Springer Nature Switzerland AG.
The registered company address is: Gewerbestrasse 11, 6330 Cham, Switzerland

For Lia, Julia, Simon, and Maartje

Preface

As we buy flowers for our family and friends, we take for granted how flowers are produced and where they come from. Indeed, we expect that flowers can be ordered online anytime and anywhere. We assume that flowers will be delivered as fresh as possible even when produced on the other side of the world. The complex production and distribution challenges of perishable products are taken for granted. Actually, few people are fully aware that high-speed flower production and trade has taken the lead in blending technology with business.

This book tells the story of *Technology Meets Flowers*. It is a great story, almost a love story, which goes back to the Netherlands and the year 1593. It reveals the birth of the bulb and flower industry in that year, when a professor of botany was appointed at Leiden University. Developments in Dutch society around that time encouraged the needed entrepreneurial spirit and initiatives for flower production and trade, and there was enough money in the hands of citizens to support flower consumption. In the seventeenth century, flowers, especially tulips, became fashionable, next to paintings by Frans Hals, Rembrandt van Rijn, and other Dutch masters. Indeed, the story of Tulip Mania in the year 1637 is retold, and it is a very different story than what you may have heard before.

However, this book not only looks back at the origin of the flower industry. It also explores several inventions in later years, such as the first small glasshouses in 1680 and larger glasshouses around 1744, the Dutch auction concept in 1887, the electric auctioneer in 1903, and the flower grower cooperative in 1911. The blending of these technological, organizational, and market concepts accelerated flower production and trade. The European market for flowers was established in 1968 and led to the production of flowers for consumers in other European countries. In 1975, standardized trolleys were introduced to speed up logistics and reduce transportation costs. The invention of the World Wide Web in 1989 created the architecture that would enable a new wave of electronic commerce and business. Electronic flower auctions were established in 1995 and showed the advantages of online pricing and trading. Web-based technologies connected flower supply with global flower demand, leading to a global market expansion. Mobile telephones and Internet connectivity fueled a mobile economy with more than five billion potential flower customers, some of whom will spend hours per day on their smart phones. Social media platforms, now with four billion active users, enable the exchange of digital images and videos and stimulate more demand and exchange. Nowadays, flowers are promoted by influencers and are popular social media content.

This is not a traditional management book for executives that describes the latest and state-of-the-art technologies and business models with examples of many different industries. Here we follow the story of one industry, the flower business and its markets, since its birth in 1593. The ups and downs and the struggles and triumphs that connected technology to business are presented and discussed. What is important here is that technology and innovation redefine the information frontier, and the frontier of achievement is extended further. Information derived from the information frontier is as perishable and time sensitive as flowers are. *Information advantage*, the value of having superior information, is a key driver for speeding up business processes in the flower business and its markets. Superior information, i.e., information that is new, fresh, and reliable, provides companies with an opportunity to win the competition in the business world. Emerging technologies provide companies with superior information, and companies can reap the benefits if they are able to blend technology with business concepts to fulfill latent customer demand.

Nowadays, modern glasshouses play a central role in the data-driven transformation of flower production. The exponential increase of computer technology, genetics, nanotechnology, robotics, and artificial intelligence contribute to a controlled production environment. Actually, you can view the flower industry as a living laboratory where these technologies are tested out. Automated and robotized glasshouses speed up production of flowers and offset carbon emissions, a welcome side effect in a world that is struggling with carbon emissions and their impact on the global climate. High-speed flower logistics with advanced distribution concepts that include last-mile distribution solutions and new ways of organizing transport and logistics to the end customer are critical because the freshness of short-lived flowers is fleeting.

Other businesses and markets can learn a lot from the production, commercial, logistical, and financial challenges of the flower business and the solutions that have been created within it. Entrepreneurs can learn about how to develop high-speed operations along the customer-driven value chain: from consumer need to flower seed. The use of digital technologies in different markets, such as media, health, transport and mobility, and food, has increased customers' expectations of fast service responses and product deliveries from the different actors in these value chains. These actors can learn from the flower business and markets and the double transformations that took place: the circular transformation and the digital transformation. Both transformations are creating a flower business that will stay within the ecological boundaries of the Earth.

Based on a solid analysis of how technologies were intertwined with the flower business and created sustainable value, this book provides lessons learned for leadership and guidance to unlock the circular and digital economy.

This book was written for four types of audience. Firstly, this book is for entrepreneurs working in the flower industry. They are eager to learn the underlying trends that will shape the transformations of the flower business and its markets, the potential value creation of emerging technologies, and the required circular and digital capabilities to reap the benefits of new business and markets. Secondly, this book is for entrepreneurs working in other sectors and industries. Many other sectors and industries are moving into customer-driven high-speed production and delivery operations. A reflection on lessons learned from the circular and digital transformations in the flower industry may help to create sustained success in other industries. Thirdly, this book is for a business school audience, both entrepreneurial executives and master's students. In my teaching at Erasmus University Rotterdam, in courses such as "Leading Transformation in the Digital Economy," "Leadership Challenges with Data Analytics," and "Digital Leadership and Change," the flower business examples and stories were always a source of inspiration and discussion, both for entrepreneurial executives and for master's students. Fourthly, this book is for anyone who may pick it up, enjoy its preface, and will start to read it.

For now, reader, you have enough information to continue reading this book. Join me on this journey and enjoy the reading!

Rotterdam, The Netherlands   Eric van Heck

Acknowledgments

The idea of writing a book came up in the spring of 2019. After 4 years as chairman of the Department of Technology & Operations Management, I was happy to be accepted as visiting scholar at New York University. I am very grateful that my wife, Lia, joined me in this endeavor. Her love, happiness, and valuable feedback, also as the first reader of the draft manuscript, are a continuous source of inspiration. We were very happy that our children, Julia, Simon, and Maartje, were able to visit us while we were staying in the City, and for their eager interest in the progress of *Tulip Time*, as the book project was called among us. Thank you!

Many people helped me with the visiting scholarship and book project. Hereby I would like to thank them all. Just before heading to New York City, Otto Koppius suggested that I join the Master Class *Malcolm Gladwell Teaches Writing*. It turned out to be an excellent suggestion. I was inspired by Malcolm Gladwell's lectures on writing nonfiction for a general audience. Actually, *Technology Meets Flowers* is an extended version of a writing assignment I began working on for his class, i.e., to write a *New Yorker*-style nonfiction article. At NYU, Rohit Deo and Alex Tuzhilin, as the current and former department chair, welcomed me to the Department of Technology, Operations, and Statistics. Vasant Dhar was an excellent host. My neighbors in the department, Anindya Ghose and Mike Pinedo, helped me to feel at home. Elisabeth Greenberg, Germaine Germanese, and Maryann Zwaryczuk were very helpful in handling the complicated US side of the visa process and ably assisted me with other administrative issues.

During our stay in Manhattan, we were very grateful to catch up with Kimberly and Ajit Kambil. Ajit was my NYU host in 1994 and I am proud of what we achieved as we worked together, intensively researching the redesign of the Dutch flower auctions. We were also fortunate to meet with our friends, Helen Shimbo and Jason Ware, for a great afternoon and evening in the City. We were very sad to learn that Helen passed away not long after in September 2019. We miss her dearly.

Many coauthors, coeditors, co-panelists, co-program chairs, senior editors, and (anonymous) associate editors and reviewers of conference papers and journal publications helped me to do the research and tell the story. I had very fine conversations about book writing or feedback on chapters with Eline van den Berg, Mayen Cunden, Magda David Hercheui, Eduardo Diniz, Nico van Hemert, Dré Kampfraath, Benn Konsynski, Martin Mocker, Joost Steins Bisschop, Tamilla Triantoro, Meditya Wasesa, Klaas Wassens, and Chen Zhang. Mary Ann Perkins was extremely helpful in editing the chapters and providing excellent suggestions to improve the storyline.

At Springer, Christian Rauscher, Prashanth Mahagaonkar, and Ruth Milewski were extremely helpful to guide me through the book editing and production process.

Technology Meets Flowers is based on research in the floral industry, in particular the "Auctioning with Advice" project sponsored by Royal FloraHolland and the "Artificial Intelligence in the Floriculture Chain" (iFlow) project sponsored by the Topsector Horticulture & Starting Materials, one of the nine top sectors of the Netherlands. I am very grateful to have led the iFlow project, which was an excellent collaboration with Eline van den Berg and Remco Wilting (Royal FloraHolland), Arjan van der Voort (Zentoo), Behzad Behdani, Jacqueline Bloemhof-Ruwaard †, Nguyen Quoc Viet, and Jack van der Vorst (Wageningen University & Research), Yixin Lu (George Washington University), Alok Gupta (University of Minnesota), and Huong May Truong and Wolf Ketter at RSM. Many conference breakfast sessions and research discussions over the years with Yixin, May, Alok, and Wolf led to very exciting research results and were an important source of inspiration for this book. In 2020, the impact of our work was recognized with the AIS Impact Award.

BIM master's students Stefan Bouts, Ronald Haring, Ricardo Prins, and Rick van Zijl contributed to the iFlow project through their thesis research. Tulsi Rakhan and Marcel van Oosterhout helped me to manage the iFlow budget and Irene Bosman created the iFlow video clip.

I am very grateful to be a member of the Business Information Management (BIM) group—a vibrant community with a world-class research and education portfolio. Research and education in the section inspired me a lot and my BIM colleagues voted for the best book title: Samaneh Bagheri, Rodrigo Belo, Tobias Brandt, Philipp Cornelius, Ayman Esmat, Yashar Ghiassi-Farrokhfal, Dominik Gutt, Els van de Kar, Jovana Karanovic, Wolf Ketter, Otto Koppius,

Yanick Kuper, Ting Li, Marcel van Oosterhout, Anna Priante, Gerrit Schipper, Haydee Sheombar, Aart Simons, Olga Slivko, Jeffrey Sweeney, Dimitrios Tsekouras, Peter Vervest, Markus Weinmann, Matthijs Wolters, Shengyun Yang, Dainis Zegners, and PhD candidates Ayman Abdelwahed, Mohammad Ansarin, Francesco Balocco, Ionannis Kanellopoulos, Agnieszka Kloc, Atabak Mehrdar, Ainara Novales, Joshua Paundra, Tamara Thuis, Huong May Truong, Charles Wan, and Zherui Yang.

At RSM, Theo Backx, Dirk van Dierendonck, Jan Dul, René de Koster, and Steef van de Velde encouraged me to go for a visiting scholarship. Cheryl Blok-Eiting, Carmen Meesters-Mirasol, Tineke van der Vhee, and Ingrid Waaijer helped me with the handling of the complicated NL side of the visa process. Ilse Lüschen and Lianne Speijer helped me with the format of the literature references and the book index.

The Wittenburg members missed my input during my time in New York City but, once back, were eager to discuss the highlights and downsides of NYC and the intriguing potential for a city of a hundred million people: Hans Abbink, Frans Copini, Nico van Hemert, Bernadette Janssen, Ton Laagland, Yung Lie, Iris Meerts, Haydee Sheombar, Floor van Spaendonck, Geerte Udo, and Siebren de Vries.

Field hockey friends were always eager to exchange jokes, pranks, and brilliant ideas: Albert Bos, Judith van Bossum, Eric Gaanderse, Monique Lander, Philip Lebbink, Tom Middendorp, Roy Osinga, Miguel Porfírio, Anne Tennekes, Petra Teunissen-de Wolf, Paul Veldhuijzen, and Gerald Wolf.

For 4 months, my rowing team at Royal Maas Yacht Club had to make do without this data-driven rower and were amazed by my once-in-a-lifetime rowing experience on the Hudson River: Brenda Brenninkmeijer, Chris van Calcar, Guus Enning, Coreille Harms, Nicoline van 't Hoff, Aeltsje Hylkema, Stephanie Leijten, Geert Meijer †, Eric van Niekerk, Thessa Noorman, Ronald Stuijfzand, and Roel van Woerden.

Friends were curious to learn about our adventures in New York City: Monique and Stan van Alphen, Wilma and Paul Gribnau, Lia Hof and Hans Bogerd, Huberdien and Pierre Hornikx, Caroline Lee and Julius van der Werf, Ingrid and Aad Jan Roos, Esther Steultjens, and Titus Nietsch. Patricia and Henk Ebeli took meticulous care of our home in Rotterdam while we were away.

Our family was not surprised that we went back to the City and were keen to hear our stories: Dorine and Jack Franken, Hilde van Heck and Geert Dirkse, Julia and Johan Jörissen, Gerdie Persoons, and Ans and Chris Wilbers.

Finally, I would like to thank my mother for her love and continuous support. My father passed away before this journey began, but he would have encouraged us to go back and stay in the City again.

The endeavor started with an empty page and magically a book was created out of it.

Eric van Heck

"What a captivating book! Eric van Heck juxtaposes two distinct histories: that of the iconic Dutch tulips dating back five centuries, and of digital technologies, considerably younger. The revolution triggered when these two elements collide has profound implications for the digital transformation of industries in general. A must-read for all interested in unraveling the impacts of ICT advances on society."
 —Ritu Agarwal *Distinguished University Professor and Robert H. Smith Dean's Chair of Information Systems, Robert H. Smith School of Business, University of Maryland, College Park, USA*

"The flower industry proves that innovations, leadership, and long-term goals are in its DNA, which has given them a dominant market position. It is the perfect example for everyone working in the corporate world and in governments."
 —Theo Backx *Executive in Residence, Rotterdam School of Management, Erasmus University, Rotterdam, Netherlands*

"*Technology Meets Flowers* is an engaging read about flowers, which play a major role in our social lives. Eric van Heck weaves in the increasing role of technology in the flower business, beginning with the engineering and genetic agricultural innovations that fueled the industry to the current day with digital platforms and auctions that are central to the industry. The stories are most engaging. I couldn't put it down once I started reading it."
 —Vasant Dhar *Professor of Information Systems, Stern School of Business, New York University, New York City, USA*

"Combining the light beauty of flowers with the harsh language of the digital universe is a masterfully executed task in this book, organized as a bouquet of algorithms, data science, and digital platforms. Mandatory reading for all those interested in the

flower business as well as for those who want to know more about the perfume emanating from digital systems."
—Eduardo Diniz *Professor and Head of the Technology and Data Science Department, Escola de Administração de Empresas de São Paulo, Fundação Getulio Vargas, São Paulo, Brazil*

"Eric van Heck is one of the most enterprising academics who has an interest in addressing relevant questions of interest for businesses through academic research. This book provides a fascinating insight into the emerging role of analytics and business decision-making in traditional businesses. His work highlights Royal FloraHolland's innovative business model and its fascinating evolution of the last three decades, from making the auction clock electronic to the latest innovation with the introduction of pre-sales. Eric is one of the most prominent academic leaders in the field who has made this fascinating world visible to people outside the business through his academic writing as well as this book. I know the book will provide managers, students, business leaders, and academics a fascinating story and tremendous insights into innovating business processes."
—Alok Gupta *Senior Associate Dean and Curtis L. Carlson Schoolwide Chair in Information Management, Carlson School of Management, University of Minnesota, Minneapolis, USA*

"This book reveals the great historical journey of Dutch Horticulture. But in the heart there are guidelines for the great digital challenges of our times. Knowing and developing competences together, in meeting points like the World Horti Center, will create the digital horticultural agenda for enterprises, research, and education."
—Nico van Hemert *Managing Partner, Strategy On Demand, Leiden, Netherlands*

"This unique book leads you through the bulb fields and auctions of the Netherlands, through history, logistics, auction design, and Internet technology, to draw lessons in business management from the study of flowers. With beautiful illustrations. A tour de force."
—John Kay *Economist, Author of Radical Uncertainty and Greed is Dead, and Fellow, St. John's College, University of Oxford, Oxford, United Kingdom*

"In his vividly written book, Eric van Heck gently leads the reader into a rich understanding of the value—and pitfalls—of the high-speed world of digital management and 'perishable' data. Rather than explaining the concepts in a dry, management-school text, he explores the application of modern technologies in fast-moving commodities markets through the historical lens of the Netherland's most famous exports—flowers and collective auctions. A must-read for anyone mystified by terms like artificial intelligence and machine learning and anyone who loves a good story!"
—Wolfgang Ketter *Professor of Information Systems, Rotterdam School of Management, Erasmus University, Rotterdam, Netherlands, and University of Cologne, Cologne, Germany*

"If one wishes to understand the history and future of markets, you must go the master, Professor Eric van Heck. His book, *Technology Meets Flowers*, is a Master Class in market evolution and market possibilities in a digital age. I can think of no better market to study than the beautiful global flower market, no better center than the Dutch marketplace, and no better insight than the decades-long research by Professor van Heck. He offers a delightful and imaginative tour through the amazing history and digital transformation of this beautiful, delicate, and globally sourced treasure. The book offers a fascinating history, current innovations, and future possibilities for the global flower market and offers insight for any evolving market. For history, economics, strategy, operations, and competitive leverage of emerging technologies—I highly recommend Professor van Heck's Master Class in a book."

—Benn Konsynski *George S Craft Professor, Goizueta Business School, Emory University, Atlanta, USA*

"This is a marvelous book! While the primary focus is the evolution and transformation of the flower industry along with the technological innovation waves, it offers valuable insights to other information-rich and time-critical industry sectors. Highly recommended for anyone who is thinking about (re)inventing business in today's hyper-competitive digital economy."

—Yixin Lu *School of Business, George Washington University, Washington DC, USA*

"A must for anyone who wants to learn from one of the great business innovation success stories of recent times—the global flower ecosystem. A fascinating compilation of case studies on innovation and the successful introduction of new technologies including information, auctioneering, and biotech."

—Martijn van de Mandele *Senior Partner, Parma Group, Leiden, Netherlands. Senior Advisor, RAND Corporation, Brussels, Belgium. Advisory Board Member, Rotterdam School of Management, Erasmus University, Rotterdam, Netherlands*

"If you want to understand the impact of information and technology on a fascinating industry, this book is a must-read. The author explains in a highly intriguing way how innovations propelled the flower industry from the sixteenth century till today. Whether you are working in the flower industry, a business student, academic, or just intrigued by the business behind flowers, you will enjoy this book!"

—Martin Mocker *Professor of Information Systems, ESB Business School, Reutlingen University, Reutlingen, Germany. Research Affiliate, MIT Sloan Center for Information Systems Research, Cambridge, USA*

"Eric van Heck's book, *Technology Meets Flowers*, is a well-succeeded mix of a scientific treatise and a romantic novel. It provided me with some enlightening insights on the leverage of logistics on information, or the other way round: the leverage of information on the logistics in the flower market. Or how the impressive progress of technology will have an impact on organizational design. However, I'll have to add

one caveat, based on my experience. Whenever I pass by a flower market, I cannot stop thinking of this book."
—Joost Steins Bisschop *Partner, Jungle Minds, Amsterdam, Netherlands*

"Professor Eric van Heck provides great insight on how technology has been impacting floriculture. He puts developments in an historical perspective and describes where the industry is heading: algorithms and data-driven ecosystems will bloom. A very enjoyable 'must-read' on how the flower industry could be exemplary of where other industries are going."
—Pascal Visée *Non-executive Board Member of Royal FloraHolland, Aalsmeer, Netherlands. Non-executive Board Member of Rabobank Group, Utrecht, Netherlands*

"A must-read, if you want to understand the key success factors of the Dutch flower industry in its four centuries development toward the current data-driven, circular, collaborative, and orchestrated network. It clearly explains the power of new technologies and data science in all stages and aspects of the global network."
—Jack van der Vorst *Board Member of Wageningen University & Research and Professor in AgriFood Supply Chain Management, Wageningen, Netherlands*

Contents

About the Author

Eric van Heck is Professor of Information Management and Markets at Erasmus University Rotterdam. He is the coauthor of *Making Markets*, among other books and articles, and the recipient of the ERIM Book Award, the ERIM Impact Award, the Outstanding Paper Literati Network Award, and the AIS Best Conference Paper in IS Education Award. In 2020, he received the AIS Sandra Slaughter Service Award, the AIS Technology Challenge Award, and the AIS Impact Award. He lives in Rotterdam.

1

People Love Flowers

1.1 Tulip Time

Waves rolled and splashed toward the shore. The force of the tide broke on the beach. White stripes, indicating breaking waves, were visible all along the shore. From the airplane, the deserted beaches appeared magnificent but silent. The adjacent pale dunes shone almost white in the brilliant sunlight, dappled with sand oats and blue sea thistle, sturdy plants that could weather the sea salt and the sand. A village with small houses and farms with cows and horses was situated nearby, below the dunes and below sea level. More inland, the landscape flattened and was divided into large agricultural plots. Suddenly, colorful lines appeared in the plots: red, yellow, purple, orange, and white, looking somewhat like colored pencils lined up in a pencil box. It was tulip time in the Netherlands. Flowers were in full bloom on this sunny day in early May. Still farther inland, lakes appeared in the landscape, and the tall white sails of boats were mere dots on the bluish surface of the water. The serpentine waterfronts of these lakes contrasted sharply with the straight, long, and rectangular agricultural plots with their vibrant stripes of color. Between the plots there were small canals. From the airplane above, it looked like a very orderly quilt pattern, but it was not just beautiful. This design had allowed the Dutch to live on and cultivate land below sea level: where other people failed, the Dutch succeeded. The French writer, historian, and philosopher Voltaire was right when he quipped "God created the world, but the Dutch created the Netherlands." The airplane began its descent. Closer to Amsterdam, an area with glasshouses was visible. Sunlight reflected off the glass, creating diamond-white sparkles. The style of the glasshouses was almost industrial, with modern windmills and cylindrical water tanks. The plane made a slow turn to the left. A broad river flowed into a wide lake, with a small island situated in it, and just beyond the lake was the city center of Amsterdam.[1]

The central station, adjacent to the river, was clearly visible. The view from above revealed the orderly design of the city, characterized by concentric circles, like tree rings. Other features were also visible: a highway went under a waterway and bridges crossed canals. Descending further over the city, more sights came into view including countless houses and canals, a soccer stadium, a student complex of colored buildings, and many green parks. The pilot executed a perfect landing, touching down on time. We have arrived in the Netherlands, the starting point of a journey that will explore the history, the present, and the future of the flower markets. Let us go.

1.2   Seduction

People all over the world love flowers. Flowers are colorful and beautiful, and some are known and beloved for their fragrance. With bright colors and strong scents, flowers are a plant's utmost attempt to stand out and attract pollinators for fertilization. Flowers seduce. People enjoy giving and receiving flowers, which bring happiness to the giver and the receiver alike. Flowers are fragile and remind us of our own vulnerability as human beings: "How fragile we are" as the Sting song goes.[2] Flowers play a prominent role in the "critical moments of life".[3] When a baby is born, friends and family arrive with flowers in hand to welcome and admire the newborn, congratulate the family, and share in their happiness. Flowers are given to show thanks to teachers when a child finishes kindergarten. Every child in the Netherlands must pass a swimming exam, and flowers are given to celebrate this achievement. At the conclusion of sports tournaments, after intense competition, be it in soccer, tennis, hockey, cricket, or baseball, flowers commemorate the victory. Flowers are exchanged at the high school prom, and flowers are given to celebrate achievements and the progression toward the next phase of life. At high school graduation ceremonies, proud parents offer flowers to symbolize their feelings. Flowers communicate emotions that people are not able to communicate easily themselves. The next big event may be a university graduation or a marriage—both are days full of flowers. Throughout a lifetime, flowers appear at birthday celebrations and other special occasions. And at the end of life, flowers will be there as family and friends mourn their loved one. Flowers adorn graveyards and memorials around the world. We see flowers placed where the name of a victim is engraved on bronze parapets surrounding the twin pools at the National September 11 Memorial in New York City. We see wreaths and flowers on the Tomb of the Unknown Soldier beneath the Arc de Triomphe in Paris or the "Bouquet of Tulips" sculpture, near the Petit Palais museum in Paris, made by Jeff Koons as a tribute to the victims of terrorist attacks at the Bataclan theater. We see the poppies people wear every year in the United Kingdom to commemorate the armistice and to remember those who died in World War One.[4] Poppies grew wild in many fields in northern France and Belgium, where some of the deadliest battles of World War One took place and many soldiers died. Poppies are tough flowers and can grow anywhere, but they are also delicate and a fitting emblem to remember those who died. Indeed, "the brief life of flowers" reminds us of our own short time on this Earth.[5]

Flowers are woven into many aspects of life. In many cultures, girls may be named for flowers, such as Daisy, Iris, Jasmin, Lily, or Rosa, and some flower varieties have been named after celebrities, such as the Marilyn Monroe rose, the Michelle Obama orchid, the Claude Monet rose, or the Franz Kafka dahlia. Every year, Saint Peter's Square in Rome is filled with Dutch flowers and plants during the *Urbi et Orbi* blessing by the Pope.

Around the world events and gatherings are organized to spread the joy and excitement of blooming flowers. Every year the return to spring is widely celebrated in Japan during cherry blossom season.[6] The Japanese have a word for it—*hanami*—that translates as "watching blossoms." It refers to the tradition of gathering beneath cherry blossom trees to picnic, drink, barbeque, spend time with friends and family, and enjoy watching the cherry blossoms. The *sakura*, as the cherry blossoms are known in Japan, start to bloom in Okinawa by January; they bloom in Kyoto and Tokyo at the end of March or beginning of April and proceed into areas at higher altitudes and northward, arriving in Hokkaido a few weeks later.

Spring is also celebrated at the Tulip Time Festival in Holland, Michigan, a town founded and largely inhabited by Dutch settlers. Its tulip festival is the largest in the United States with around five million planted tulips. The festivities include tulip parades, shows, concerts, and fireworks. Around the world, there are thousands of these festivals, among them the Portland Rose Festival in the United States, the Chelsea Flower Show in England, the Mangaung Rose Festival in South Africa, the Singapore Garden Festival, the Indonesian Tomohon International Flower Festival, the Hong Kong Flower Expo, the Melbourne International Flower and Garden Show, the Flowers Festival in Medellín, Colombia, and Expo Flora in Holambra, Brazil (a moniker formed by combining the first letters of Holland, America, and Brazil). In Zundert, the Netherlands, the largest flower parade of the world, Corso

Zundert, is held on the first Sunday of September. For over 80 years, 20 heralds compete against each other to build the most beautiful float. One float—nine meters high and 19 m long—can hold 500,000 dahlias and represent a mythical figure or action scene. And in Lisse, the Netherlands, Keukenhof can be visited, a park with 7 million spring-flowering bulbs, with a total of 800 varieties of tulips. Keukenhof, opened in 1950, is considered the most beautiful spring garden in the world; see Fig. 1.1.[7]

Next to receiving and giving flowers, or watching them blossom, many people also take great pleasure in gardening. Last year in December, I planted around 80 bulbs (snowdrops, tulips, daffodils, and common grape hyacinths) in my small garden and was delighted when the snowdrops appeared as the first sure sign of spring. England has an ideal climate for gardening, and it is among the top gardening countries in the world. Some have said that gardening is "the great British art," and the aesthetic of English country and cottage gardens is echoed in gardens in countries around the world.[8] Japan also has a culture of gardening, and Japanese Zen gardens are considered as places of meditation and reflection.[9] The Japanese stone garden has circular gravel figures, rocks, moss, small trees, and flowers. It reflects nature in harmony. I have visited the Ryoanji Temple Zen Garden in Kyoto, an excellent example of Japanese gardening that gave me a Zen experience and revealed the power of gardening to me in a new way.

Fig. 1.1 Keukenhof in Lisse, the most beautiful spring garden in the world. https://news.cision.com/keukenhof/i/200419llt8509,m23651. With permission by Keukenhof

1.3   Inspiration

Flowers clearly have great social and cultural power, and they are beloved by all. The by-products of flowers are no less valuable. Some varieties of *papaver*, within the poppy family, are the principal source of opium, the dried latex produced by the seed pods. Opium can be used to produce morphine, thebaine, and codeine, among other drugs. Opiates are sedative and are highly valued for medical treatment. The struggle for control of trade in opiates has made its mark on world history. Opium and war were often intertwined, as they were in the Opium Wars between China and Western countries in the nineteenth century. Nowadays, opium production and trafficking remain tied to international conflict. Afghanistan, Columbia, Mexico, and Myanmar control advanced opium production areas and are key players in the illicit drug economy.[10]

The medical value of poppies is but one example of the expanding use of flowers, herbs, plants, and mushrooms to promote health and well-being.[11] The range of uses extends from edible flowers in your vegetarian lunch or dinner, to the use of flower extracts in your tea to sleep better, and to the use of cannabis for all kinds of purposes. Research has shown that having flowers and plants in your office has an effect. It may improve the oxygen level— although experiments in offices at my department did not corroborate that effect—and may make people a little happier and also slightly more productive.

Another by-product of flowers is related to a very different advanced industry. Flower scents, with their aroma components, can deter leaf-eating insects and attract pollinators, such as insects or birds, that move pollen around. Only recently, French researchers identified "precisely which genes make a rose smell so sweet, and where to tinker in the genome to enhance its distinctive scent."[12] Although the rose genome had been mapped before, the new map indicates which genes tend to travel together—scent and color, for example—and which genes are responsible for continuous blooming, among other traits. The study also revealed "a detailed family tree of the rose, and how it differs from its closest cousin, the strawberry, and its more distant apple and pear relations." The new map will be very helpful to edit the genes of roses not only to enhance scent and color production, but also to reduce the need for pesticides and water.

Flower fragrances, natural or synthetic, are used in well-known perfumes, and fragrances have become a multibillion dollars industry. Take, for example, the famous Chanel No. 5. In 1921, Gabrielle Bonheur "Coco" Chanel asked a perfumer to create a scent "that smells like a woman, not a flower bed."[13]

Chanel No. 5 has "a highly complex blend of aldehydes and florals—including rose, ylang-ylang, jasmine, lily of the valley, and iris—layered over a warm, woody base of vetiver, sandalwood, vanilla, amber, and patchouli—this perfume satisfies Chanel's request that No. 5 smell like a 'composition' rather than any single flower."

Flowers were and are sources of inspiration for many painters, writers, and poets. Numerous examples come to my mind. Claude Monet visited the Netherlands several times and in April 1886 he wrote, "I came here at the invitation of a gentleman I did not know, an admirer of my paintings, who intended to show me the bulb cultivation, the enormous fields in full flower: they are quite admirable, but drive the poor painter mad; it cannot be conveyed with our poor colors".[14] A great example is his painting "Tulip Fields at Sassenheim"; see Fig. 1.2.

Fig. 1.2 "Tulip Fields at Sassenheim" painted by Claude Monet in 1886 https://www.clarkart.edu/ArtPiece/Detail/Tulip-Fields-at-Sassenheim. With permission by Clark Art Institute

In the center of the painting there are different tulip beds, in the background a farm, and tulips in the foreground floating in the canal. He was attracted by the regular lines of the bulb beds, as well as by the petals floating past in the canals at flower-harvesting time, which were "like rafts of color, yellow splashes arriving in the blue reflection of the sky." Color followed a similar pattern, "from the grays and purple-browns of the farm to the green of the tulip leaves, then to the saturated crimsons, yellows, and whites of the blooms themselves, with the final flourish of a dense blue footbridge at the left-hand corner." Other paintings by Monet were inspired by his own garden in Giverny, near Paris. You can still visit Monet's gardens, which include a Japanese bridge over a pond full of floating lilies. It was this pond with lilies that inspired Monet to paint the impressive Water Lilies—*Nymphéas*—compositions that are shown in Musée de l'Orangerie in Paris.[15]

Vincent van Gogh's sunflower paintings are another favorite. The paintings show sunflowers in extreme yellow and orange colors, and the images seem to radiate the intensity of not only the sun and its flowers, but the artist himself.[16] Vincent wrote in Arles about two of his sunflower paintings, in a letter dated January 22, 1889, to his brother, Theo[17]:

I have good and bad luck in my production, but not bad luck *alone*. If, for example, our Monticelli bouquet is worth 500 francs to an art lover, and it's worth that, then I dare assure you that my sunflowers are also worth 500 francs to one of those Scots or Americans. Now, to be sufficiently heated up to melt those golds and those flower tones, not just anybody can do that, it takes an individual's whole and entire energy and attention.

Poets and writers were inspired by flowers. Take the famous tragedy of Romeo and Juliet written by William Shakespeare and produced in 1597. The dialogue in Act II, Scene II[18]:

Juliet:
  "Tis but thy name that is my enemy;
  Thou art thyself, though not a Montague.
  What's Montague? it is nor hand, nor foot,
  Nor arm, nor face, nor any other part.
  Belonging to a man. O! be some other name:
  What's in a name? that which we call *a rose*.
  By any other name would smell as sweet;
  So Romeo would, were he not Romeo call'd,
  Retain that dear perfection which he owes.

Without that title. Romeo, doff thy name;
And for that name which is no part of thee,

Romeo:
Take all myself.
I take thee at thy word.
Call me but love, and I'll be new baptiz'ed.;
Henceforth I never will be Romeo."

It meant that what matters is what something is, not what it is called. In line with Shakespeare's thought, but with a slightly different explanation, are the famous words from Gertrude Stein's poem *Sacred Emily*, written in 1913 and published in 1922[19]:

> *Rose is a rose is a rose is a rose*
> Loveliness extreme.
> Extra gaiters,
> Loveliness extreme.
> Sweetest ice-cream.
> Pages ages page ages page ages.

When asked what she meant by this line, Stein said that in the time of Homer or of Chaucer, "the poet could use the name of the thing and the thing was really there." As memory took it over, the thing lost its identity, and she was trying to recover that: "I think in that line the rose is red for the first time in English poetry for a hundred years."

Flowers are symbols for emotions that we as humans would like to communicate, and sometimes are not able to communicate directly. We move into the field of floriography, the language of flowers.[20] It began to develop in the United Kingdom, of course, during the period of Queen Victoria's reign (1837–1901): the Victorian age. Long before messages were exchanged via social media, messages traveled with flowers that were exchanged as gifts. To decode the message, one had only to refer to a Victorian flower dictionary for the meaning of each flower, for example, alstroemeria for "devotion," chrysanthemum for "truth," crocus for "youthful gladness," daffodil for "new beginning," scarlet geranium for "stupidity," iris for "message," lily for "majesty," poppy for "fantastic extravagance," red rose for "love," snowdrop for "consolation and hope," sunflower for "false riches," and tulip for "a declaration of love." Nowadays, each flower is associated with many more meanings, even competing and conflicting meanings. The language of flowers is complicated but fun, so please check with the one that bought you scarlet geraniums.

1.4 Value Network

Most people buy flowers in their own neighborhood, perhaps at a corner shop or at the local farmer's market. In the East Village neighborhood of Manhattan, there are many options. In East 7th Street there is the Popup Florist and within three blocks there are 15 other options to buy flowers, ranging from a specialized flower shop, Sunny's Florist, at 2nd Avenue, to small flower kiosks in different retail and grocery shops; see Fig. 1.3.

Some flowers arrive in these shops from local producers in the United States. Many flowers are imported from Canada, Columbia, Ecuador, Mexico, and the Netherlands and are flown in via John F. Kennedy Airport (JFK) in New York City. The supply chain of flowers connects Dutch growers to the New York retailers and their consumers.[21] It begins in the evening, when a Dutch flower grower cuts a group of gerberas. These are transported to the temperature-controlled distribution warehouses in Aalsmeer, one of the largest trading complexes in the world. Early the next morning around 4 AM, inspectors determine the quality of the produce, and data are uploaded to potential buyers. At 7 AM, part of the lot of gerberas is sold via a Dutch auction system to the highest bidder: a flower exporter. The flower exporter makes a deal with an importer in the United States and the gerberas are transported to Schiphol airport. The flight departs around 2 PM for JFK and arrives at 4 PM local time. The importer clears the product with the border authorities, and around 8 PM the flowers are delivered by a local transporter to a retail florist in the East Village. It is a very long trip for a perishable product, and

Fig. 1.3 Flower retail outlet in the East Village, New York City. Author's own image

yet this example illustrates how a supply chain functions for goods that are produced and sold as a singular product (in this example, the gerbera flower).

In practice, most flowers are sold in bouquets, and gathering flowers into a bouquet is a great value creator. How does it work? Suppose that the importer decided to create bouquets for the New York market and purchased roses, gerberas, daffodils, decorative greenery, and tulips with a total purchase value of $10 per bouquet. The importer will sell these bouquets to retail shops for $20, and the retail shop will sell the bouquets to the end customer for $40. Voila! This is the essence of the flower value chain.

An intriguing question is *where* the bouquet-making process could be done, and there are four options. The group of growers who combine their different products have the first opportunity to create the bouquet. The second opportunity is held by the exporter, who could combine purchases from different growers. The importer has the next opportunity to combine purchases from different export and domestic sources. The final opportunity to create a bouquet is at the retail shop. Which option do you—as an end customer—prefer? Indeed, customers tend to prefer the bouquet at the lowest price and the highest freshness level. Each of the four options exists and has different advantages in the complex global network of interactions among growers, exporters, importers, retailers, and end customers.

There are further considerations as well. Locally produced bouquets will travel a shorter distance and will have a lower carbon footprint with a higher freshness level. But a local bouquet will have less variety. Globally produced bouquets will travel via transport trucks, cargo planes, cargo trains, and cargo ships, adding to their carbon footprint. Longer transport distances can reduce the freshness level (depending on how cool the transport is), but these bouquets could include a great variety of flowers. One of the main challenges of the future is to optimize these factors to reduce production and transportation costs and increase customer value through higher variety and freshness, all the while reducing the carbon footprint.

1.5   Flower Demand

Let us explore the trends that shape global flower markets. Interestingly, flower consumption trends are aligned with more fundamental trends in demographics. In 2019, there were around 7.7 billion people in the world, led by China (1.4 billion) and India (1.3 billion) and followed by the United States,

Indonesia, Brazil, Pakistan, Nigeria, Bangladesh, Russia, Mexico, Japan, Ethiopia, and the Philippines.[22] The populations of Russia and Japan are expected to decline in the near future, but in the next 30 years (by 2050), the global population is expected to increase to 9.8 billion and climb to 11.2 billion by 2100.

Demand for flowers is also aligned with trends in economic development. People tend to buy flowers once they have attained decent work and income, shelter, enough to eat, and the ability to pay for other necessities, such as their children's education. People who are able to save money for luxuries are able to buy flowers and ornamental plants. At the national level, once the indicator of income per capita reaches a certain threshold, people start purchasing flowers. Economic development is expected to be positive in Asia, meaning that many more families will generate enough income to start purchasing flowers. The total value of flower consumption in Asia is forecasted to grow 80% in the next 10 years.

Flower consumption is also aligned with worldwide migration to cities. In 2018, 55% of the world's population lived in cities, including megacities, such as Tokyo (37 million), New Delhi (29 million), Shanghai (26 million), Mexico City (22 million), and São Paulo (22 million). The population of North America is the most urbanized of any region in the world at 82%. It is expected that in 2050, 2.5 billion *more* people will live in cities, or 68% of the world's population. More megacities will be developed, and it is projected that India will add 416 million urban dwellers to its cities, while China will add 255 million, and Nigeria will add 189 million. These population forecasts are astounding, especially when compared to the forecast for the Netherlands, which has 17 million total inhabitants and is expected to have 18 million inhabitants by 2050.

In the future, cities will be larger but also "greener," with green walls and roofs, urban jungles, and parks. There will be new ways of cultivating interior and exterior gardens, including the urban usage of flowers, plants, and trees. At Erasmus University Rotterdam, an advanced analytics tool for the city of Rotterdam was developed that measured and predicted progress in the construction of "green" roofs. Trees and plants on top of a building absorb sunshine, micro-dust, and rain and therefore improve the micro-climate around the building. Transportation to and from cities and the "last mile" of distribution and delivery need to become carbon neutral, by shifting to electric trucks, cars, and motors, and bicycles. Solar and wind energy and smart electricity grids will act as *virtual power plants*, to store electricity when the wind blows and the sun shines and to use the electricity when there is no wind or sun.

New algorithms were developed to connect the supply of and demand for renewable energies (wind, solar) with the storage capacity of electrical cars.

Another intriguing development is the online behavior of the millennial generation (people born between 1985 and 2000). Millennials shop more online, and they use advanced social media tools to search, observe influencers, and purchase flower products. Online purchasing and payments will grow very steadily, enabled by mobile phones with digital wallets and advanced payment systems. Customers and companies will tap into the value creation opportunities of mobile smart phones.[23] It is estimated that around five billion people have mobile devices, and over half of these connections are smart phones.

Mobile payments are increasing in popularity. In China, for example, payments are enabled via WeChat, an online social chat platform. Facebook and a consortium of companies, such as Booking, Spotify, and Uber, announced the development of Libra, a new digital currency, for online payments. New personal assistants, such as AliGenie (Alibaba), Alexa (Amazon), and Google Home, will allow you to order anything, including flowers, from your kitchen. On-site retail shops are also innovating at a rapid pace. Some retail stores track their customers' location through their mobile phones using advanced location analytics, with so-called bluetooth beacons.[24] These beacons can accurately detect location to within a few inches and emit one-way messages when you (and your mobile phone) are nearby. As you approach the flower kiosk in the retail store, a push notification is sent to your mobile phone with a coupon offer for a discount on the purchase of your next bouquet of flowers.

1.6   Global and Local Markets

These societal and technological trends will have a profound impact on the global flower business. Before the impact is explored in greater detail in the upcoming chapters, a first review of the size of the global flower industry and the main players will be given.

Cut flowers, cut foliage, and flower bulbs are traded globally, mainly from south to north, while more bulky plants, such as potted plants and nursery products, are traded mainly regionally.[25] Overall, 80% of the total flower and potted plant production is local and sold in the country where it is produced (local for local), while the other 20% is traded internationally. The total worldwide value of flower and potted plant consumption was around $70 billion in 2017 and will grow to $100 billion in 2027. For years, the Netherlands was the global market leader, with a share of 60%, but it has declined and is expected to decline further to 35% in 2027, but with a continued market growth in absolute terms. The relative market growth decline of the Netherlands has to do with the expected sharp increase in total global market growth, with a spectacular forecasted growth in Asia at 80%, and in Europe and North America at a relatively modest 20% by 2027. The key players are Colombia and Ecuador for both the North and South American markets. In Colombia, the areas around Medellín and in Ecuador around Quito are flower production centers. (For the position of locations, see the included Map of the World and the Netherlands at the end of this chapter.)

In the United States, the area of California, especially around San Diego, is a flower production center and Portland is famous for its International Rose Test Garden. In Brazil, the city of Holambra is the center of flower production. Kenya and Ethiopia are centers for the African and European markets. In Kenya, it is the area nearby Naivasha and in Ethiopia the area around Addis Ababa. India, China, Japan, and other Asian countries produce for Asian markets, and flower production centers include Kunming in China, Kolkata in India, and Nagoya in Japan, among others. The new trade agreement between the European Union and Japan will expand opportunities to export to Japan. Increasing expenditure in China will also provide opportunities for trade, but it is uncertain which countries will respond to market growth in China.

With regard to global logistics, the nodes in the supply network are home to innovation. Kenya and Ethiopia will set up direct air freight lines to their export destinations. Sea transport, with temperature-controlled containers, is being developed by Colombia and Vietnam, which will bring more destinations within their reach. China is working hard to establish a global infrastructure network—the Belt and Road Initiative (BRI) as the new silk road—that will connect China to Asia, the Middle East, Africa, Europe, and the Americas. An example is a cargo train trial in 2018, with 41 containers, that departed from Changsha, in the province of Hunan, and arrived in Tilburg in the Netherlands.[26] The total distance was 12,912 km; it took 17 days and the journey went through Inner Mongolia, Russia, Belarus, Poland, and Germany. New infrastructure developments will impact the long-term global supply and demand for flowers.

To be clear, not all is rosy in the flower business, where raw capitalism has resulted in horrendous working conditions and very low wages for laborers, mostly women and young children. Exceptionally high levels of pesticides are used, which poison the soil and the natural environment, and a tremendous amount of water is required for production. Some countries that produce flowers already have to deal with extreme dry periods due to global climate change, and water may be diverted from local food production to sustain the production of flowers. Flower production is moving into parts of Africa and South America, where local laws on labor conditions and pesticide usage are more relaxed and monitoring is weak. Nevertheless, recent global initiatives were developed to improve work conditions, establish a guaranteed minimum wage of $1.90 per day—just at the international poverty line set by the World Bank—ban pesticide usage, and reduce water usage.[27] New initiatives, such as the Floriculture Sustainability Initiative (FSI2020) or the IDH Sustainable Trade Initiative certificates, will help to transform the global flower business.

Actually, the Dutch are still a strong key player in the global flower markets, with a business ecosystem of seed and bulb production, flower and plant production, logistics and distribution, auctions and sales, and research and development. Within this business ecosystem, Royal FloraHolland organizes the exchange of flower and plants for around 5406 suppliers and 2458 buyers.[28] In 2019, around 12 billion products were exchanged with a total turnover of € 4.8 billion. There are around 100,000 transactions a day and products are sold via auction sales and direct sales. There are 35 auction clocks with on-site and online bidding. The product portfolio includes more than 20,000 species of flowers and plants. The top five export countries are Germany, the United Kingdom, France, Italy, and Poland. The top five import countries are Kenya, Ethiopia, Israel, Belgium, and Germany. The top five flower varieties are rose, chrysanthemum, tulip, gerbera, and lily.[29] Millions of transactions cater to flowers for Valentine's Day, International Women's Day, and Mother's Day.

1.7   Three Questions

Technology Meets Flowers focuses on three fascinating questions. The first question has to do with the Dutch: why do the Dutch play a central role in the global production, sales, and distribution of flowers?

The Netherlands is partly situated a couple of meters below sea level and does not have the greatest weather in terms of sunshine and rain. Most people around the world probably know that the Dutch play some role in the flower industry. They would have seen pictures of colorful tulip fields with a Dutch windmill in the background, and they might have heard about the impressive export figures of Dutch flowers to other countries around the world. Some might have learned about Tulip Mania and how the Dutch went almost bankrupt in the seventeenth century, although the story in itself is a hoax as will be discussed later. Tourists to the Netherlands may have visited the floating Amsterdam flower market (known locally as the *Bloemenmarkt*) or Keukenhof in Lisse. Visitors to these impressive Dutch sites are easily hooked on the flower markets. *Technology Meets Flowers* will unravel the origins and history of the bulb and flower industry in the Netherlands dating back to the sixteenth century when the seed was planted with the appointment of a professor in botany at the University of Leiden. The development of the flower industry and the role the Dutch played highlight the surprising factors that contributed to the Dutch becoming global leaders in the flower markets. Although the elevation below sea level and the weather, soil, and natural conditions do play a role, the greatest factor was the Dutch way of organizing with a continuous debate among many stakeholders to create impact with the invention and adoption of new technologies.

The second question has to do with the complexity of the flower markets: how are the flower markets able to produce and distribute fresh flowers at such a high speed and global scale?

The short life of flowers lasts for around 5–10 days. As we buy flowers for our family and friends, do we stop to consider where they come from and how they are produced and transported? We take it for granted that fresh flowers can be ordered anytime and delivered anywhere, even when they are grown on the other side of the world. The high-speed flower markets take a front-runner position in creating sustainable value for customers with advanced emerging digital technologies from robotized glasshouses to the use of algorithms driven by artificial intelligence (AI) for flower production and distribution.[30]

The complex production and distributional challenges of these perishable products will be explained in detail. Future challenges will be explored where new customer demands—driven by a continuous growth of the world's population—will be balanced with the supply of new types of flower offerings created with advanced emerging genetic and digital technologies within the ecological boundaries of the earth. The genetic revolution will create a potential Cambrian explosion of flower types.[31] Genetic technology will expand the flower portfolio that will be offered by growers and create the opportunity for personalized flowers. Automated and robotized glasshouses will speed up production of flowers and help to offset carbon emissions from other sectors.

Carbon consumption is an indispensable strategy in a world that is struggling to curb high carbon emissions and mitigate the impact on the global climate. The working of the high-speed flower markets where advanced data-driven decision tools support sellers, auctioneers, and buyers will be investigated. High-speed flower logistics will be explained with advanced algorithms that include last-mile distribution solutions and new ways of organizing transport and delivery to the end customer.

Most end customers live in large cities and increasingly order products online via their mobile phones and laptops. Online ordering leads to a greater demand for the last-mile distribution of flowers, which is just one element in the complex distribution portfolio of megacities including more critical resources such as energy, water, and food.

The third question has to do with other sectors and industries, such as higher-speed sectors and industries, like food, health, energy, water, tourism and travel, transport, and mobility, but also lower-speed industries such as manufacturing or the construction industry: what can they learn from the circular and digital innovations that have taken place or will take place in the high-speed flower markets?

These other sectors and industries, with intertwined relationships and blurring borders, will experience a similar circular and digital transformation with a rise of circular business models with advanced usage of emerging technologies such as artificial intelligence, genetics, nanotechnology, and robotics. The focus will be on controlling finite materials and the usage of renewable resources with recycling, refurbishing, and re-using that will preserve and enhance natural capital. Actually, you can view the flower industry as a living laboratory where these circular business models and digital technologies are tested out.

The circular and digital transformation with a shift of the information frontier to circular information where circular and digital capabilities will be the key components for the future will be revealed in a chapter on the circular and digital future. Other sectors and industries can learn a lot to balance the ecological limits with the commercial, logistical, and financial challenges that entrepreneurial firms in the high-speed flower markets have overcome and the solutions that were created.

1.8 Map of the World and the Netherlands

Author's own illustration. Created with mapchart.net ©

Notes

1. The island is called "Pampus" and is a man-made island with a late nineteenth-century sea fort located in the IJmeer. There is a well-known Dutch expression, "laying for Pampus," which is used to refer to a person knocked out and lying down. It stems from the time ships had to wait for high tide at Pampus before they could enter the harbor of Amsterdam.
2. Quote in the song by Sting (1988). Quote "How fragile we are."
3. Stafford, F. (2018). Quote "critical moments of life" (p. 6).
4. Remembrance poppies, including the footnote, in BBC (2017, November 10).
5. The quote "the brief life of flowers" refers to Stafford, F. (2018).
6. Cherry-blossom in Japan in Whiteaker, C, Katanuma M. & Murray P. (2019, April 7) and Rizzo, C (2019, April 5).
7. One can visit flower fields in the Keukenhof park in Lisse. Due to higher temperatures in the winter of 2020, the park had to plant 30% more bulbs to be sure that tourists will be able to view many blooming flowers after its opening by the end of March. If you plan to visit, first check the current blooming time, as it depends on the weather conditions. It is advised to visit the Keukenhof for taking selfies, but not the open tulip fields where visitors may damage flowers, in Picheta, R. (2019, April 24).
8. English gardening and the English garden in Mount H (2015, May 16).
9. The Japanese garden in Kyuhoshi (2019).
10. Opium production in Afghanistan in Felbab-Brown V. (2017 November 21).
11. Medicinal flowers and plants in Foster S, Duke J (2014).
12. Rose scents and the genome sequence in Weintraub K. (2018, April 30).
13. Chanel and its fragrances in Helbig C (2019, Dec 09).
14. Quotes and description of Claude Monet's "Tulip Fields at Sassenheim" in Lees S (ed.) (2015). Quotes "I came here," "like rafts of color," and "from the grays and purple-browns".
15. Claude Monet and his paintings in Musée de l'Orangerie (2020).
16. The number of different seed spirals on a sunflower's face follows the Fibonacci sequence 34 and 55, or 55 and 89, or 89 and 114, for four out of five sunflowers. The sequence is also found in other patterns of life. The Fibonacci sequence is a set in which the next number is the sum of the previous two numbers (0, 1, 1, 2, 3, 5, 8, 13, 21, 34, 55, 89, 144, 233, ….). The Fibonacci sequence is named after the Italian mathematician, who introduced the sequence to Western European mathematics in his book *Liber Abaci* in 1202. Thanks to Joost Steins Bisschop for suggesting the link to the mathematical pattern in sunflowers, based on Bohannon J (2016, May 17).
17. Quote in a letter written by Vincent van Gogh to Theo van Gogh, 22 January 1889, Arles, in Jansen L, Luijten H, Bakker N (eds) (2020). Quote "I have good and bad luck." Vincent van Gogh refers here to two canvases: "Still Life:

Vase with Twelve Sunflowers" and "Still Life: Vase with Fifteen Sunflowers." These paintings are now on display in the Alte Pinakothek, Munich, and in the National Gallery, London. Allocation of the two canvases, The Vincent van Gogh Gallery, F 456/JH 1561 and F 454/JH 1562. http://www.vggallery.com/painting/p_0454.htm

18. The Romeo and Juliet dialogue in Shakespeare W (2004).
19. Gertrude Stein's poem *Sacred Emily*, published in Stein G (2011). Quotes in the meaning and origin of the expression: A rose is a rose is a rose "the poet could use the name of the thing" and "I think in that line the rose" in https://www.phrases.org.uk/meanings/15900.html. Accessed 15 July 2020.
20. Victorian flower dictionary with examples from Kirkby M (2011).
21. Some elements of the flower supply chain are from From Place to Space (Chapter 2) and Using B2B Markets in the Supply Chain (Chapter 5), Kambil A, van Heck E (2002). The flower supply chain and its logistics in Croke, D. (2018, April 28).
22. World population data is in United Nations (2017, June 21).
    United Nations (2018, May 16).
23. Around 4.8 billion people have a mobile phone nowadays, which is 62% of the world population. For more insights on how to unlock the mobile economy, see Ghose A (2017).
24. The beacon store example is in Kwet M (2019, June 16).
25. Flower industry data is in the reports by Van Rijswick C (2016, November).
    Van Horen L, Bac A (2017, September).
    Van Horen L (2017, December).
26. Changsha train to Tilburg in Van Leijen M (2018, August 21).
27. For the international poverty line, see World Bank Press Release (2015, October 15).
28. Data of the Dutch flower business ecosystem is based on Royal FloraHolland (2019a, b).
29. Overview of flower trends and the floral top 5 is in Veld A (2019, May).
30. *Technology Meets Flowers* is based on the results of several external funded research projects in particular the "Artificial Intelligence in the Floriculture Chain" project (in short: iFlow) in collaboration with Royal FloraHolland, Zentoo, Wageningen University, and Rotterdam School of Management of Erasmus University. The iFlow project was part of the Topsector Horticulture and Starting Materials, one of the nine top sectors of the Netherlands. In 2020, the Association of Information Systems (AIS) awarded the iFlow project, with its AIS members Alok Gupta, Wolfgang Ketter, Yixin Lu, May Truong, and Eric van Heck, with the AIS Impact Award.

The goal of iFlow is to develop innovative solutions that powerfully will renew the commercial process of day trading in combination with the logistics process. An important issue in this is how to combine best pricing with the optimal organization of the supply chain. Both the auction process, the sales that take place via digital transaction systems, and the logistics chain process (fast delivery from grower to buyer at minimal costs) will be supported with advanced decision-support systems, inspired by artificial intelligence. Van Heck E, Ketter W, Lu Y, Gupta A, Truong M (2020, March 12).

31. The original term "Cambrian Explosion" refers to the sudden appearance in the fossil record of complex animals with mineralized skeletal remains. It represents an important evolutionary event in the history of life on Earth.

References

BBC (2017) Remembrance poppy: controversies and how to wear it. BBC, November 10. http://www.bbc.co.uk/newsbeat/article/41942346/remembrance-poppy-controversies-and-how-to-wear-it. Accessed 2 Sept 2020

Bohannon J (2016) Sunflowers show complex Fibonacci sequences. Science, May 17. https://www.sciencemag.org/news/2016/05/sunflowers-show-complex-fibonacci-sequences#:~:text=Count%20the%20clockwise%20and%20counterclockwise,large%20sunflowers%E2%80%9489%20and%20144. Accessed 27 Oct 2020

Croke D (2018) The logistical dance that gets all those flowers to market in Europe…and elsewhere. FreightWaves, April 28. https://www.freightwaves.com/news/dutch-flower-market-logistics. Accessed 2 Sept 2020

Felbab-Brown V (2017) Afghanistan's opium production is through the roof—why Washington shouldn't overreact. Brookings, November 21. https://www.brookings.edu/blog/order-from-chaos/2017/11/21/afghanistans-opium-production-is-through-the-roof-why-washington-shouldnt-overreact/. Accessed 2 Sept 2020

Foster S, Duke J (2014) Peterson field guide to medicinal plants and herbs, 3rd edn. Houghton Mifflin Harcourt, Boston

Ghose A (2017) Tap: unlocking the mobile economy. MIT, Cambridge

Helbig C (2019) Review of Chanel no. 5 perfume: is it worth the hype? Byrdie, December 09. https://www.byrdie.com/chanel-no-5-review-of-chanel-no-5-perfume-346120. Accessed 1 Sept 2020.

Jansen L, Luijten H, Bakker N (eds) (2020) Vincent van Gogh, The Letters, Letter No. 741. http://www.vangoghletters.org/vg/letters/let741/letter.html. Accessed 13 July 2020

Kambil A, Van Heck E (2002) From place to space. In: Making markets: How firms can design and profit from online auctions and exchanges. Harvard Business School Press, Boston

Kirkby M (2011) A Victorian flower dictionary: the language of flowers companion. Ballantine Books, New York

Kwet M (2019) Retail stores track your every move. New York Times, Sunday Review, 5, June 16. https://www.nytimes.com/interactive/2019/06/14/opinion/bluetooth-wireless-tracking-privacy.html

Kyuhoshi (2019) Japanese gardens–history, types, elements, and more. https://www.kyuhoshi.com/japanese-gardens/ Accessed 2 Sept 2020

Lees S (ed) (2015) Nineteenth-century European paintings at the Sterling and Francine Clark Art Institute. Tulip fields at Sassenheim. Yale University Press, Yale, vol 2, pp 534–536

Mount H (2015) There's nothing like the glory of our gardens. The Telegraph, May 16. https://www.telegraph.co.uk/gardening/chelseaflowershow/11610142/Theres-nothing-like-the-glory-of-our-gardens.html. Accessed 7 Sept 2020

Musée de l'Orangerie (2020) History of the water lilies cycle. Paris. https://www.musee-orangerie.fr/en/article/history-water-lilies-cycle. Accessed 14 July 2020

Picheta R (2019) Dutch tulip growers beg selfie-taking millennials to stop trampling their flowers. CNN travel, April 24 2019. https://edition.cnn.com/travel/article/netherlands-tulip-selfies-scli-intl/index.html. Accessed 2 Sept 2020

Rizzo C (2019) Japan's cherry blossoms are in full bloom. Travel + Leisure, April 5. https://www.travelandleisure.com/attractions/festivals/tokyo-japan-cherry-blossom-peak-season-sakura. Accessed 2 Sept 2020

Royal FloraHolland (2019a) Facts and figures. https://www.royalfloraholland.com/en/about-floraholland/who-we-are-what-we-do/facts-and-figures   Accessed 7 Sept 2020

Royal FloraHolland (2019b) The strengths of the marketplace. Annual Report 2019. https://www.royalfloraholland.com/media/14287960/royal-floraholland-annual-report-2019.pdf. Accessed 7 Sept 2020

Shakespeare W (2004) Romeo and Juliet. In: Folger Shakespeare Library, Simon & Schuster, New York. The dialogue is in Act II, Scene II

Stafford F (2018) The brief life of flowers. John Murray Press, London

Stein G (2011) Geography and plays. Traveling Press, El Paso, pp 173–174

Sting (1988) Fragile. In: Nothing Like the Sun, Music album

United Nations (2017) World population projected to reach 9.8 billion in 2050, and 11.2 billion in 2100, June 21 2017. https://www.un.org/development/desa/en/news/population/world-population-prospects-2017.html. Accessed 2 Sept 2020

United Nations (2018) 68% of the world population projected to live in urban areas by 2050, May 16 2018. https://www.un.org/development/desa/en/news/population/2018-revision-of-world-urbanization-prospects.html.   Accessed 2 Sept 2020

Van Heck E, Ketter W, Lu Y, Gupta A, Truong M (2020) Optimise floriculture and make it more sustainable with AI algorithms. RSM discovery, March 12 2020. https://discovery.rsm.nl/articles/427-optimise-floriculture-and-make-it-more-sustainable-with-ai-algorithms/. Accessed 8 Sept 2020

Van Horen L (2017) Flourishing flowers, promising plants. Rabobank Research, December 2017. https://research.rabobank.com/far/en/sectors/regional-food-agri/Flourishing_flowers_promising_plants_Changes_in_consumer_behaviour.html. Accessed 7 Sept 2020

Van Horen L, Bac A (2017) Volop kansen voor de Nederlandse Sierteelt (Many opportunities for Dutch horticulture), Rabobank Research. https://www.rabo-

bank.nl/images/pdf_rabobank_volop_kansen_nederlandse_sierteelt_
sep2017_29924822.pdf. Accessed 7 Sept 2020

Van Leijen M (2018, August 21) First train Changsha-Tilburg hits the tracks, RailFreight, August 21. https://www.railfreight.com/beltandroad/2018/08/21/first-train-changsha-tilburg-hit-the-tracks/?gdpr=accept. Accessed 3 Sept 2020

Van Rijswick C (2016) World floriculture map 2016: Equator countries gathering speed. Rabobank Research, November 2016. https://research.rabobank.com/far/en/sectors/regional-food-agri/world_floriculture_map_2016.html.   Accessed 7 Sept 2020

Veld A (2019) Floral oasis. Holland Herald, pp 28–38, May 2019. https://www.holland-herald.com/archive/#2019-5_28. Accessed 3 Sept 2020.

Weintraub K (2018). How a rose blooms: Its genome reveals the traits for scent and color. New York Times, April 30. https://www.nytimes.com/2018/04/30/science/rose-genome-gene-editing.html. Accessed 2 Sept 2020

Whiteaker C, Katanuma M, Murray P (2019) Understanding the business of Japan's cherry-blossom season. Bus Stand, April 7 2019. https://www.business-standard.com/article/international/understanding-the-business-of-japan-s-cherry-blossom-season-119040700068_1.html. Accessed 2 Sept 2020

World Bank Press Release (2015) World Bank forecasts global poverty to fall below 10% for first time; major hurdles remain in goal to end poverty by 2030. World Bank Press, October 15 2015. https://www.worldbank.org/en/news/press-release/2015/10/04/world-bank-forecasts-global-poverty-to-fall-below-10-for-first-time-major-hurdles-remain-in-goal-to-end-poverty-by-2030.   Accessed 3 Sept 2020.

2

Tulip Bulbs

2.1 Tulip Fields

It is easy to travel by train within the Netherlands. At Schiphol Airport, you can catch a train in the station hall. You will see the yellow train ticket booths and screens display departure information for the different destinations. The Dutch train network is dense and carries 1.3 million passengers every day. An excellent short train ride, around 20 min, is from Schiphol Airport to the city of Leiden. You will travel through the area of tulip fields, blooming at the end of April and beginning of May, with short stops in Hoofddorp, Nieuw Vennep, Sassenheim, where Claude Monnet painted his "Tulip fields at Sassenheim," and Leiden central station. Leiden is a very interesting city and, for the Dutch, an important one. On the west side of its central station, you can see the buildings of the Leiden University Medical Center. On the east side, you can walk via the "Stationsweg"—the station road (*weg* is the Dutch word for road)—to the historic city center. You would enjoy the walk into this charming city as you congratulate yourself for learning your first Dutch word.

2.2 Bourgeois Deal

Leiden has played an important role at crucial moments in Dutch history. The Netherlands—as a unified country with a plural name—was established after a very turbulent and long war with Spain that lasted for 80 years. The States General of the Burgundian Netherlands was established in 1464 as an

© The Author(s), under exclusive license to Springer Nature Switzerland AG 2021
E. van Heck, *Technology Meets Flowers*, https://doi.org/10.1007/978-3-030-69303-9_2

assembly of 17 provincial states of an area that comprised the major parts of present-day Belgium, the Netherlands, Luxembourg, and Hauts-de-France.

The Dutch War of Independence (1568–1648) started as a revolt of these 17 provinces but continued with the seven Northern provinces known as the Republic of the Seven United Netherlands or the Dutch Republic.[1] The Act of Abjuration (in Dutch: *Plakkaat van Verlatinghe*) was signed in 1581 as the declaration of independence based on a decision by the States General. William of Orange (1533–1584) led the Dutch revolt against the Spanish Habsburgs. During the Dutch revolt the Siege of Leiden turned out to be a turning point in the revolt for independence. The Siege of Leiden occurred in 1573 and 1574, when the Spanish General, Francisco de Valdez, attempted to capture the rebellious city.

Every year the city celebrates the end of the Siege of Leiden on October 3. Free herring and white bread are distributed to the citizens of Leiden. The victory over Spain had an enormous positive impact on the power position of William of Orange, it buttressed the fighting spirit of the Dutch rebels, and the citizens of Leiden earned a reputation for perseverance.[2] To recognize the city's sacrifice in the siege, William of Orange founded Leiden University a year later in 1575 as the first university of the Netherlands.[3] It took many more battles before the long struggle for independence finally concluded and the Dutch republic was formally recognized by the Spanish Empire in 1648 at the Treaty of Münster.

The tumultuous context of the 80-year war for the independence of the Netherlands was matched by great uncertainty in other dimensions of life: religion, power, institutions, and business. From a religious point of view, there was a clash between the Catholics and the Protestants. Although the Netherlands was a Calvinist-run society, it tolerated other religious groups, such as Catholics (reluctantly), sects of Protestantism such as Lutherans and Mennonites, and Jews. People of these groups brought their capital and contacts to the Netherlands. Refugees fled the Spanish-dominated regions and found shelter in the Northern Netherlands. The nation of the Netherlands formed in a more decentralized way, as a republic of federalized states instead of as feudal states with powerful monarchies that ruled other European countries. The Dutch distributed power among the towns and states. There was no real aristocracy, but town-dwellers were led by oligarchies of wealthy merchants. These merchants were in business, but also took care of public services and were active as mayors or as financial controllers of towns and cities. New institutions for commerce were established: "the foundation of a chamber of assurance in 1598, a new commodity exchange in 1618, a public exchange bank, the Wisselbank, in 1609, and a lending bank in 1614—attracted capital and mercantile interest from all over Europe".[4] The profitable East India Company (VOC) in 1602 and the rather less successful West India Company (WIC) in 1621 stimulated global trade. Capital was easily available, and many investment options were possible, such as in trade and manufacturing, in drainage projects to reclaim land from sea, and to invite painters for group painting and art projects. Urban life, through "both trade and immigration, was becoming more cosmopolitan and cultured. Amsterdam in particular was becoming a center of the world."

All of these were signs that a fundamental transformation of society was underway. More than 400 years later, a professor in economics, history, English, and communications at the University of Illinois in Chicago connected all the dots. Professor Deirdre McCloskey, in her monumental trilogy of books, *Bourgeois Virtues*, *Bourgeois Dignity*, and *Bourgeois Equality*, described the fundamental shift from a feudal society to a bourgeois society.[5]

The feudal society was based on the "Aristocratic Deal":

You honor me, an aristocrat by natural inequality, and give me the liberty to extract rents from you in the first act, and in all subsequent acts. I forbid you under penalty of death to seek competitive 'protection'. By the third act of the zero-sum drama, if you have behaved yourself, and have pulled your forelock or made your curtesy as I ride by, I will not at least have slaughtered you.

That was the power of the feudal lords over the peasants. Liberty and dignity yielded the "Bourgeois Deal":

You accord to me, a bourgeois projector, the liberty and dignity to try out my schemes in voluntary trade, and let me keep the profits, if I get any, in the first act—though I accept, reluctantly, that others will compete with me in the second act. In exchange, in the third act of a new, positive-sum drama, the bourgeois betterment provided by me (and by those pesky, low-quality, price-spoiling competitors) will make you all rich.

With the benefit of hindsight, the results of this transformation are evident around the world, "starting in Holland in the sixteenth century and spreading to England in the eighteenth, and now, two hundred years on, spreading to China and India."[6] McCloskey's analysis attributed dramatic results to the *Bourgeois Deal*. She observed that "the average income over time resembles an ice-hockey stick, with tens of thousands of years spent tracing the long, horizontal handle. Then finally, after 1800, history reached the business end of the hockey stick and shot up the blade." For centuries, the average human being made, earned, and consumed around $3 a day (expressed in present-day US prices and allowing for inflation and relevant exchange rates among currencies). Today, "the world average, including even the very poor, has reached $33 per day." "Since 1800 the ability of humans to feed and clothe and educate themselves, even as the number of humans increased by an astonishing factor of seven, has risen, per human, by an even more astonishing factor of ten. Do the math, then, of total production. We humans now produce and consume *seventy*—7 × 10—times more goods and services worldwide than in 1800." Thus, McCloskey refers to the period after 1800 as "the Great Enrichment," but it began "with bourgeois dignity in Holland after 1600." In Dutch society at that time, trade and commerce had become prestigious and success enabled many people to make money and climb the social ladder. The trade of tulips became a logical component of that economy and society.

2.3   True Monarch of Flowers

In 1593, 18 years after the Siege of Leiden, its university attracted the most famous botanist in Europe, Carolus Clusius.[7] His official name was Charles de l'Ecluse (1526–1609).

He was born in 1526 in Arras in what is now northern France, which at that time was the county of Artois of Spanish Netherlands. He initiated studies in Latin and Greek, civil law, theology, and philosophy, but Clusius became very attached to plants and the emerging field of botany and decided to study medicine at the University of Montpellier. Following his studies, he never practiced medicine as a physician, but was employed by the Fugger banking family as a tutor of one of their sons and as an agent for a plant collection expedition to Spain. As an active participant of the expedition, he collected plants, described them in detail, and categorized them. He befriended Ogier Ghiselin de Busbecq, a writer and herbalist, and crucially, a diplomat who served three generations of Austrian monarchs. Busbecq was appointed as ambassador to the Ottoman Empire, which at that time was under the rule of Suleiman the Magnificent and covered most of Southeast Europe, parts of Central and Eastern Europe, Western Asia, North Africa, and the Horn of Africa. Over the years, Clusius gained experience collecting plants, amassed a large network of correspondents, and kept a close friendship with Busbecq.

Eventually, Clusius was offered a very prestigious position. In 1573, at the age of 47, Clusius became the prefect of the imperial medical garden in Vienna. The garden was owned by Emperor Maximillian II, the Holy Roman Emperor. With the appointment, Carolus Clusius gained recognition, a budget, and the responsibility of cultivating both the imperial garden and the field of botany. Clusius had a wealth of impressive botanical knowledge and served as a source of inspiration for many botanists in Europe. He asked his friend Busbecq—with his contacts in the Ottoman empire—to send him bulbs and seeds and he began to enlarge and rearrange the imperial garden. He traveled extensively throughout Europe to collect new plant specimens, to exchange knowledge, experience, plants, and bulbs, and to provide purchase and planting advice to bourgeois society. Clusius was not an "isolated genius," but worked with everyone from ruling princes and the leading figures of the European aristocracy, to diplomats, humanists, fellow physicians and naturalists, printer-publishers, artists, and apothecaries.[8] His network of correspondents extended all over Europe, "from England to Hungary and Austria, from Greece and Italy to Poland, and from Spain and Portugal to the Northern Netherlands, France, Germany, and Norway," and he wrote letters in six languages: Latin, French, Italian, German, Spanish, and Dutch, in order of importance. When Clusius's reputation as a botanical expert grew, his network of correspondents expanded further until "he could be in touch, directly or indirectly, with all the then relevant experts on living nature in Europe." In 1602, Emanuel, Prince of Portugal, addressed Clusius as "the true monarch of flowers."

Unusually, he preserved many letters that were sent to him from about 1560 until his death in 1609. There are roughly 1300 extant letters that Clusius received from all around Europe from more than 330 correspondents, and there are around 200 extant letters sent by Clusius himself. All the extant letters have been researched and digitized, and they were made searchable online with the help of the Clusius Project (2005–2009) with funding from the Netherlands Organization for Scientific Research. The extant letters are but a fraction of those sent to him. Clusius and his network of hundreds of men and women all over Europe helped to shape knowledge through the careful and meticulous exchange of information, via letters, about varieties, growing conditions (soil, water, and weather), medical usage of plants, or about the beauty and color of flowers. Based on this "collective enterprise," the academic field of botany and the flower bulb industry were established.

From the 330 correspondents, I have chosen three key players in the life of Clusius: Charles de Saint Omer (1533–1569), Marie de Brimeu (around 1550–1605), and Johan van Hoghelande (1546–1614). Charles de Saint Omer was the first patron of Clusius. Marie de Brimeu represents his extensive network of female correspondents. She had a long and intensive correspondence with Clusius from the 1560s until her death in 1605, and she encouraged him to move from Frankfurt to Leiden and helped him attain a professorship at Leiden University. Johan van Hoghelande was "in a class of his own" and a very good friend of Clusius before and during the time when he lived in Leiden. You can find a summary of their correspondence with Clusius in the Chapter Notes. Both de Brimeu and van Hoghelande, and some others, were representatives in Leiden of the elite gardening and botanical culture of the Southern Netherlands that helped to further establish Clusius' reputation. His work was already well known before he arrived in Leiden. Actually, during the 1560s Clusius helped with the development of the *Libri Picturati A18–30* (as it is called) as one of the most remarkable European collections of watercolors depicting *naturalia* of the sixteenth century; see Fig. 2.1.[9]

A book based on his expedition to Spain and Portugal was published in 1576.[10] Over 200 rare and exotic plants in Spain and Portugal are described in the book, which includes detailed illustrations. And here for the first

Fig. 2.1 Tulips (*Tulipa gesneriana*) were introduced into the Netherlands by Carolus Clusius via the *Hortus botanicus* Leiden Jan de Koning, Gerda van Uffelen, Alicja Zemanek, and Bogdan Zemanek (eds), *Drawn After Nature, The complete botanical watercolours of the sixteenth-century Libri Picturati* (KNNV Publishing, 2008), page 54. With permission by KNNV Publishing

time—although in the appendix—the tulip (in Latin: *Tulipa*) was presented, categorized, and illustrated. The illustrations were printed via woodcuts, a relief printing technique. To make a woodcut, the negative space around an image is carved away from the surface of a block of wood, and then ink is applied to the surface to transfer the image to paper. The woodcuts were used in later books by Christopher Plantin, who at that time was a famous printer in Antwerp. Clusius' other major work, published in 1583, was on the description of plants of Austria and Hungary, including the potato. These books and illustrations helped Clusius to spread his work and they also increased his fame. In today's terms, we can think of Clusius as a "brand name" and can see him as an "influencer" within his vast network of correspondents. The network of correspondents was a "collective enterprise," where men and women shared their passion for gardening, as well as information, plants, and bulbs. The letters were useful for the "accurate description and illustration based as far as possible on first-hand experience in the service of precise identification." There was competition, for sure, to be the first person to discover a new variety or to grow a rare, exotic plant in difficult weather conditions. Clusius had an important role in his network. If he referenced someone—nowadays like a citation in the academic literature—the person would be very honored; he or she would gain some notoriety and be motivated to help Clusius further with his work. Clusius was "interested in scoops, scientific *primeurs*: he continued to add appendices with newly discovered plants or animals to his publications more or less as long as the printer-publisher allowed him."

Clusius arrived in Leiden in 1593. Leiden University wanted to establish an academic garden so that medical students could learn about the use of medicinal herbs and plants. Clusius was appointed as honorary professor of Botany at the university and became *prefect* (director) of the first botanical garden in the Netherlands: the Hortus botanicus in Leiden. One can still visit the Hortus botanicus with its Clusius Garden and Clusius statue. The statue reflects a serious looking rugged gentleman with a beard. With his experience as prefect of the imperial garden in Vienna and his scholarly work and reputation in Europe, he was very well suited for this new position. The position included a salary of 750 guilders a year plus travel expenses. The appointment of Carolus Clusius—as it turned out much later—was the start of a flourishing Dutch bulb industry.

In 1593, Clusius was 67 years of age. Although he was not in very good health, he continued to use his knowledge, experience, and extensive networks of contacts to further his research, educate others, and add to his growing collection of plants. He selected plants from his own collection for the botanical garden in Leiden, with a special focus on tulips. The initial garden was small—about 31 by 40 m, and it contained more than 1500 plants after Clusius was appointed as prefect. From his own bulb collection, he planted tulips in 1593, and those came into flower in the spring of 1594, the first time that tulips bloomed in the Hortus botanicus. Some tulips were single-color varieties; others were variegated (i.e., with striking color patterns). At that time Clusius developed a tulip taxonomy. Taxonomy is the science of naming, defining, and classifying groups of organisms or artifacts on the basis of shared characteristics. Usually, a taxonomy theory is the start for explanatory or predictive theories. In 1951, an amended version of the taxonomy consisting of 32 pages, illustrated with six woodcuts, and including two indexes was published for the first time as *A Treatise on Tulips*. The English translation has been used since 1951 as a reference guide for the Dutch bulb growers. The introduction emphasized the exceptional breakthrough established by Clusius[11]:

> Among these mediaeval plants, there were a few 'florist flowers' *in statu nascendi* (in the state of being born), such as Hollyhock, Wallflower, Stocks, Carnations, and Violets; a few hardy perennials like Columbine, Monkshood, Periwinkle, Peony, Cowslip, *Iris germanica*, double Daisies and Buttercups, Sweet Williams, and Rose Champion, three Lilies—foremost the splendid and ancient Madonna-lily—and about as many Roses, some annuals like Cornflower and Marigold, and there almost all the fragrant herbs and subshrubs … But there were no Tulips, no Crocuses (except from the true Saffron), no bulbous Irises, no Hyacinths, scarcely any Snowdrops or Daffodils, no Lilacs, nor Mock Oranges, no Anemones, and no Sunflowers.

Clusius wrote of "the exotic plant which, in good reason, is held in high esteem by all plant lovers on account of its considerable variety in flower color, and which is called by the people *Tulipa*, and by learned men *Lilionarcissus* [*Tulipa Gesneriana L.*]."

The taxomony, *A Treatise on Tulips*, identified three types of tulips, based on their flowering time: the early tulip, the late tulip, and the intermediate tulip. Specific tulip types were discussed in great detail such as the Apennine tulip, the Narbonne tulip, the Spanish tulip, the Byzantine tulip, the Persian tulip, and the tulip of Caccini. Each tulip is presented with characteristics such as flowering time, size, color, and shape of segments, filaments, anthers, and claws.[12] Sometimes the origin of the bulb and its conditions and its growing pattern are recorded. The following description of an intermediate tulip shows the detailed descriptions Clusius gave in his taxonomy:

Of the middle-sized intermediates with very large flowers, [Fig. 14] few varieties have been observed by me.

1. One of these is of a very pale yellow colour, nearly like boiled sulphur, for which the reason the Austrian ladies surname it 'Schwefelfarb', that is sulphur coloured. All its segments are pointed, the claws soot-stained. The generous Dame von Heysenstain used to have a single bulb of it, imported from Byzantium, an offset of which she gave me, but although it flowered and produced viable seed in the year 1586, the bitter winter which followed has ruined it along with the mother plant. The seed, which I had sown the next year, I left in my small garden in Vienna.
2. The next one has a flower of an elegant light-yellow shade, all segments of which are pointed; the claws are black and so are the anthers, the filaments are stained with soot. In the year 1589 this variety bore a flower with me consisting of 16 segments, and an offset of it had 13 of them, but the next year the mother plant had only eight and the offset six segments.
3. The flower of the third variety is variegated yellow, that is to say a mixture of yellow and red, and consists of six large, pointed, light yellow segments with red veins, occasionally sparsely scattered, at times densely crowded, running radiately from the black claw all over the length of the segment and spreading towards the sides.

Clusius also made a note on, what he observed as, "self-colored" tulips; see Fig. 2.2:

For I had, in the year 1585 and in several following years, tulips which in preceding years had borne flowers of a fine red, but which then became an intermixed miscellany of reds and yellows, sometimes the yellow occupying the middle of the segments, sometimes the red, or both colours being arranged in rays, diverging along the edges. Similarly, a yellow tulip has shown yellow and red, and a purple one white and purple colours, variously intermixed and disposed in rays in the length of the segment. And this also I have observed, that any tulip thus changing its original colour is usually ruined afterwards and wanted only to delight its master's eyes with this variety of colours before dying, as if to bid him a last farewell.

When you read the text, it is clear that Clusius struggled with this coloring phenomenon. He looked for an answer, but it remained a mystery to him. Why did one bulb produce a single-color tulip, and why did the other, sometimes from the same parent bulb, bloom with a variety of colors? Clusius was not able to answer these questions before he died at the age of 83 in 1609. He was buried in de Lieve Vrouwekerk (Our Lady's Church) in Leiden, which

Fig. 2.2 "Self-colored" tulips in my garden. Author's own image

was demolished in 1819.[13] The Pieterskerk now stands in its place and a memorial plaque for Clusius is there to this day.

2.4   Tulip Breaking Mystery

But what were the underlying causes of the phenomenon known as "breaking" in tulips, or the changes in coloring year on year that were seen as a mystery in the lifetime of Carolus Clusius? Was it caused by the type of tulip? Was it the soil, the weather, the lack of a specific nutrient? In fact, it was none of these, but it would take more than 300 years for the cause to be discovered through a series of experiments that began in 1927.

Gregor Mendel conducted "pea plant experiments between 1856 and 1863 and established many rules of heredity that are referred to as the laws of Mendelian inheritance."[14] Mendel worked with "seven characteristics of pea plants: plant height, pod shape, pod color, seed shape, seed color, flower position, and flower color." Taking seed color as an example, Mendel showed that "when a true-breeding yellow pea and true-breeding green pea were crossbred their offspring always produced yellow seeds. However, in the next generation, the green peas reappeared at a ratio of one green to three yellow."

To explain this phenomenon, Mendel coined "the terms "recessive" and "dominant" in reference to certain traits. In the presented example, the green trait, which seems to have vanished in the first filial generation, is recessive, and the yellow is dominant." You might remember the discussions in your high school biology classes about a brown-eyed parent, a blue-eyed parent, and their blue-eyed children. The principles derived from Mendel's research have become the foundation of modern genetics. In 1900, three independent researchers—Austrian agricultural botanist Erich Tschermak, German botanist Karl Correns, and Dutch botanist Hugo de Vries—published responses to a rediscovered 35-year-old paper by Gregor Mendel titled *Experiments on Plant Hybridisation* (1865) that led to the development of modern genetics.[15] The work of Mendel was first introduced into England in 1900 by Cambridge biologist William Bateson. Its original reception was controversial, leading Bateson to publish a short follow-up book, *Mendel's Principles of Heredity: A Defence*, in 1902.[16] Bateson also coined the word "genetics." Bateson was the first director of the John Innes Horticultural Institution, founded in 1910 with a bequest from John Innes, which included the manor house at Merton Park, England. Bateson led the institution until his death in 1926. John Innes was a merchant and philanthropist. In 1910, Merton Park was part of Surrey, but nowadays it is a borough of London and hosts the Wimbledon tournament. In the 1960s, the institution was relocated to Norwich, Norfolk, England, and it is known as the John Innes Centre.[17] The aim throughout the work of this institution had been "the standardization of materials and methods so that growers anywhere may rely upon reproducible results of proved excellence. It is a further and a large step in the direction of what is, after all, the goal of every grower—complete control over every phase of a plant's growth to the greater benefit of man's nutritional and esthetic needs."

Experiments on the cause of breaking in tulips began at the John Innes institution in 1925. The leading researcher was Dorothy Cayley. She had extensive in-depth knowledge and experience in a wide array of fields such as biochemistry, horticulture, mycology, plant genetics, and preventive medicine. As shown by Mendel, plant experiments were a great way to discover causality. Field experiments were a new research method at that time. By the beginning of the twentieth century, science was much more advanced than in Mendel's time. (I will give some extra attention to experimental design, because it is a very useful approach for modern corporations. Amazon and Google execute thousands of field experiments every day.)

Cayley had been born to British parents in 1874 in Ceylon. At the age of seven, she returned to England with her family. She was educated at Stamford High School, and then she moved to Germany where she studied music. For a while, she studied science at London University before going to University

College in Reading. Cayley was especially interested in plant diseases and soils and entered the board of education's examination in horticulture, where she earned first-class honors, a medal, and a diploma. She also took first-class honors in the Royal Horticultural Society Examination and was appointed as the superintendent of the gardens that belonged to the Botanical Department at Reading. Cayley's meandering education had some similarities with the path of Clusius, who also pursued a range of studies before he entered the field of botany. They both enjoyed the practice of gardening and the more practical science of horticulture.

In 1927, Cayley undertook the first series of experiments that would make her world famous. The complex research topic was to uncover the causality underlying breaking in tulips. She went on to publish two ground-breaking papers where she explained the experiments and results. Dorothy Cayley published her results in *Annals of Applied Biology* in 1928 and 1932, respectively.[18] In the introduction of her first paper "'Breaking' in Tulips," she started with a clear description of the problem at hand:

> It is a well-known fact that when tulips are raised from seed, the flowers for the first years are of a uniform "self" colour, the colour of course being different according to the variety. These self-coloured seedlings are known as breeders. At any time these breeders are liable to "break". The flowers become variegated to bi-colours, the original self colour or a darker shade of the same being restricted to splashes, stripes, or lines, somewhat irregularly distributed on a white or yellow ground as the case may be.

And she presented a probable line of thinking:

> Thus the active agent which brings about "breaking," whatever it may be, virus or enzyme, can inhibit the formation of anthocyanin sap colour in certain areas in the flowers, and also affect the chloroplasts in the lighter areas of the leaves.

And later on, she defines the object of study:

> With the object of finding out whether "breaking" in tulip is or is not caused by disease, or some such transmissible variegation as described by Hertzsch in *Abutilon*, a series of experiments was started in September 1927.

Her research method included ingenious experiments with "plugging" and "crafting" of bulbs of the May flowering tulip called *Bartigon*, a self-colored variety which does not break very readily. The experimental design was well established in the horticultural sciences and the John Innes institution was a front-runner in the careful design of these plant experiments. By using plant experiments, science was done at the explanatory theory level, instead of the descriptive taxonomy theory level that was known at the time of Clusius. (Thinking in an experimental way is very useful in the age of artificial intelligence and the digitizing world; see Chaps. 6 and 7) However, experiments in the field were (and still are) not easy. Indeed, there were challenges during the execution of a series of experiments running between 1927 and 1931. During storage three aphids were found on one bulb, the injecting of bulbs took longer, and the filtrate was not so fresh for some bulbs as for others (and the filtrate results were negative at the end). Also, a mild form of parroting in the plots of bulbs plugged with tulip tissue with breaks was recorded in 1928. And in the summer of 1930 fasciation was observed in different species of plants. It became also clear that the close juxtaposition of treated plots to plots showing breaks accounted for a certain percentage of breaks in the second year. And at the end of the experiments, it became clear that the recording of the exact position of the various laterals and bulbils would have been very helpful, but this was not known at the setup of the experiments. In short, there were many hurdles (in science this is usually the case, but setbacks are rarely included in smoothly written academic journal articles). Indeed, Cayley needed stamina and a clear focus on the details, both in the experimental design and in its execution. Nine experiments were carried out and the experimental results by Dorothy Cayley are presented in the Table 2.1.

Please have a look at the data. For each experiment, there is a row of data that includes the number of bulbs planted, the description of the treatment, the total number of Bartigon plants which flowered, the number of breaks, and the percentage (number of breaks divided by the total plants flowered).

Take a couple of minutes to formulate two conclusions based on the data.

What are your two conclusions?

Indeed, the first conclusion is that "injections with filtrate" (treatment 3, 5, and 6) do not lead to breaking. The second conclusion is that all other treatments will lead to breaking, but with different degrees. The highest level of breaking is in experiment 1; the lowest level is in experiment 2. You also might have noticed that these experiments have a relatively low level of flowered plants compared to the number of bulbs planted—and you may wonder what is the reason for that. Further, the total number of bulbs in the experiment is relatively low.

Cayley formulated the results as follows:

The above results show that the percentage of "breaking" in Bartigon can be increased artificially on an average of 26 percent. During the course of one growing season by means of bringing the internal tissues of an "unbroken" bulb in contact with freshly cut living tissue from a "broken" bulb, when both are in

Table 2.1 "Breaking in Tulips" experiments

Experiment	No. of bulbs	Treatment	Total plants flowered	"Breaks"	%
1	50	Bulbs only plugged "broken" tissue	15	6 Slight	40.0
2	50	Bulbs with 1 lateral. Bulb and lateral plugged "broken" tissue	20	3 Slight	15.0
3	50	Lateral only plugged "broken" tissue	2	0	0
4	30	Bulbs wit 2 laterals. Bulb and 1 lateral only plugged "broken" tissue	9	2 Slight 1?	22.2
5	70	Bulbs only injected with filtrate	23	0	0
6	50	Bulbs with 1 lateral. Bulb and lateral injected with filtrate	23	0	0
7	60	Bartigon grafted "broken" Sulphur	47	13	27.6
8	30	Bartigon grafted "broken" Kroeschler	19	4	21
9	20	Bartigon grafted "broken" kaleidoscope	16	5	31.2
Total	410		174	33	19
Total[a]	240		126	33	26.3

Adapted from Cayley DM (1928) "Breaking" in Tulips, Annals of Applied Biology 15(4), p 538
[a]Not included the 50 untreated bulbs (experiment 3) and 120 bulbs with filtrate injections (experiment 5 and 6)

dormant condition. The degree of breaking appears to be proportional to the amount of infected tissue introduced, the bulbs plugged with small plugs of "broken" tissue showed only slight but quite definite "breaks"; whereas two bulbs, one "broken" and the other not, when cut vertically so as to leave the growing points intact, and the halves of each bulb tied together, produced much heavier "breaking".

She concluded that the "virus or enzyme infection" was sap-transmissible, probably transferred by an insect, and the degree of breaking was proportional to the amount of infected tissue introduced. The causality was made clear, but what transmitted the infection from a broken tulip to an unbroken tulip?

2.5   Mystery Solved

In 1928, the same year of Cayley's first paper, D. Atanasoff in Bulgaria was able to show that breaking could be induced in the tulip by needle inoculation with freshly expressed unfiltered sap from the shoots of narcissus and hyacinth affected with mosaic, a plant virus. In 1929, further experiments were carried out on Bartigon bulbs by A.W. McKenny Hughes at the John Innes institution.[19] Four types of aphids were placed on bulbs that were known to be broken. After colonizing the bulbs, the aphids were transferred to separate unplanted bulbs. Each bulb was covered with a lamp glass or glass tube with a muslin top. The results showed that self-breaking could be selectively transmitted by the green peach aphid or the peach-potato aphid—a small green aphid that is a pest for peach trees—and by the aphid that is found in dense colonies on the upper parts of the flower stem of wood avens and on the undersides of the leaves of chervil. Peach trees, wood avens, and chervil were commonly grown in seventeenth-century Holland. The transfer of the virus was non-persistent, meaning that the viruses were attached to the distal tip of the stylet in the aphid's mouthparts and were transferred to the next plant the insect fed on. The virus does not affect the seed that produces a bulb, only the bulb itself, its leaves and blooms, and its daughter offsets. Other results were that the pest *Anuraphis tulipae* (B. de Fonsc) is a definite vector in the bulb store but not on the growing plant and that at a certain stage of growth tulips ceased to be susceptible to the infection of the virus.[20]

The tulip breaking virus (TBV)—the official name—is one of the five plant viruses of the family Potyviridae that cause color-breaking of tulips. These viruses infect plants in only two genera of the family Liliaceae: tulips (*Tulipa*) and lilies (*Lilium*). The virus infects the bulb and causes the cultivar to "break" its lock on a single color. It results in intricate bars, stripes, streaks, featherings, or flame-line effects of different colors on the petals. Symptoms vary depending on the plant variety and the age at the time of the infection. Different types of color breaks depend on the variety of the tulip and the strain of the virus. Carolus Clusius would have loved to learn of this reason for the mysterious color changes he observed, and he would have been happy to know that even advanced scientists had struggled to find the answer.

2.6 Bulb Breeding

Interest in producing and selling tulip bulbs spread to more and more people in the Netherlands. It turned out that the area between Leiden and Haarlem—with a string of villages, including Oegstgeest, Voorhout, Noordwijk-Binnen, Sassenheim, Lisse, Hillegom, Heemstede, Overveen, Heemskerk, and Uitgeest—was very well equipped to grow bulbs in the open air. The west wind blew in from the North Sea, but it was actually the quality of the sandy soil that stimulated flower bulbs to grow so well. Bulbs do not grow well in wet soil. In sandy soil, rainwater drains easily, and the groundwater is deep in that region. Bulbs also like lime in the soil and the proximity to the sea meant there was a lot of shell dust to go around. If we go back around 11,000 years (why not?), global warming in the Holocene period (indeed already then) gradually caused the sea level to rise by 30–40 m, forming what we know today as the North Sea. Between 5000 and 2000 years ago, sand dunes formed in the area. Later the sea level declined and the area between the old sand dunes filled with peat, a brown deposit resembling soil that was formed by the partial decomposition of vegetation under wet conditions. The old sand dunes were excavated and the remaining sandy soil turned out to be ideal for growing tulip bulbs, probably because the soil conditions were quite similar to the original Turkish, Spanish, or Persian soil conditions. The soil was a mixture of white and black sand.

In the early spring, the soil was heavily fertilized and turned over. You might guess that the next step would be to start planting the bulbs, but that is not the case: one started with potatoes. After harvesting the potatoes (as we have seen, potatoes were also identified and categorized by Clusius), the tulip bulbs were planted in October. During winter the bulbs were covered to protect them from the cold winter conditions, and in February the bulbs started to bloom. In March and April—depending on the weather conditions (temperature, moisture)—the flower fields were in full bloom. When the bulbs finished flowering, the leaves were cut off, but the bulbs stayed in the ground and continued to grow until June. Around that time the bulbs were harvested and put in storage to be dried. These were in-house storage facilities or more advanced wooden barns with open windows where the sea wind would dry the bulbs. Finally, in August and September bulbs were inspected, graded, and packaged to be transported to foreign customers in countries around the world. It is peculiar that the soil cannot accommodate these bulbs every year—it must be 1 year on, 1 year off—and therefore the bulb growers need twice as much land to sustain their production volume.

As said before, the appointment of Carolus Clusius as professor of Botany at Leiden University was the beginning of the bulb industry in the Netherlands. Nowadays, the Dutch bulb industry produces around 8.5 billion flower bulbs every year, of which around 3 billion are tulip bulbs. If each tulip bulb is planted four inches apart, they would circle the globe at the equator seven times. (Clusius would have been utterly astonished at these numbers.) Next to tulips, the greatest bulb quantities are lilies, hyacinths, daffodils, gladioli, dahlias, and crocuses.

Today there are around 1500 bulb growers who specialize in one or more kinds of cultivars. The bulbs are sold to trading companies for export markets and local markets, to forcing companies that produce cut flowers, and to breeding companies that focus on product development, i.e., the design of new cultivars. The breeding of new cultivars has always been a very time-consuming, trial-and-error process, but it can yield highly desired colors, shapes, or other plant characteristics. For example, tulip breeders were unable to produce an entirely blue flower until recently. Breeding can also improve the bulb's growing capacity and resistance to diseases and mechanical processing.

The making of a new tulip cultivar is done by crossing two different tulips.[21] The pollen of one tulip (the father) is lubricated on the pistil of the other tulip (the mother). The pollen of the father germinates inward to the fruiting principle of the mother where fertilization takes place. The pistil gradually changes into a huge seed box containing hundreds of seeds. All these seeds are potentially new tulips and are harvested in the summer. Seed pods are stored and dried in the bulb shed and they are opened in the fall. All seeds are sown in bins and placed in a sheltered place where they are not bothered by the weather. Here all the energy of the seed can be used to develop into a mini tulip bulb called a tulip globule. The growth period lasts from autumn to the following summer.

In the summer, all newly developed globules are carefully removed from the bins. The harvest differs per container. Not all tulip seeds will develop into a new bulb. It can happen that out of one hundred seeds only one has grown into a globule, and not every cross produces a successful new cultivar. The one-year-old bulbs are planted outside in the ground for the first time in the fall. When the one-year-old tulips emerge in the spring, the growth looks like grass. It is not until the fifth year of the life of the tulip bulb that there will be a flower to show the result of the crossing. From this moment it is important to make a good selection. Breeding is "the art of throwing away." Seedlings develop in the fourth, fifth, and sixth year, and in the seventh year all seedlings are flowering and can be selected. From the eighth year until the fifteenth year it is about testing, propagation, promotion, marketing, and naming.

2.7   High Tech Genetics

Recently, I visited the Indoor AgTech Innovation Summit in New York City and was flabbergasted by the new breeding and artificial intelligence techniques that are being developed by startup companies. They combine research in genetics with machine learning and high-resolution video images, and, therefore, create a link between the genotype and the phenotype of flowers, plants, and crops.

The terms genotype and phenotype were coined in 1903 by Wilhelm Johannsen, a Danish botanist, plant physiologist, and geneticist. The genotype refers to the genetic makeup of an organism; in other words, it describes the complete set of genes of an organism. A gene is a small, sequence section of deoxyribonucleic acid (DNA) that codes for a molecule that has a function. DNA is composed of two chains that coil around each other to form a double helix carrying genetic instructions for the development, functioning, growth, and reproduction of all known organisms and many viruses. There are four chemical "letters" or nucleotides (A, T, C, and G) used to spell out all this genetic information in "words" of three letters each. An organism's genome is simply a list of the exact order of every single letter in this DNA instruction code. The phenotype refers to the actual physical features shown by the organism. The phenotype is the result of the genotype, the environment, and interactions of the genotype with the environment.

The search for genomes started with the Human Genome Project, an international scientific research project with the goal of determining the sequence of nucleotide base pairs that make up human DNA, and of identifying and mapping all of the genes of the human genome from both a physical and a functional standpoint.[22] The project started in 1990 and the human genome was determined in 2003. It turned out that the human genome consists of around three billion nucleotides or "letters."

After mapping the human genome, other organisms were investigated with astonishing results. For example, what do you expect would have the largest genome?

You may be surprised to learn that "a rare Japanese flower named *Paris japonica* sports an astonishing 149 billion base pairs, making it 50 times the size of a human genome—and the largest genome ever found."[23] However, bigger is not always better. The researchers warn that "big genomes tend to be a liability: plants with lots of DNA have more trouble tolerating pollution and extreme climatic extinctions—and they grow more slowly than plants with less DNA, because it takes so long to replicate their genome."

A consortium of three leading Dutch organizations, BaseClear, Dümmen Orange, and Generade, announced on October 31, 2017 in Leiden, the city of Carolus Clusius, that they identified the DNA sequence of the tulip genome.[24] The tulip genome contains large sections of identical DNA which occur extremely frequently. By isolating these sections in an intact form and reading them with the help of a DNA sequencing technology, so that the ends have a unique DNA sequence, it is possible to map the entire genome. The genome size of the very common garden tulip *Tulipa gesneriana* is "estimated at approximately 34 giga base pairs, nearly 11 times larger than that of humans." The tulip genome reveals "how the DNA determines the characteristics of a tulip. DNA patterns that are linked to desirable characteristics will soon be used in advanced breeding so that these characteristics can be combined to give new, improved varieties. With this knowledge, new tulip varieties which are resistant to common diseases can be developed faster and in a more targeted way. This will also reduce the use of plant protection products." Hans van den Heuvel, Director of Research and Development at Dümmen Orange, explained, "The tulip genome makes the human genome look tiny: the entire human genome fits into one tulip chromosome. With the technology that was available at the turn of the century, this job would have taken over 100 years, an impossible task. But now we can do it in a matter of days. Data analysis is in full swing and there is no doubt that it will produce information which will transform tulip breeding, making it faster, more predictive and above all 'greener' because we will focus on varieties that can be grown sustainably."

Another breakthrough was reported in bulb propagation by the Dutch consortium of IribovSBW and Dümmen Orange.[25] The newly developed laboratory-based propagation process uses starting material from one single tulip bulb. After about one year, the tissue culture-derived small bulbs were allowed to further develop in a soil mixture to get to bulb sizes ready for flowering. In the spring of 2018, successful flowering trials took place in the open field at the Hobaho Ornamental Crops Trial Centre in Lisse, the Netherlands. The tissue culture method increases the multiplication rate of a single tulip bulb from three to several thousand per year. This ground-breaking result brings new opportunities for the tulip sector.

Once the DNA sequence of the tulip genome is known, one can develop and link genomic selection with phenotype prediction. For example, Computomics, a startup company in Tübingen, Germany, predicts phenotypes from genome-wide markers and offers CropScore, a large-scale phenotyping service.[26] In a greenhouse, seeds or bulbs are planted, and CropScore uses cameras to capture detailed video images to monitor flowers or plants. The physical features can be detected in real time. For a client, "15,000 plants were monitored in detail 24 h a day and germination rate, root growth, biomass, and necrotic tissue were recorded year over year." Automated image analysis with machine learning technology can speed up the seed selection process dramatically. Both Carolus Clusius and Dorothy Cayley would be very impressed.

Notes

1. For an overview of the formation of the Dutch Republic and the Dutch Golden Age (seventeenth century), see Israel J (1998).
2. Indeed, the citizens of Leiden earned a reputation for perseverance. The Spanish had surrounded the city, but it was protected by huge defensive walls and low-lying boglands that could be easily flooded by opening dikes and letting the seawater in. To free the city, a plan was set in motion. It began with breaking the dikes and allowing the sea to flood the low-lying land, which would force the Spaniards to fall back as the water advanced. A rebel fleet of more than 200 small vessels stocked with provisions and manned by 2500 Dutch seamen was prepared to sail for the city. The wind was against them, however, which caused the water to flow back to the sea. The water level was too low for the vessels to sail. During these months of the siege, 6000 citizens, half of the population of Leiden, died of infectious diseases, such as the black plague, or of malnutrition. Eventually, a storm set in, causing the water level to rise and allowing the small vessels to sail once again. Faced with the rising water and the coming Dutch vessels, General Valdez ordered a retreat in the night of October 2, 1574. The sound of a terrible crash convinced the Spanish army that another dike had been broken, and they hastened their departure. In fact, part of the city wall of Leiden had fallen, having been eroded by seawater. The Spanish army retreated, unaware that the city was completely vulnerable to attack. The next day, the Dutch rebels arrived with herring and white bread to feed the citizens of Leiden. According to legend, an orphan boy went to explore the vacated camp of the Spanish army and found a pot full of *hutspot*—a carrot, onion, and beef stew with pepper, nutmeg, ginger, eggs, and white bread—that the Spaniards had left in their haste to escape the rising waters. So, that evening the citizens also feasted on *hutspot*, which remains a popular Dutch meal to this day.

   Interestingly, the *hutspot* recipe was already in 1611 in use as *uspot* in a famous Spanish cookbook by the chef of the Spanish King Filips II, in Martinez Montiño F (2015). Thanks to Nico van Hemert for suggesting the source of the *hutspot* story and recipe.

   For the role of Leiden in the Dutch revolt, see Dash M (1999).
3. The current king of the Netherlands, Willem-Alexander of Orange, graduated at Leiden University, established by William of Orange, one of his ancestors. Another student was the painter Rembrandt van Rijn. He was born in Leiden and registered at Leiden University on May 20, 1620, at the age of 14. He studied—for some time—literature and theology.
4. The unique characteristics of the Dutch republic that was established around 1600 are in Goldgar A (2007). With quotes: "the foundation" (p. 9), and "both trade and immigration" (p. 9).

5. Deirdre N. McCloskey with her monumental work (in total 1974 pages) published in a trilogy. McCloskey D (2006, 2010, 2016). With quotes: "You honor me" (p. 22), "You accord to me" (p. 21), "starting in Holland" (p. 23), "the average income" (p. 24), "the world average" (p. 6), "Since 1800" (p. 7), "with bourgeois dignity" (p. XXII).

I attended a keynote of professor Deirdre N. McCloskey in the Smyrna Church in Gothenburg on Friday July 8, 2011. The crowd were participants of the 27th EGOS colloquium that was held in Sweden. PhD candidates and professors from around the world discussed their latest research results on organizational theory. Her keynote speech was entitled *"Bourgeois Dignity: Why Words Mattered to the Modern Economic World"* and it was one of the most brilliant addresses I have ever seen. She began with the question "who has some royal blood?" (As you might know the Netherlands is a small country, everybody is linked to everybody within 16 generations, and there is enough evidence of many bastard children from the royal family.) I raised my hand. On the other side of the church, another attendee also raised a hand. She was, probably, directly related to the royal family of Sweden. Anyway, Professor McCloskey made clear that the power of the royals, around 1500, started to crumble and was over. "Your time is gone" she said as she pointed to the two "royals" in the audience. She continued vividly with the development of the society and economy where a fundamental transformation was on its way.

6. McCloskey refers to Holland, but Holland was only one of the seven provincial states of the Republic of the Seven United Netherlands. The other states are Friesland, Gelderland, Groningen, Overijssel, Utrecht, and Zeeland.

7. Work and life of Carolus Clusius is based on several sources Dash M (1999); Goldgar A (2007).

8. Letters and correspondents in a detailed study by Egmond F (2016). The correspondence with Charles de Saint Omer in "The Garden of Europe: Botany as a Courtly Fashion in the Southern Netherlands," pp. 14–18, with Marie de Brimeu in "Female Experts: Elegance and Rivalry" pp. 59–63; with Johan van Hoghelande in "Town and Gown: Leiden and the Convergence of European Cultural Traditions," pp. 164–169; and "Conclusion," pp. 209–219, with quotes "isolated genius" (p. 5 and 219), "from England to Hungary" (p. 6), "he could be in touch" (p. 6), "The true monarch of flowers" (p. 1), "in a class of his own" (p. 164), "most famous market of Europe" (p. 11), "stayed for months" (p. 15), "A man not only" (p. 16), "not only an intelligent" (p. 59), "his patroness" (p. 49), "such as the persistent thefts" (p. 61), "but it seems to me" (p. 63), "a class of his own" (p. 164), "A man most diligent" (p. 164), "domestic" and "can only be" (p. 166–167), and "he had more than 2000 tulips," "one of the special sites," "quite a few visitors" (p. 167), "were pulling ropes" (p. 165), "how to take care" (p. 166), "I was glad" (p. 166), "collective

enterprise" (p. 209), "accurate description" (p. 215), "interested in scoops" (p. 217).

The respective role of Clusius and Saint Omer in Egmond F (2008), with quotes: "professional" (p. 14), "some 122 illustrations" (p. 16), "have been crucial" (p. 20), "one of warfare" (p. 20).

Based on Florike Egmonds' work the following summary provides a detailed insight in the correspondence of Carolus Clusius with Charles de Saint Omer (1533–1569), Marie de Brimeu (around 1550–1605), and Johan van Hoghelande (1546–1614).

By the 1560s, the Southern Netherlands was the unrivaled center of botanical and horticultural matters in all of Europe. Plants and flowers from all around the world were bought to this "most famous market of Europe," and were cultivated there, in spite of the adverse climate, but thanks to the hard work, diligence, and perseverance of the inhabitants. In what has been named Bruges humanism, many active patrons played a central role in developing the passion for gardening. One of them was the wealthy nobleman, Charles de Saint Omer, a patron and friend of Clusius. Saint Omer owned extensive gardens and parks, farms, mills, various feudal landholdings and rights, as well as a town house in Bruges. Little is known about his life prior to the mid-1560s. He had given up his military career because of his poor health. Upon retiring to his estate and castle in Moerkerke, close to Bruges, he devoted himself to the arts and sciences, in particular to the study of nature.

After Clusius' journey to Spain in 1564–1565 he visited Saint Omer and "stayed for months on end at the castle, where he saw various exotic substances, such as true cinnamon." In 1566, Clusius gave seeds of the Brazilian pepper to Saint Omer, who managed to cultivate a pepper plant in his garden, which even flowered in the autumn.

Saint Omer became famous with the *Libri Picturati A18–30* (as it is called) as one of the most remarkable European collections of watercolors depicting *naturalia* of the sixteenth century. There is sufficient evidence that Saint Omer brought the core of the collection together probably between 1562 or 1563 and 1568, with assistance and advice from Clusius. The albums had been commissioned by Saint Omer, whom Clusius described as:

> A man not only most expert in matters of plants and who had the plants themselves, birds, and quadrupeds depicted with outstanding skill in lively colors, but also very interested in the nature of all sorts of wonderful things.

The collection includes more than 1400 watercolors of flowers, plants, fungi, animals, birds, and insects. A considerable number of watercolors were painted by Jacques van den Corenhuyse. The watercolors were used as "documentation" of plants grown in Saint Omer's own garden and of the birds and some "curious" animals and as a kind of home encyclopedia including pictures, copies of pamphlets of exotic plants and animals sent to Saint Omer,

Clusius, or one of their friends. The annotations in the "professional" hand on the group of 625 botanical watercolors were probably made by Clusius. Furthermore, "some 122 illustrations in Clusius' printed works are directly based in the *Libri Picturati* collection."

Actually, Saint Omer's albums of watercolor paintings were discovered in the 1970s in the Jagiellonian Library in Kraków, Poland. An annotated version was published in 2008. Some factors "have been crucial in hiding the origins of the collection from the sight of modern scholars" for more than 400 years. The early death of Saint Omer—at the age of 36—prevented him from completing and possibly from publishing his album. The context of the 1560s in the Southern Netherlands was "one of warfare and plundering, of incipient civil war, and religious strife." During those times it was reported that collections, printing presses, and gardens were destroyed. Upon Saint Omer's death, his estate changed hands, property was divided and sold, and somehow, the albums ended up in an archive in Poland. Meanwhile, because so many records and collections were destroyed during that period in the Netherlands, anyone interested in Clusius' references to the unpublished albums might have had good reason to assume they were no longer in existence. For the time being, the library in Poland did not know how the albums originated until the 1970s, when the connection back to Saint Omer was discovered.

Forty-two women were in direct contact with Clusius, and 25 of them were either friends or relatives. Clusius never married and there is no evidence that he had affairs, lovers, or children. Nearly all of the women wrote to him about plants and gardening, and sent him packages with bulbs, seeds, cuttings, or pictures of plants. These packages were transported via a postal network of post riders, sometimes using the faster diplomatic post channel. Marie de Brimeu was Clusius's best known and lifelong friend. Twenty-seven of her letters to Clusius have been preserved, all but one from the period 1592–1605. She was a very enthusiastic grower of tulips and other rare flowers and shrubs. She created several superb gardens, both in the Southern and Northern Netherlands, and she corresponded with a number of plant lovers and gardeners. Brimeu's letters show her to have been "not only an intelligent and resolute, sometimes imperious, melancholy and probably quite headstrong woman, but also a cultured one who wrote a beautiful and elegant French." She openly acted as "his patroness – pulling strings at the court of The Hague to get Clusius appointed at the University of Leiden – she never patronized him in her letters, and always wrote to him in terms of great respect and friendship."

Brimeu lived a turbulent life in line with the turbulent war with Spain. She was born into an aristocratic family in the Southern Netherlands and she grew up in the Bruges and Malines area. She inherited the county of Megen in 1572 from an uncle and married twice. The county of Megen was a

Catholic enclave separated from, but dependent on, the Dutch republic. (As a side note: Around 1620, one of my ancestors, Jan van Heck, lived in the county of Megen, in a small village called Berghem near Oss, in the province of North Brabant).

Brimeu was a supporter of Protestantism and the Dutch Revolt. She converted her (second) husband to Protestantism, but the conversion did not last. She left him and lived alone as a wealthy and independent woman. From 1590 to 1593, she stayed in Leiden in a house with a garden adjacent to the plot where the first botanical garden in the Netherlands would be established a few years later. Shortly, after Clusius arrived in Leiden in October 1593, she was invited by the Dutch Estates General to move to the Hague, and she later moved to Liège where she died in April 1605. She was buried in Megen.

Several things about gardening can be gathered from Brimeu's letters— "such as the persistent thefts from both her own and Clusius' gardens, the sending of seeds, rare plants and plant portraits back and forth between them, the location of the Leiden garden she put at his disposal, and the importance she attached to gardening." She took enormous pleasure in gardening and tried to become an expert in it, with the help of Clusius and others. She even had thought to model her garden in terms of colour variety upon a tapestry sent to her by Clusius and she also considered having a painting made of her Leiden garden, so that Clusius—then still in Frankfurt—could have a better idea of it and give her more specific advice. She was interested, for instance, in color changes from one generation of tulips or other bulbs to another, and hoped that experience over time would teach her more about this phenomenon: "but is seems to me that there are some that have changed colour into another kind than last year and I did not know at all that this happened, but experience teaches many things" (letter, May 24, 1593).

Johan van Hoghelande was, as said before, in a class of his own. One of his frequent visitors described him as:

> A man most diligent in making notes about plants, who had devoted himself completely to these matters, both because of his deafness which forces him to abstain from social intercourse and because he does not have any public or private business to occupy him (letter, February 19, 1591).

Hoghelande was a wealthy landowner from Zealand. He was born in Middelburg, which at the time was an important port city with sea connections to the Middle East and the Far East regions. These connections were used to obtain exotic plants and bulbs. He left around 1580, probably on account of the war, and moved to Leiden. He remained a Catholic which was possible in the religiously tolerant, but dominantly Protestant, city of Leiden. There he owned one "domestic" garden in the city and one outside Leiden which "can only be classified as an impressive, botanical garden where he grew rare plants and experimented." There is evidence that in 1600 "he had more than 2000 tulips" in his gardens. His garden was "one of the special sites of Leiden" and Hoghelande mentioned in his letters "quite a few visitors who came to see his garden, some even from abroad."

Both Hoghelande and Brimeu "were pulling ropes behind the scene in Leiden to get Clusius appointed there." Once Clusius arrived in Leiden, in 1593, they had many conversations and discussions. Clusius communicated with the deaf Hoghelande by writing on the tablets that were carried by the latter. In terms of botanical and gardening knowledge the exchange between Hoghelande and Clusius covered a wide field. Clusius sent Hoghelande "rare plants and a few exotica: from tulip seeds and bulbs (marked by labels and color marks on their paper wrapping), tubers of cyclamen, and 'leontopeta-lum', to seed of Persian peonies, an opuntia cactus and American potatoes." By June 1591 Hoghelande had five potato plants growing in his garden. More advice about "how to take care of plants that had come from a very different climate" was welcome:

> I was glad that you gave me advice on how to take care of the *papas ameri-canas*. I wish you had also done the same for the laurocerasus [Prunus laurocerasus, cherry laurel]. Because we often take so much care of our rare plants that the same thing happens to us that happens to a monkey with its young, for I fear that is what happened to my *charam*. For it needed cool conditions instead of hot ones (letter, June 9, 1591).

9. Egmond F (2008).
10. The most important works of Carolus Clusius are: Clusius C (1576, 1583, 1601).
11. Clusius' observations on tulips has been translated and annotated by Van Dijk W (1951). With quotes: "Among these" (p. 5), "the exotic plant" (p. 13), "Of the middle-sized" (pp. 40–41), "For I had, in the year 1585" (pp. 16–17).
12. A segment is a part or subdivision of an organ, e.g., a petal is a segment of the corolla. The stamen is the male organ of a flower, consisting (usually) of a stalk called the filament and a pollen-bearing head called the anther. The stalk is the supporting structure of an organ, usually narrower in diameter than the organ itself. The claw is a narrow, stalk-like, basal portion of a petal, sepal, or bract.
13. In the early seventeenth century, the church was attended by the Pilgrims, who left Leiden in 1620 and traveled via Southampton, United Kingdom, to board the Mayflower, sailed to America, and settled in Plymouth Colony.
14. The work and life of Gregor Mendel are in Wikipedia https://en.wikipedia.org/wiki?curid=12562. Accessed 24 Nov 2020.
    With the quotes "pea plant experiments," "seven characteristics," "when a true-breeding yellow pea," and "the terms 'recessive' and 'dominant'".

15. The paper by Mendel GJ (1865).
16. Bateson W (1902).
17. The history of the John Innes Centre including the role of William Bateson and Dorothy Cayley is from "The history of plant science and microbial science at the John Innes Centre," John Innes Centre, 1900–2019, with the quote: "If the Quick Fund were used."

    https://www.jic.ac.uk/about-us/history-of-plant-microbial-science-at-john-innes-centre/

    Accessed 2 Sept 2020

    Another pioneer at the center was Dr. Rose Scott-Moncrieff. Scott-Moncrieff went on to publish a series of ground-breaking papers in the 1930s identifying some of the enzymes in the biochemical pathways of pigment biosynthesis in flowering plants and the genetic basis for these biochemical activities. Her work was recognized as fundamental in establishing the emerging field of biochemical genetics.
18. Breakthrough work on breaking in tulips was published by Cayley DM (1928, 1932). With quotes: "It is a well-known fact" (p. 529), "Thus the active agent" (p. 529), "With the object of finding" (p. 531), "The above results" (p. 536), Bulb illustrations (p. 532), and Table (p. 538).
19. Atanasoff D (1928).

    McKenny Hughes AW (1930, 1931, 1934).
20. McWhorter FP (1938).
21. The traditional breeding strategy is from the tulip breeder and grower company Ligthart Bloembollen. https://www.ligthartbloembollen.nl/veredeling/ With the quote: "the art of throwing away." Accessed 3 Sept 2020.
22. The Human Genome Project in Green ED, Guyer MS, and National Human Genome Research Institute (2011, February 10).
23. The gen and genome explanation and the largest genome in Pennisi E (2010, October 7). ScienceShot: Biggest Genome Ever, with quote: a rare Japanese flower, *Sciencemag*. https://www.sciencemag.org/news/2010/10/scienceshot-biggest-genome-ever

    Barnett J (2019, May 6).
24. The tulip genome project is in Van der Sar M (2017, October 31). With quotes "estimated at approximately," "how the DNA determines," and "The tulip genome.".
25. A new method to significantly speed up the propagation of tulip bulbs in Straver N (2018, July 26).
26. The genomic selection and phenotype prediction as a service are based on: Prediction of Phenotypes and Scalable Phenotyping with CropScore, with the quote "15,000 plants were." Computomics (2019).

References

Atanasoff D (1928) Mosaic disease of flower bulb plants. Bull Soc Bot Bulgarie, II

Barnett J (2019) Who's got the biggest genome of them all?, That's Life Science, May 6. http://thatslifesci.com/2019-05-06-Biggest-genome-of-them-all-JBarnett/

Bateson W (1902) Mendel's principles of heredity: a defence. Cambridge University Press, Cambridge

Cayley DM (1928) "Breaking" in tulips. Ann Appl Biol 15(4):529–539

Cayley DM (1932) "Breaking" in tulips. II. Ann Appl Biol 19(2):153–172

Clusius C (1576) Rariorum aliquot stirpium per Hispanias observatarum historia. Christoffel Plantin, Antwerp.

Clusius C (1583) Rariorum aliquot Stirpium, per Pannoniam, Austriam, & Vicinas Quasdam Provincias Observatarum Historia. Christoffel Plantin, Antwerp

Clusius C (1601) Rariorum plantarum historia. Christoffel Plantin, Antwerp

Computomics (2019) Prediction of phenotypes and scalable phenotyping with CropScore. https://computomics.com/. Accessed 2 Sept 2020

Dash M (1999) Tulipomania: The story of the World's Most coveted flower and the extraordinary passions it aroused. Three River Press, New York City

De Koning J, Van Uffelen G, Zemanek A, Zemanek B (eds) (2008) Drawn after nature, the complete botanical watercolours of the 16th-century Libri Picturati. KNNV, Zeist

Egmond F (2008) The making of the Libri Picturati A16-30. In: De Koning J, Van Uffelen G, Zemanek A, Zemanek B (eds) Drawn after nature, the complete botanical watercolours of the 16th-century Libri Picturati. KNNV, Zeist, pp 13–21

Egmond F (2016) The world of Carolus Clusius: natural history in the making, 1550–1610, perspectives in economic and social history, vol 6. Routledge, London

Goldgar A (2007) Tulipmania: money, honor, and knowledge in the Dutch Golden Age. The University of Chicago Press, Chicago

Gray SM, Banerje N (1999) Mechanisms of arthropod transmission of plant and animal viruses. Microbiol Mol Biol Rev 63:128–148

Green ED, Guyer MS, National Human Genome Research Institute (2011) Charting a course for genomic medicine from base pairs to bedside. Nature, 470, February 10.

Israel J (1998) The Dutch Republic: its rise, greatness, and fall 1477–1806, Oxford history of early modern Europe. Clarendon Press, Oxford

McCloskey D (2006) The bourgeois virtues: ethics for an age of commerce. The University of Chicago Press, Chicago

McCloskey D (2010) Bourgeois dignity: why economics can't explain the modern world. The University of Chicago Press, Chicago

McCloskey D (2016) Bourgeois equality: how ideas, not capital or institutions, enriched the world. The University of Chicago Press, Chicago

McKenny Hughes AW (1930) Aphis as a possible vector of breaking in tulip species. Ann Appl Biol 17(1):36–42

McKenny Hughes AW (1931) Aphis as vectors of 'Breaking' in tulips. Ann Appl Biol 18(1):16–29

McKenny Hughes AW (1934) Aphis as vectors of breaking in tulips II. Ann Appl Biol 21(1):112–119

McWhorter FP (1938) The antithetic virus theory of tulip-breaking. Ann Appl Biol 25(2):254–270

Meerman J (ed) (2015) De Kleine Geschiedenis van de Nederlandse Keuken, Ambo Anthos, Amsterdam

Mendel GJ (1865) Versuche über Pflanzen-Hybriden (Experiments concerning plant hybrids). In: Verhandlungen des naturforschenden Vereines in Brünn [Proceedings of the Natural History Society of Brünn] IV, pp 3–47

Pennisi E (2010). ScienceShot: biggest genome ever, with quote: a rare Japanese flower. Sciencemag, October 7. https://www.sciencemag.org/news/2010/10/scienceshot-biggest-genome-ever. Accessed 2 Sept 2020

Straver N (2018) Breakthrough in tulip bulb propagation. Dümmen Orange, July 26. https://www.dummenorange.com/site/en/news-archive/detail/breakthrough-in-tulip-bulb-propagation/en-111-271. Accessed 2 Sept 2020

Van der Sar M (2017) Dutch consortium unravels first tulip genome. Dümmen Orange, October 31. https://www.dummenorange.com/site/en/news-archive/detail/dutch-consortium-unravels-first-tulip-genome/en-111-224. Accessed 2 Sept 2020

Van Dijk W (1951) A treatise on tulips, printed for the associated bulb growers of Holland. John Enschedé en Zonen, Haarlem

3

Glass City

3.1 Urban Landscape

The twenty-six minutes journey from Schiphol Airport to Rotterdam on the intercity direct train offers spectacular views. From your seat you can see airplanes landing at Schiphol Airport and you can watch as the high-speed train from Paris races along its tracks. Here and there in the greenish landscape, old windmills regulate the water level in the lower land and new windmills provide electricity to the grid. In the last part of the journey near Zoetermeer, the landscape becomes more and more industrial with long stretches of glasshouses reaching very close to the train tracks. Some of the glass roofs are whitened to reflect the radiation of the sun. The windows of some of the glasshouses are wide open, as if to wave to the passengers as their train rushes past. The open windows allow the colder outside air to lower the temperature in the glasshouse. Adjacent to the glasshouses, cylindrical water tanks store rainwater that was collected from the glass roofs. The glass city covers a very large area with the municipalities of Westland, Midden-Delfland, Pijnacker-Nootdorp, Lansingerland, Zuidplas, and Waddinxveen. You might wonder how these glasshouses work and why they are here within the urban landscape of Amsterdam, the Hague, Rotterdam, and Utrecht, called the *Randstad*.

Let us explore the world of the Dutch glass city.

3.2 Orangeries

As we have seen, Carolius Clusius was instrumental in setting up the Hortus botanicus at Leiden University when he was appointed as prefect in 1593, together with Dirk Cluyt (1546–1598), an apothecary from Delft, followed by the physician Petrus Paauw (1564–1617) after Cluyt passed away.[1] Paauw, who "already taught medical botany, acted as perfect of the *hortus* and also took care of the on-the-spot teaching of medicinal plants," and the hortus became the center of botanical research. Initially, the board of the university wanted to establish a *hortus medicus* with a focus on medicinal herbs, but gradually Clusius, Cluyt, and Pauw built a *hortus botanicus* into "a botanical garden which included rare plants from various parts of Europe and the Levant as well as some living exotica from other continents." The garden was designed in a renaissance style with four quadrants (in Latin: *quadrae*), each divided into long, small beds (*areae*), and each bed divided with numbered boxes (*areolae*). The first garden was small (about 31 meter by 40 meter), consisted of around 1400 boxes, and contained 1060 different species of which about one-third were medicinal. The set of four quadrae was "surrounded by beds along the walls of the garden." By 1594, the garden was ready and Clusius presented a plan to the board of the university, including an inventory with 1585 items, the *Index Stirpium*. Tulips were "amongst Clusius's favorite plants; no less than 216 of the 1585 items were plants with bulbs. Two beds were entirely devoted to tulips, containing not only early and late tulips of all kinds and colours, but also '*Tulipae selectorum generum a me collectae*'." The detailed plan of the garden at that time shows "a true plantman's garden, with low irises along one path, *Hepatica* and *Primula* at the heads and feet of the long and narrow plant beds, and a jumble of spring and summer bulbs in some of the beds. Roses, peonies (*Paeonia*), irises (*Iris*), tulips (*Tulipa*), composites (*Asteraceae*), umbellifers (*Apiaceae*), *Boraginaceae* and ferns were planted together."

In 1601, a stone building, the *ambulacrum,* was constructed. It is a covered gallery cum conservatory that was running on one side of the garden, where "potted plants could be protected from inclement weather and many exotic *naturalia* and *artificialia* were on show." The only surviving tree from that period "is the *Laburnum*, allegedly planted in that same year."

Clusius urged the Dutch East India Company (VOC) to collect tropical plants and (dried) plant specimens from the Indies, but his request did not lead immediately to a large influx of tropical plants. Often these were collected by doctors stationed at trading posts, who were looking for edible and medicinal species and were amazed by the variety and exotic flora of these regions. Early additions to the garden included cinnamon, peppers, and aloe, among others. Later under the directorship of Herman Boerhaave (1668–1738) many tropical and subtropical plants from South Africa, Asia, and Japan were received and catalogued.

The first glasshouse in the Hortus appeared around 1680, because many tropical plants could only survive in a glasshouse where they could be sheltered from the cold and wet climate in the Netherlands.[2] A hortus map of 1719 showed several small glasshouses, the first of these were heated with peat. The monumental Orangery was built between 1740 and 1744.[3] After 1777, several small glasshouses were built in the garden. The Victoria glasshouse was opened in 1801. In this cast-iron and round glasshouse with an onion-shaped roof, "many shades of green and a variety of leaves form the backdrop for a diversity in flowers, orchids, exotic arums, and the Victoria amazonica." Victoria amazonica has a circular green leaf and thrives in the Amazon River and Brazil. Victoria amazonica flowered in July 1872 for the first time in the Hortus. Legend has it that the Victoria amazonica only flowers once a year, but that is not true. If all the requirements are met, in terms of temperature, light, and humidity, the plant will form a new flower approximately every seventh or eighth night, usually in June, July, or August. Tropical orchids, ferns, cactuses, palms, and bromelia were kept in separate glasshouses. In 1937, the construction of the current glasshouse complex started, containing several glasshouses and different climate zones. These glasshouses were heated with coal. Underneath one of the glasshouses was a special room to keep the coal, which was delivered by boats. In 1965, coal was replaced by oil and a big tank was placed underground for this purpose. In harsh winters, up to 200,000 liters of oil were spent on heating, which proved to be quite costly during the oil crisis in the 1970s. The glasshouse complex was renovated again in 1983, when the roofs were replaced by synthetic material, the heating transitioned to gas, and all the fuel and water lines were placed above ground for easier access and maintenance. Due to an increasing number of visitors, the Winter garden was renovated and reopened in September 2019. A walkway was created that visitors will use to view the plant collection from above and a balcony was constructed so that visitors can view the Orangerie, the tropical glasshouse complex, and the ancient trees.

3.3   Flowering Plants

The short life cycle of plants is intriguing and complex. The purpose of glass-houses is to create optimal conditions for the development and growth of plants. It is important to distinguish between the phases of a plant's *growth* and *development*. Growth has to do with the increase in size, length, area, or weight of the plant. The main factors that will contribute to growth are light and carbon dioxide. Keep in mind that plants consume carbon dioxide. Development has to do with the initiation of new organs on the plant (e.g., leaves or flowers), and it indicates the transition from one phase to the next in the life cycle. It is defined as "the systematic movement along the genetically programmed sequence of events during the life cycle, of which the main influencing factor is temperature".[4]

Flowering plants are the most advanced and widespread, because they attract pollinators and spread seeds. The major stages of the flower life cycle are "the seed, germination, growth, reproduction, pollination, and seed spreading stages".[5] The plant life cycle starts with the seed stage. Every seed holds a miniature plant called the embryo. It stores food to sustain the plant when it produces its first leaves. The seed also has the beginning of a root system. When a seed falls on the ground, it needs warmth and water in order to germinate (also called sprouting), and some seeds need light: this is the germination phase. After a few days in the soil, the seed absorbs water and swells until its coat splits. The stem pushes through the soil toward the light along with its first tiny leaves. The tiny root pushes down toward water and nutrients. Soon the initial leaves fall off and the first true leaves start to emerge. The growth phase has begun.

It is crucial that the seed is planted in the right place and at the right time and that the plant can produce its own food. The process of food production is called *photosynthesis*. Plants contain chloroplast in the leaves which convert the energy from the sunlight, carbon dioxide, and water into sugars, which they use as food. You might remember, from high school, the following chemistry formula that captures the photosynthesis: $6\ CO_2 + 6\ H_2O \rightarrow C_6H_{12}O_6 + 6\ O_2$. C stands for carbon, O for oxygen, and H for hydrogen. The numbers indicate the number of atoms of each element. Under the condition of sunlight (or artificial light) 6 atoms of carbon dioxide (CO_2) and 6 atoms of water (H_2O) are transformed into 1 atom of sugar ($C_6H_{12}O_6$) and 6 atoms of oxygen (O_2). The photosynthesis formula is the most important formula of all plant life.

Plants store the sugars in their roots and stems. The root system continues to develop and anchor the plant in the ground, and growing root hairs will help the plant to better absorb water and nutrients. The stem grows longer toward the sun and transports water and food between the roots and the leaves. Plants perform an amazing act of lifting themselves up toward the sun (or artificial light).[6] Sugars and starches are changed into energy used to make new plant growth. New leaves grow from the top of the stem. After a while, flower buds develop. Some plants will flower within days, but others will take months or years. In the reproduction phase the bud opens and inside is a tiny but complete flower. The sepals look like little green leaves at the base. The flower is the sexually reproductive part of the plant.[7] The petals of the flower are often very noticeable, brightly colored, and strongly scented in order to attract pollinators. The female part of the flower is "called the pistil and has four parts: stigma, style, ovary, and ovules. The male part of the flower is called stamen and consists of the long filament and the anther, where pollen is made. In the center of the flower, there is a long slender tube called the style." On top of the style is the stigma that may be sticky, hairy, or shaped in a way that it helps to better trap pollen. Once the pollen is trapped "it travels down the style to the rounded part at the base, called the ovary, where eggs are waiting to be fertilized. The fertilized eggs become seeds in this stage of the flower life cycle. In fruit producing plants, the ovary ripens and becomes fruit. Some flowers have only male parts, and some have only female parts. In others, the male and female structures are far apart." In the pollination phase, "insects, birds, animals, wind, water, or other pollinators carry the pollen from the male flowers or the male parts to the female flowers or female parts. Without pollinators, there would be no seeds or new plants in these plant species. Even flowers that can self-pollinate benefit from being fertilized by pollen from a different plant, called cross-pollination, because this will result in stronger plants." There are different strategies to seduce pollinators: brightly colored petals, strong smell, nectar, and pollen. Pollen can stick to the legs and wings of insects that go from flower to flower for nectar and pollen. Pollen can stick to the fur of animals or the clothes of humans. It can be caught by the wind and carried to other flowers. The final stage of the life cycle is the seed spreading stage. Seeds can be scattered by the wind, animals may bring seeds to other places, or humans may spread seeds by planting gardens. Once the seed falls to the ground, the plant cycle starts all over again.

3.4 Glasshouses

Entering a glasshouse is exciting: the temperature is mostly hot and humid. It will remind you of the climate of a tropical country. All over the world, glasshouses are built to protect crops, increase productivity, and make more efficient use of water, light, energy, and fertilizer. When a crop is sheltered, the whole internal climate will differ from outside conditions. Let us explore the Dutch glass city that is home to Jac.Oudijk Gerbera's, a modern glasshouse firm; see Fig. 3.1.

The Oudijk family is situated in Moerkapelle, in the Dutch province of South Holland.[8] The directors are the brothers Dirk-Jan and Laurens Oudijk and with their team they produce mini gerbera all year round. The gerbera is a flower plant of the Asteraceae – the daisy family – and named after the German botanist and medical doctor Traugott Gerber (1710–1743). Gerbera is native to tropical regions in South Africa, Africa, and Asia. The first scientific description was made by J.D. Hooker in 1889 when the *Gerbera jamesonii* was described. Gerbera is also commonly known as the African daisy. The breeding of gerberas started at the end of the nineteenth century in Cambridge, England, when two South African species were crossed into a hybrid, today known as Gerbera hybrida. Nowadays, Gerbera is in the top 5 of the most traded flowers worldwide. Gerbera species bear a large capitulum with striking two-lipped ray florets in yellow, orange, white, pink, or red colors.

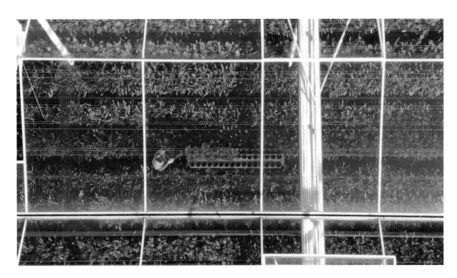

Fig. 3.1 A view from above into Jac. Oudijk's glasshouse https://www.jacoudijk.nl/videos With permission by Jac. Oudijk Gerbera's

The capitulum, which has the appearance of a single flower, is actually composed of hundreds of individual flowers. The flower heads can be as small as 7 cm (Gerbera mini "Harly") in diameter up to 12 cm (Gerbera "Golden Serena") or even 15 cm. At Jac.Oudijk Gerbera's they specialized in Germinis, the little sister of the Gerbera. They produce 61 varieties of Germinis in many different colors. In 2014, they entered into an consortium with sixty other growers under a new brand label called Decorum Plants & Flowers to ensure the quality, reliability, and sustainability of their flower products and communicate that message to their customers (exporters and retailers) and the customers of the customers (the end consumers).

The two glasshouses are impressive. In total there are seven hectares full of long stretches of different varieties of Germinis. These are flower plants with stems of around one meter. Jac.Oudijk Gerbera's provided their products via a web shop that has direct links to buyers. Its financial transactions are processed via the Floriday platform of Royal FloraHolland. As a grower Jac. Oudijk Gerbera's is a member of the Royal FloraHolland cooperative and the important requirement for members is to process all transactions (direct sales and auction sales) via the grower cooperative. At the web shop potential buyers can review and order Germini products. Around 70–85% of the production is picked in an order-driven way. The remaining part of the production will be sold via the auctions of Royal FloraHolland (and will be discussed in Chap. 4).

Early in the morning the orders come in and the order picking list is made of the incoming orders and demanded products per order. There will be two order picking rounds in the morning. The first one started at 9:30 AM. The products for each order were picked manually. The employees walked next to the Germini beds and picked and cut the best Germinis. These Germinis were put in cone-shaped, vertical metal cylinders of electric, robotized cars. This logistical system was a crucial component for the overall success of the glasshouse company. Flexibility, speed, and reliability were the key words for the adoption of this logistical system. The individual electric cars are fast – they drive 4 km per hour and are able to drive in 4 minutes from the picking areas to the packaging and control area. The cars followed an induction route that is built in the floor of the glasshouse; see Fig. 3.2.

Computer chips are also built in to be used for regulating the traffic of the 60 electric cars. There are buffer lanes where the cars can be stored. From the buffer lanes the car will drive to one of the five processing areas. The car knows how to drive to the requested processing area. At the arrival area, employees print a sticker on the spot for each bucket or box with the product name, order and customer information, a quick response (QR) code for internal use,

Fig. 3.2 Electric robotized cars run on solar energy and transport Germinis https://www.jacoudijk.nl/videos With permission by Jac. Oudijk Gerbera's

and a bar code for the customer. The robotized cars drive automatically to a central packaging station where the Germinis are processed. All products are order-produced, e.g., the customer (a wholesaler or a retailer) can indicate the type of Germini, the order size, single color, mixture of colors or a theme-related mixture (like for Mother's day), the order size, and the type of packaging. The customer can request the Germinis in a box or in a bucket with water. Germinis can be individually packaged or packaged as a bouquet wrapped in plastic.

The processing includes several steps such as quality control, sorting, and packaging. Some parts of the process are fully automated. The level of automation in glasshouses is very high, due to the high capital investments and the high labor costs. Flowers can be sorted by using high-speed cameras with sensing and recognition technology to identify the type of Germini. For bundles, automated machines cut the flower products at the right length and bundle them based on the order specifications. The individual packaged Germinis are still processed manually.

The buckets are processed through a fast and reliable system of conveyor belts that deliver the buckets to one of the five destination areas. Each destination area can hold the orders of five customers, and the orders of around 55 customers are processed each day. Finally, the last quality control process is done by employees. They check the delivery details and put the orders in trucks to be transported to the customers. Expected delivery times are almost always met by this unique system.

3.5   Data-Driven Production

Growers like to use glasshouses to control both the *growth* and *development* of produce such as vegetables and flowers. Let us first explore the complexity of the growth and development of plants and review some of the knowledge and insights that are available, for example, in the seminal work by Cecilia Stanghellini, Bert van 't Ooster, and Ep Heuvelink at Wageningen University & Research.[9]

The *growth* cycle of a plant follows a sigmoid curve or S-shaped curve.[10] In the first phase there is gradually an exponential growth, then a linear part, and finally a slowdown in growth. The leaf area is an important driving variable for plant growth, as only light intercepted by green leaf area results in photosynthesis and growth. One can calculate the relative growth rate (RGR) as "the increase in plant weight per unit of weight and per unit of time." The relative growth is the product of three components: a photosynthetic component, a component reflecting leaf thickness, and a partitioning component, i.e., a variable that indicates the fraction of the total plant growth that is partitioned to the leaves. The RGR is higher "when the rate of increase plant weight per unit of leaf area, also called Net Assimilation Rate (NAR), is higher, when leaves are thinner or when a larger fraction of the total plant growth is partitioned to the leaves."

Growth is usually expressed as an increase in dry mass. The sugars produced in the process of photosynthesis must be transformed into structural biomass, such as proteins, lignin, and organic acids. The highest priority is to maintain the existing biomass, so part of the produced sugars is burned again in maintenance respiration. The remainder of the sugars will be used for dry mass production. The conversion efficiency is "about 0.7 for most glasshouse crops, which means that 1 gram of sugars (remaining after use for maintenance respiration) results in 0.7 gram of dry mass. The loss is called growth respiration. A linear relationship between dry mass production and the cumulative intercepted light sum has been observed for many crops. The slope of this relationship is called the crop Light Use Efficiency (LUE)." It can be used to directly calculate the crop growth rate from the amount of intercepted light.

The *development* of plants primarily depends on temperature. There is a linear relationship between the temperature and the leaf initiation and unfolding rate. A fixed temperature sum, in degree days, is known for each specific plant variety and that sum can be used to calculate the needed heat to speed up the development of the plant. The development rate "is equally related to the day and night temperatures, and therefore to the 24-hour mean temperature, as observed for tomato, cucumber, chrysanthemum, and Easter lily." However, the minimum temperature is also relevant. At temperatures lower than this minimum, no development takes place. Most growers will measure and control the air temperature, but "it is the plant or organ temperature that is relevant for the development and growth." The meristem temperatures that determine the rate of leaf initiation may deviate greatly from air temperature. The leaf area increase (LAIn) is often calculated as "a function of the plant developmental stage and this is determined by the temperature sum. In the glasshouse, this simple relationship does not hold true, because the grower can regulate the temperature *independently* from the light level."

One way of controlling the production is the advanced use of glasshouses – also called protected cultivation, controlled environment agriculture (CEA), or greenhouse horticulture. Let us explore the different factors that contribute to the growth and development of the different varieties of Germinis that are produced by Jac.Oudijk Gerbera's.

What are the Factors That Jac.Oudijk Gerbera's Can Control with a Glasshouse?

There are *five factors* that they can control: light, temperature, carbon dioxide, humidity, and drought and salinity (or saltiness). Solar radiation reaching the Earth's surface has wavelength from approximately 300 to 2500 nm. This is called "light," the *first* control factor, although, strictly speaking, light is what we can see with our eyes, between 380 and 750 nm. For crop production "it is necessary to split the solar spectrum into three wavelengths ranges (wavebands): UltraViolet (UV), the range between 300 and 400 nm, Photosynthetic Active Radiation (PAR), the range between 400 and 700 nm, and Near InfraRed (NIR), the range between 700 and 2500 nm. PAR is the part that plants use for photosynthesis and half of the energy is in the PAR range and half in the NIR range."

As natural light is partially scattered in the atmosphere, solar radiation at the Earth's surface also has a spatial distribution; in daytime we get light from all spots in the sky. From the spot where the sun is, we get direct radiation; the rest is diffuse radiation, i.e., solar radiation scattered by the atmosphere. The lower the sun's elevation on the horizon, the longer the path of its light in the atmosphere and the larger the fraction of diffuse radiation. This is a consequence of latitude (high latitude has a low sun elevation), season, and time of the day. The scattering effect can be increased by clouds, water vapor, and smog. In the Netherlands, only "20% of global radiation is direct in winter, in summer it is 35%. In Arizona 80% of the radiation in summer is direct and in winter it is still 70%, while in Southern Italy it is 60% in summer and 40% in winter."

The glasshouse cover, glass or plastic or other materials, always does three things: reflects, absorbs, and transmits the solar radiation. Transmission should be as high as possible and reflection and absorption should be as low as possible. Reflection can be modified by coatings or structures on the surface of hard materials. Growers in regions with dark winters increasingly use supplementary light. By using supplementary light "growers are able to raise and control both crop production and product quality. Growers can produce year-round to meet the market demands, improve the efficiency of investments and have a more regular labour demand. High Pressure Sodium lamps (HPS) and Light Emitting Diodes (LED) lighting is often used for supplementary light."

Besides light intensity and day length (the period during which the plant receives natural or artificial light), the light color (spectrum) is also important. With LEDs, the grower "can determine the exact color of the additional light. HPS lamps, on the other hand, have a high component of yellow-red light. Red light has the highest level of photosynthesis efficiency that will result in higher levels of yield. However, leaves acclimate to the growth light spectrum and hence short-term spatial effects on leaf photosynthesis may differ from the long-term response. A higher fraction of blue light results in more compact plants, and the role of green light might enhance stem elongation, carbon dioxide assimilation, and biomass production and yield."

On a cloudy day it looks as if light comes from all angles. This is called diffuse light. Compared to direct sunlight on a cloudless day, diffuse light is more equally distributed in the crop, both horizontally and vertically, and it increases production. Most research on diffuse light is done in the Netherlands, where materials to diffuse the light are rated in comparison to clear glass. Only recently has it been possible to diffuse the light more without impacting total light intensity. Nowadays, both diffusing glass and coatings scatter the light but barely affect the intensity, because an anti-reflection coating is simultaneously applied to the surfaces of glasshouses.

This brings us to the *second* control factor: temperature. The temperature regime or pattern is another crucial variable. It makes a difference whether the temperature will be kept constant, e.g., 21 °C in a day/night regime of 25/17 °C or even the reverse regime of 17/25 °C. The difference between day and night temperature is called difference (DIF) and the reverse regime is called negative DIF. Growers "use negative DIF to reduce elongation and obtain more compact plants. Also the regime during the day is important, a Drop in the temperature during a brief period (called DROP) can reduce plant elongation. In general, full grown crops react more to the long-term average temperature." The strategy of defining and controlling the desired average temperature over a longer period, such as a day, several days, or a week, is called temperature integration. Glasshouse temperature is regulated to save energy over a longer period of time. When the sun heats up the glasshouse, the energy is free, and the temperature can be allowed to rise slightly above daytime setpoint. If the grower must use heating the next day due to more wind or more clouds, a lower temperature can be maintained while continuing to realize the desired long-term average temperature.

Shading can cool off the glasshouse when ventilation cannot cool the glasshouse sufficiently. The most widely used shading method is whitewash, a white paint that reflects a fraction of the sun's radiation. Usually, it is applied in late spring and early autumn and at the end of these periods is washed away. The temperature reduction is "30% to 50% and the paint has a scattering effect, so the light in the glasshouse is diffuse. Shading by means of moveable screens is another option and has the advantage that they can be folded away whenever the temperature allows for it – such as in the morning, evening, or on cloudy days."

The *third* control factor is carbon dioxide. Raising the carbon dioxide concentration in glasshouses stimulates crop growth dramatically. Carbon dioxide enrichment is very common. It improves "yield by 15% to 30% and will lead to better plant quality. There is also an interaction effect among light, carbon dioxide, and temperature. Carbon dioxide works even better when light and temperature are at higher levels."

Humidity, the amount of vapor in the air, is the *fourth* control factor and an important aspect of the air in glasshouses. The crop puts water vapor into the glasshouse air via transpiration.[11] The temperature of the air can be measured, but temperature does not measure an important aspect, namely the latent heat of humidity. The water vapor in the air contains a lot of energy. The amount of vapor that air can contain increases exponentially with its temperature. Therefore, if warm humid air is cooled down, there will be a certain temperature at which the air cannot hold all the water in vapor form and part of it will condense – the dew point. Humidity represents "latent heat: maintaining the right level of humidity, for example through natural ventilation, costs energy, because humid warm air is removed from the glasshouse. Extremely high humidity can cause problems, because the plant cannot transpire enough, and water flow is absent. It means that no calcium is transported to the leaves. As a result, the leaves will be smaller and there will be less light interception and less photosynthesis. The other extreme is low humidity, leading to the closing of stomata to reduce transpiration and higher resistance for carbon dioxide, and a reduction of photosynthesis."

Different air treatments can be used, such as heating, cooling, ventilation, mixing of two air flows or volumes, and (de)humidification. Ventilation not only removes energy from the glasshouse, it also removes vapor, when the outside air is less humid than inside air. Ventilation also affects the photosynthesis rate, indirectly, via the inflow or outflow of carbon dioxide within the glasshouse. Open ventilation also "allows a way in for unwelcome pests and a way out for predators that may have been introduced for biological control." Ventilation throws away excess energy that might be useful later.

The *fifth* control factor is drought and salinity. The response to water and salt stress is identical: both limit the plant's uptake of water. Droughts limit the uptake of water, but it is also limited when soil is saturated with water, because plants do not have enough oxygen to use the water and the roots do not function well. Both extreme situations will lead to lower yield.

Data-driven climate control programs are highly sophisticated decision support tools that growers can use to achieve an optimal climate inside a glasshouse. Modern climate computers aid in achieving temperature integration with the lowest possible energy costs, using a combination of screens, ventilation, and heating to maintain the average temperature. The grower will determine a number of target variables such as air temperature, humidity, carbon dioxide concentration, and light. Based on sensing technology, the climate control software program determines the current levels of the target variables. With the help of models and algorithms, it analyzes and specifies optimal levels of the target and identifies improvements that the grower needs to agree upon and execute. The climate control program continues to gather data on air temperature, humidity, carbon dioxide concentration, and light, which are used to check if the target levels are met. Once the newest plant yield data are analyzed one can determine if the response was successful and a new cycle of sensing, storing, analyzing, responding, and learning from the response can start. In Chap. 6, this cycle and its relationship with algorithms are explained in more detail. The newest approach is to develop and use three-dimensional plant models to predict the growth and development of plants. Nowadays, *digital twins,* e.g., the digital replica of a living (such as a plant or animal) or non-living (such as a bridge or building) physical entity, are used to model and simulate these entities. For example, by using a three-dimensional (3D) light model in combination with a 3D model of the plant, the lighting system in a glasshouse can be optimized.

3.6   Laboratories for Innovation

Jac. Oudijk Gerbera's collaborated with Wageningen University & Research to tackle the fungal disease Botrytis, also known as grey mould or gray mold.[12] One symptom of Botrytis is a brownish color of the flower petals of the produced Germinis, and this is not appreciated by customers. The normal strategy to tackle this fungal disease is to simultaneously heat and ventilate the glasshouse. The lower humidity level will break down the development of the fungus, but this is a costly solution because the heat is immediately lost by ventilation. A better solution had to be found. The solution was to invest in a dehumidification system to control the humidity of the air in a glasshouse. How? Indoor air will be mixed with outdoor air or with sensible and latent heat with a heat pump. The energy savings, the amount that was not needed for heating, were reported in the order of 700,000 m^3 natural gas. Natural gas was not burned and therefore carbon dioxide was not produced that led to a carbon dioxide reduction of 1.3 million kg per year for seven hectares of glasshouses.

Due to the competition, glasshouse firms continue to innovate for more efficiency. Recently, new lighting innovations are explored, such as new LEDs provided by companies like Samsung or Signify. These new LEDs can provide a wider spectrum of artificial light and stimulate the growth and development of plants in an energy-efficient way.

Glasshouses are also laboratories to test out new digital technologies, such as drones. One of the startup companies is PATS.[13] PATS is specialized in the usage of drones in glasshouses. Bram Tijmons, a Business Information Management (BIM) master alumni of Rotterdam School of Management, cofounded PATS, together with his brother Sjoerd Tijmons and Kevin van Hecke. PATS will revolutionize and automate insect control. Instead of using a lot of biopesticides or chemical pesticides to kill insects, PATS will use autonomous and bat-like drones. PATS has focused on moths, because their offspring, caterpillars, can cause considerable damage to the crops, such as gerberas or chrysanthemums. Base stations are equipped with monitoring cameras that will scan the interior of glasshouses. Once a flying moth is detected, a drone is immediately activated and directed toward the moth. The drone is the size of your hand with four drone propellers; see Fig. 3.3.

Fig. 3.3 Drones for automated insect control in glasshouses https://pats-drones.com/ With permission by PATS

The drone collides with the insect, and the drone's rotating propellers incapacitate the moth. The swift bat-like action takes just a few seconds. Once the insect has been eliminated, the drone returns to the charging station to recharge for the next mission. Usually, the micro drones are active between sunset and sunrise, because moths are nocturnal, i.e., active during the night.

There are several algorithms used by the base station, the drones, and the charging station. Algorithms will help to detect the movement of insects, the type of insects, and the required action (destroy or not) given specific parameters that can be specified by the grower. Actually, algorithms can support the decision-making of the growers with regard to the decline of the moth population and the effectiveness of the PATS drones. Some of the PATS algorithms use advanced techniques, such as machine learning. Machine learning is derived from the functioning and the learning capability of the human brain. "How do you identify a moth in the darkness?" is an interesting question that you can ask yourself. To understand the detection, visualization, and the reaction initiated by your brain was very helpful in the development of a new field called artificial intelligence (AI) with the subfields machine learning (ML) and deep learning (DL). Chapter 6 will discuss the challenges and usage of ML and DL algorithms in the floral business.

3.7   Urban Cities

Why is the Dutch glass city typically found close to other cities including Rotterdam, Utrecht, Amsterdam, and the Hague? To find the answer, we turn to Johann Heinrich von Thünen (1783–1850), a brilliant German economist and landowner in the nineteenth century. He developed a theory of spatial economics and economic geography combined with the theory of rent that we know as Von Thünen's model of land use.[14] He theorized that the use of a piece of land is a function of the cost of transport to the market and the land rent a farmer can afford to pay, which is determined by the yield of the produce. The model described six concentric rings of agricultural activities around a core, the city center. Von Thünen predicted that dairy and intensive farming, such as horticulture, would take place in the first ring, as vegetables, fruit, milk, and flowers must be delivered swiftly to the markets in the city and, therefore, would be produced close to the city. Timber and firewood, produced for fuel and building materials, would be found in the second ring. Wood for heating and cooking was, at that time, very important, but wood is heavy and difficult to transport so the allocated space for it is close to the city. The third ring consisted of the production of grain. Grain lasts longer than dairy products and is lighter; therefore, transportation costs were lower and it could be located further from the city. The fourth ring was grassland which was alternately cultivated and grazed. The fifth ring was a three-field economy with fallow land. In the sixth ring, livestock were fattened and transported to the city center where consumption took place.

Von Thünen's model of land use is based on some basic assumptions that do not completely hold in the current economy, including a localized economy around a city with no connections to the rest of the world, nineteenth-century costs and transport speeds that focused on walking or horse-driven carts, and the lack of advanced cooling for storage and transportation. However, some aspects of von Thünen's land use concept are still visible in modern land use, and indeed, the Dutch glass city is located near Rotterdam, the Hague, Amsterdam, and Utrecht.

Beyond Von Thünen's model of land use, there are other factors that play a role in the location of the Dutch glass city. The most important factor is an unexpected surprise. Under the glass city, several small gas fields were discovered, such as in Delfgauw, 's-Gravenzande, Naaldwijk, Maasland, and Monster. From a depth of 3 km, gas is pumped to a distribution station and it is cleaned of gas condensate, water, and other residues. And that natural gas bulb is used to heat the glasshouses in the glass city. Flowers are produced from natural gas.

Interestingly, the formation of natural gas started 350 million years ago. At that time, the Netherlands consisted of swampy forests. The forests disappeared and thick layers of sand and salt covered the remaining vegetation. Under the high pressure of these layers of the earth, the forest remains first turned into peat and later into coal. The pressure eventually caused the coal seam, a dark brown or black banded deposit of coal that is visible within layers of rock, to become warmer and natural gas was created. Plant remains were transformed into an underground natural gas supply, and now glasshouses can be heated with natural gas and flower plants can be cultivated year round. The Dutch miracle covered in one sentence.

A second surprise will be instrumental for the future of the Dutch glass city. In the industrial cluster near the Port of Rotterdam, the largest port in Europe, heat is a by-product of the processes of chemical plants and refineries, and the heat has not yet been captured or used. But in the future, the heat that is now wasted will be transported to the glass city where it will be reused.[15] A heat network will be established from the port cluster to the Hague, the so-called pipeline through the Middle, with a branch coming to Delft for the heat supply to the glasshouse horticulture of the glass city. Plans and investments have been made for the period 2020–2030, and 2–3 million tons of carbon dioxide can be saved per year by reducing the need to burn natural gas.

A third surprise movement is that the industrial cluster produced not only heat but also carbon dioxide. The carbon capture utilization and storage (in short CCUS) is an emerging technology that will be able to store carbon dioxide and use it at a later stage.[16] Several companies in the port cluster would like to supply their carbon dioxide to a collective pipeline that runs through the Rotterdam port area. A compressor station will pressurize the carbon dioxide and a pipeline will carry it to an empty gas field beneath the North Sea, 20 km off the coast. There, carbon dioxide will be injected into a sandstone reservoir under the seabed. It is expected that the reservoir will be able to store 2–2.5 million tons of carbon dioxide per year. The carbon dioxide captured from the Rotterdam port area could be used to grow plants faster in glasshouses of the glass city.

3.8   High Tech and Carbon Neutral

In the United States, coal mines are being shut down in the eastern part of Kentucky. Coal is out as energy source, and natural gas, wind, and solar will take over. With the closing of mines in Kentucky, unemployment in the area increased, the standard of living fell, economic activity slowed down, and young, educated, and talented people relocated to more prosperous areas. In 2019, unemployment in Kentucky had risen to 13%, well above the national average of 4%. In search of better opportunities, many young people have departed for big cities in other States with cool startup centers, jobs, and decent salaries.

In the little village of Morehead, 220 km east of Louisville, Jonathan Webb enthusiastically pointed to the horizon overlooking grass, sand, and fields of cornflowers and described a future he envisions: "This is where it will happen; 25 hectares of glass and steel. The largest high-tech greenhouse in the United States. Maybe the beginning of a new East-Kentucky. We have the opportunity to lead the country to a new future."[17] (In the United States a glasshouse is usually referred to as a greenhouse, but they are similar.) Apart from a University of Kentucky baseball cap, Webb looked like a typical young entrepreneur, dressed in jeans and a blue T-shirt, and sporting a hipster beard and a trendy pair of glasses. His most striking feature, however, was his determination to develop high-tech horticulture in Kentucky. "We would like to achieve here what has been done in the Netherlands" said Webb, who visited Wageningen University & Research to explore the opportunities. In 2017, Webb acquired €85 million for a startup company called AppHarvest. By 2019, 600 containers carrying the latest greenhouse technology were on their way to Morehead, including LED technology from the world leader in lighting, the Dutch lighting company Signify, a split-off from the well-known Royal Philips, which nowadays is positioned as a multinational health company. The Dutch company, Dalsem, would build the AppHarvest greenhouse when the materials arrived. The $97 million greenhouse will use digital monitoring, sunlight, and artificial light with the latest LED technology, recycled rainwater, and non-chemical growing practices.

The greenhouse will have 285 employees and ship 45 million pounds of fresh produce annually, primarily tomatoes, to grocery stores from Atlanta to New York, and as far west as Chicago and St. Louis. Webb made a strategic decision to launch his startup in rural eastern Kentucky rather than in technology hubs near San Francisco, New York, or Boston. The transit time from Kentucky to grocery stores in major markets like Chicago or New York is about one day – far shorter than competitors. It can take up to five days for products from Canada or Mexico to travel cross-country, and the produce of these two countries accounts for more than half of the $3 billion fresh tomato market in the United States. Tomatoes grown in the AppHarvest greenhouse will have lower transit costs and emissions and have longer shelf life once they arrive.

AppHarvest will meet the highest standards with regard to food safety, product freshness, environmental quality, and energy consumption. The greenhouse will run on recycled rainwater, which allows for significant savings for a large-scale agriculture operation. Kentucky has seen increasingly wet and rainy weather over the past few years, and the AppHarvest initiative is in part a bet that this trend will continue, making the region a more hospitable place for building an Ag Tech hub. With 70% of freshwater going toward agriculture globally, according to the World Bank, farming in the United States must adapt to the more sustainable methods AppHarvest is developing.

The greenhouse will use a hybrid LED system, utilizing Signify's Philips GreenPower LED Toplighting Compact and Agrolux High Pressure Sodium (HPS) lighting. The LED system is 40% more energy efficient than traditional greenhouse lighting, and it disseminates less radiant heat.[18] During fall and spring, LEDs will be used to grow more produce. HPS lamps will be used during colder months, in addition to the LED system. The heat from the HPS system will help warm the greenhouse and reduce natural gas usage. By separating heat and light, Philips GreenPower LED Toplighting Compact gives growers independent control over their greenhouse climate.

3.9 Innovate and Digitize

Glasshouse companies have begun using advanced information and communications technologies (ICT) to improve the performance of their business. Wageningen Economic Research (WER) completed a detailed analysis of the impact of ICT on the performance of firms in three horticulture subsectors: vegetables, potted and bedding plants, and cut flowers. The results of the WER study revealed several lessons to be learned.[19]

The first lesson is that "larger firms have more financial power to innovate. Product innovation has to do with developing new cultivars, while process innovation has to do with using renewable energy, the use of robots to harvest fruits or vegetables, and precision farming. Innovative firms are larger than less innovating firms; they have younger CEOs, and these firms have a higher income. For innovative horticulture firms the overall turnover is around €2.3 million, with 19 employees, the age of the youngest CEO is 43, and the yearly income of an employee is €89,000. For the less innovative horticulture firms the overall turnover is around €1.8 million, with 8 employees, the age of the youngest CEO is 45, and the yearly income of an employee is €51,900." The second lesson is that "horticulture firms are highly mechanized but the business management systems that provide ICT support to office procedures such as order processing, stock management, certification processes, and production planning are still in their infancy in Dutch horticulture." Even the systematic approach "to managing and using information for decision-making processes is somewhat rudimentary." The third lesson is that "the use of ICT and expansion of the firm size appear to go hand in hand with improved economic results. ICT is especially useful for maintaining an overview of increasingly complex business procedures and is a great tool for saving time. As horticultural holdings continue to grow, a concurrent growth of ICT use is to be expected."

The fourth lesson is that "ICT alone is not a guarantee for improved economic results. Economic results are determined by many different factors; the use of ICT is only one of these. Furthermore, investments in ICT only show their impact on business procedures and economic results after some time. This delay will not affect all businesses in the same way. The use of ICT is often paired with broader innovations and can result in changes in the behavior of employers and staff." The fifth lesson is that firms "with better ICT support show a higher level of profitability. Larger firms have a more mature ICT support system for purchasing, stock management, order processing, labour registration and energy management. This may be attributed to larger companies having more comprehensive and complex business procedures. Purchasing and labour registration do not yet score highly in terms of ICT support. Companies with more ICT support for these aspects have higher profitability. Considering that these companies are also larger, this higher profitability may also be explained by the business size and the use of ICT as a tool for support."

The sixth lesson is that most horticulture firms "benefit from using business management systems. It will give them extra insight into business procedures and simplifies administration. Currently, management processes are mainly supported by general software such as Excel spreadsheets. Vegetable glasshouses have the most systematic system of management (the highest organizational maturity) and pot plant and bedding plants horticulture have the most structured decision-making."

The seventh and last lesson is that firms with "the highest profitability will invest predominantly in cost management. If horticulturalists invest in ICT in the next few years, the firms with the highest profitability will give preference to investing in cost accounting, labour registration and energy management. Larger businesses are likely to give priority to ICT investments in sales, purchasing, distribution/transport, stock management, order processing, labour registration and shipping records."

3.10   Vertical Farming

For the next step in the controlled production of flowers and vegetables we have to travel to Japan. Keihanna Science City is a science and technology district in the green Keihanna hills between Kyoto, Osaka, and Nara Prefectures in western Japan. Its industrial buildings are home to university research centers, such as the Experimental Farm by Kyoto University's Graduate School of Agriculture, technology companies, and startups that are not yet well known. From the outside the buildings look almost like a normal industrial area, not particularly spectacular. However, the companies working here are developing very spectacular technologies and business ideas. Spread Co. is one of the most exciting companies in the world that started in Keihanna Science City.[20] Spread Co. develops the world's largest automated leaf-vegetable factory. The factory is not a glasshouse anymore; it only uses artificial light, but is situated in a high-rise building without any windows, also called vertical farming. The term vertical indicates that plants are grown on stacked racks. Like the floors of a vertical, high-rise building, these racks are put on top of each other. The company's vertical farm could mark the turning point for vertical farming by keeping production cost low enough to compete with traditional farms on a large scale. For some time, vertical farms that grow produce indoors in stacked racks without soil have been presented as a solution to the rising food demand in the world's expanding cities. Japan is a densely populated country with an aging population of over 137 million people, and its largest conglomerate of cities is the Tokyo-Kanto Metropolitan Area with over 37 million people. The problem has always been reproducing the effect of natural rain, soil, and sunshine at a cost that makes the crop competitive with traditional agriculture. Spread Co. is among the first firms that "claim to have cracked that problem using a mix of robotics, technology, and scale. Spread's new facility in Keihanna Science City will grow 30,000 heads of lettuce a day on racks under custom-designed lights using LED. A sealed room protects the vegetables from pests, diseases, and dirt. Temperature and humidity are optimized to speed the growth of the greens, which are fed, tended and harvested by robots."

Spread President Shinji Inada won the Edison Award in 2016 for his vertical-farming system. It is expected that the new factory, called Techno Farm, will "more than double the company's output, generating ¥1 billion in sales a year from growing almost 11 million lettuces. Spread sells lettuces for ¥198 a head to consumers, about 20–30% more than the normal price for conventionally grown varieties. Consumers pay the premium because the pesticide-free vegetables are increasingly seen as an alternative to often more expensive organic foods, which must be grown outdoors in soil. Japan's hot summers and high humidity also make organic plants more vulnerable to insects and diseases."

Spread's Shinji Inada, a former vegetable trader, "founded his company in 2006 and opened his first facility the following year in Kameoka. The company spent years refining systems for lighting, water supply, nutrients and other costs. The plant finally turned its first profit in 2013." Its new Techno Farm "will push efficiency further, yielding 648 heads of lettuce a square meter annually, compared with 300 heads at its Kameoka farm and only 5 in an outdoor farm. It will use only 110 milliliters of water per lettuce – 1% of the volume that is needed outdoors – as moisture emitted by the vegetable is condensed and reused."

Power consumption per head "will also decrease, with the new factory using custom-designed LEDs that require about 30% less energy. A collaboration with telecom company NTT Weston an artificial intelligence program to analyze production data could boost yields even more. Spread Co. has not disclosed the cost of producing lettuce at its farms, but Japanese researchers estimate that the cost to produce one head of lettuce at the existing Kameoka building is about ¥80 – among the lowest in the world. Production costs at the new Techno Farm are expected to come close to parity with outdoor farms within about 5 years."

But extreme weather events and climate change, "major disrupters of traditional agriculture, are making vertical farming competitive even sooner. Japan's hottest-ever summer in 2019, with its heavy rains, typhoons and flooding, sent supermarket lettuce prices soaring to more than double the level at which Spread sells its products."

Around the world, many existing vertical farms are located in climates that are inhospitable for vegetable farming and have high transport costs to import fresh produce, or in places where pollution concerns created a demand for "clean" food. Other high-rise farms "have appeared in office towers or condos as part of the design. In Tokyo's Ginza shopping area, vertical farms arise in buildings to supply lettuces exclusively for restaurants and bars. The higher demand for these novel and organic lettuce products will compensate for the higher production costs compared with vegetables grown in outdoor farms.

The real race though, is to go global. Spread plans to export its farming system to more than 100 cities worldwide, competing with companies in Japan, China, and the United States." The examples of the vertical farming in fresh produce, with its combination of robotics, artificial intelligence for sensing and control, and scale, will have a spillover effect to the horticulture world of the glass city.

Notes

1. The role of Carolus Clusius and the Hortus botanicus in the study by Egmond F (2016), with quotes "already taught," "a botanical garden," "potted plants," p. 158.
   The early history of the Hortus botanicus Leiden in Van Uffelen G (2008), with quotes "surrounded by beds," "among Clusius's favorite plants," and "a true plantman's garden, p. 56, and "is the *Laburnum*," p. 57.
2. The construction of glasshouses in the Hortus botanicus in Van Uffelen G, Kessler P.J.A. (red) (2015). With the quote: "many shades".
3. In France, glasshouses were called orangeries, since these were used to protect the orange trees from freezing. The Orangerie built in 1617, now Musée de l'Orangerie at the Palace of the Louvre, was inspired by the Italian Renaissance gardens and inspired many orangeries around Europe, such as the Versailles Orangerie (1686) in Versailles, the Orangery (1760) in Moscow, the Chrystal Place (1851) in Hyde Park, London, and the Orangerieschloss (1864) in Potsdam.
4. The explanation of growth and development of flower plants in Stanghellini C, van't Ooster B, and Heuvelink E (2019). With the quote: "the systematic movement," p. 27.
   Economics, with its focus on growth, could learn from plant science with its fundamental distinction between growth and development. Most economists (and politicians) are very fond of the concept of gross domestic product (GDP). GDP indicates the monetary value of all products and services that are produced in a country over a period of time. It estimates the economic size of the country and its growth rate. For example, the GDP of the Netherlands was around €900 billion at the end of 2018, with a growth rate of 2.7% over the year 2018. Development, the transition toward new forms of economic activities such as the transition to a circular and digital economy, is not taken into account or wrongly defined in the GDP figures. For a discussion about GDP and its measurements, see Brynjolfsson E, Saunders A (2009, October 1).
5. The stages of the plant cycle are in Avas Flowers (2019). With the quote: "the seed, germination".
6. Stems are in competition for light and therefore the longer plants will get out of the shadow of adjacent plants and get more sunlight or artificial light.

Flower plants are in that sense like the skyscrapers of New York City, where *air rights*, contractual agreements that protect the construction of the neighboring high-rise buildings, allow skyscrapers to get enough light and an unobstructed view.

7. Crucial details of the flower life cycle are in Avas Flowers (2019). With the quotes "called the pistil and has four parts," "it travels down the style," "insects, birds, animals".

8. The Jac.Oudijk Gerbera's glasshouse operations in Vakblad onder Glas (2017, March 18) and in the company website Jac. Oudijk Gerbera's (2020a, b).

9. The explanation of growth and development of flower plants and its control in glasshouses is in the excellent book by Stanghellini C, van 't Ooster B, Heuvelink E (2019). With quotes "the increase in plant weight," p. 33, "when the rate," p. 35, "about 0.7 for most glasshouse crops," p. 47, "is equally related to," p. 31, "it is the plant or organ temperature," p. 32, "There are five factors," p. 133, "it is necessary to split," p. 55, "20% of global radiation," p. 59, "growers are able to raise," p. 136, "can determine the exact," pp. 213–214, "use negative DIF," p. 148, "30% to 50% and the paint," pp. 62–63, "latent heat: maintaining," pp. 155–156, "yield by 15% to 30%," p. 151, "allows a way in for unwelcome pests," p. 111.

10. The sigmoid curve or S-shaped curve is seen in many phenomena, from plant growth, the adoption of innovations, or the distribution of winning bids in flower auctions. Pedro Domingos called, in his book Domingos P (2015) *The Master Algorithm,* the sigmoid curve "The Most Important Curve of the World." The curve will be discussed in more detail in Chap. 6.

11. Crop transpiration and evaporation were identified and measured by Howard Penman in 1948. The Penman equation describes the evaporation from open water surface, bare soil, and grass. Variations of Penman's equation were developed to measure the potential evapotranspiration of vegetated land areas and crop transpiration. My first academic paper was about Penman's equation to predict evapotranspiration of the Susquehanna river basin area; see Ray NR, Lambregts A, Van Heck E, Steenhuis TS (1982).

12. Jac.Oudijk's efforts to tackle Botrytus in collaboration with Wageningen University in the company's website and videoclips. Jac. Oudijk (2020a, b).

13. The use of drones in glasshouses in BNR Zakendoen (2019, July 19). And in PATS (2020).

14. Von Thünen's model of land use is in Von Thünen JH (1826).

15. The heath network in Mackor R. (2019, September 10).

16. The Carbon Capture Utilization and Storage (CCUS) technology in the Port of Rotterdam CO_2 Transport Hub and Offshore Storage project. Porthos (2020).

17. The story of Jonathan Webb and the AppHarvest glasshouse development in Morehead (Kentucky) in Sisson P (2019, June 28).
    Schneider K. (2019, September 3), with quotes: "This is where it will happen" and "We would like to achieve here."

Persson M. (2019, October 8).
18. Details of the lighting system are in Philips Lighting (2019, August 16).
19. The lessons learned are based on research by Wageningen Economic Research (WER) on the use and impact of ICT in glasshouses in Bondt N, Robbemond R, Ge L, Puister L, Verdouw C (2016). (Summary in English) with quotes: "still in their infancy in Dutch horticulture," "to managing and using information," "especially useful for maintaining," "determined by many different factors," "a more mature ICT support system," "extra insight into business procedures," "with the highest profitability".

The WER research report provides a detailed analysis of how the extent of ICT use (ICT maturity) correlates with the size and profitability of the horticultural firm. The level of ICT maturity and its relationship with profitability and size of the firm is analyzed in terms of correlation. A higher level of ICT maturity in "purchasing" and in "labor registration" correlates well with a higher level of profitability of the firm. A higher level of ICT maturity in "purchasing," "stock management," "order processing," "labor registration," and "energy management" correlates well with a larger horticulture firm.
20. The story of vertical farming in Japan and the Spread Co. Company in Takada A. (2018, November 1). With quotes: "claim to have cracked," "more than double," "founded his company," "will push efficiency further," "will also decrease," "major disrupters," and "have appeared in office towers.".

References

Avas Flowers (2019) The stages of the flower life cycle. Avasflowers.net. https://www.avasflowers.net/the-stages-of-the-flower-life-cycle Accessed 2 Sept 2020

BNR Zakendoen (2019, July 19) Pitch by Bram Tijmons, CEO and Co-Founder of PATS

Bondt N, Robbemond R, Ge L, Puister L, Verdouw C (2016) Nut van ICT-gebruik voor inbouwondernemers, Wageningen Economic Research Report. https://library.wur.nl/WebQuery/wurpubs/fulltext/390645 Accessed 2 Sept 2020

Brynjolfsson E, Saunders A (2009, October 1) What the GDP gets wrong, why managers should care, MIT Sloan. Manage Rev 51(1):95–96. https://sloanreview.mit.edu/article/what-the-gdp-gets-wrong-why-managers-should-care/ Accessed 2 Sept 2020

Domingos P (2015) The master algorithm, how the quest for the ultimate learning machine will remake our world. Penguin Books, London

Egmond F (2016) The world of Carolus Clusius: natural history in the making, 1550–1610, perspectives in economic and social history, vol 6. Routledge, London

Jac. Oudijk Gerbera's (2020a) Tailored to every customer requirements with maximum service. https://www.jacoudijk.nl/?lang=en Accessed 2 Sept 2020

Jac. Oudijk Gerbera's (2020b) Our company video's. https://www.jacoudijk.nl/videos?lang=en Accessed 2 Sept 2020

Mackor R (2019, September 10) Havenwarmte straks naar Den Haag en Westland (in Dutch), Nieuwsblad transport. https://www.nieuwsbladtransport.nl/havens/2019/09/10/havenwarmte-straks-naar-den-haag-en-westland/ Accessed 2 Sept 2020

PATS (2020) PATS – Bat-like drones for insect control. https://pats-drones.com/ Accessed 2 Sept 2020

Persson M (2019, October 8) In het arme steenkool zwarte Kentucky gloort een gouden toekomst (in Dutch), De Volkskrant, pp 10–12. https://www.volkskrant.nl/kijkverder/v/2019/in-het-arme-steenkoolzwarte-kentucky-gloort-een-gouden-toekomst/?referer=https%3A%2F%2Fwww.google.com%2F Accessed 2 Sept 2020.

Philips Lighting (2019, August 16) Signify helps AppHarvest to increase yields in 25-hectare greenhouse. https://www.lighting.philips.com/main/products/horti-culture/press-releases/signify-helps-appharvest-to-increase-yields-in-25-hectare-greenhouse Accessed 2 Sept 2020

Porthos (2020) CO_2 reductie door opslag onder de Noordzee. https://www.portho-sco2.nl/ Accessed 2 Sept 2020

Ray NR, Lambregts A, Van Heck E, Steenhuis TS (1982) Long-term prediction of evapotranspiration by means of a simplified application of Penman's equation. Cornell University, Department of Agricultural Engineering, Ithaca (USA)

Schneider K (2019, September 3) from a greenhouse large enough to feed the eastern seaboard. New York Times. https://www.nytimes.com/2019/09/03/business/appharvest-greenhouse-kentucky-agriculture.html Accessed 2 Sept 2020

Sisson P (2019, June 28) Will Kentucky's 'giga-greenhouse' revolutionize high-tech farming? Curbed. https://www.curbed.com/2019/6/28/19102684/tech-kentucky-farming-agriculture-appharvest Accessed 2 Sept 2020.

Stanghellini C, van't Ooster B, Heuvelink E (2019) Greenhouse horticulture, Technology for Optimal Crop Production. Wageningen Academic Publishers, Wageningen

Takada A (2018 November 1) As high-rise farms go global, Japan's spread leads the way. The Japan Times. https://www.japantimes.co.jp/news/2018/11/01/business/tech/high-rise-farms-go-global-japans-spread-leads-way/ Accessed 2 Sept 2020.

Vakblad onder Glas (2017, March 18) Gerberateler kiest zelfde systeem orderver-werking als bij potplanten (in Dutch) https://www.onderglas.nl/gerberateler-kiest-zelfde-systeem-orderverwerking-als-bij-potplanten/ Accessed 2 Sept 2020

Van Uffelen G (2008) The Libri Picturati and the early history of the Hortus botanicus Lieden. In: De Koning J, van Uffelen G, Zemanek A, Zemanek B (eds) Drawn after nature, the complete botanical watercolours of the 16th-century Libri Picturati. KNNV Publishing, Zeist, pp 55–58

Van Uffelen G, Kessler PJA (red) (2015) 425 Jaar Hortus botanicus Leiden, Hortus botanicus, Leiden.

Von Thünen JH (1826) Der Isolirte Staat in Beziehung auf Landwirtschaft und Nationalökonomie. Wirtschaft & Finan, Hamburg

4

Dutch Flower Auctions

4.1 The Year 1637

In the cold and rain of February 1637, tulip bulb dealers traveled via muddy roads to Alkmaar, a town nowadays famous for its traditional cheese market, for an auction organized by the board of the city's orphanage. One of the most valuable collections of tulip bulbs had come into the possession of the board of the orphanage, and tulip bulbs were serious business. The auction was organized for the benefit of the seven orphans of Wouter Bartolomeusz Winckel, a very rich tavern keeper who had died the year before.[1] Winckel left behind "more than seventy fine or superbly fine tulips, representing about forty different varieties, together with a substantial quantity of pound goods totaling about thirty thousand aces of lower-value bulbs."[2] Auctions were used to determine the price and awarded the bulbs to the highest bidder. They were typically held in taverns and in other public places. The auction of Winckel's tulip bulbs was held on Thursday, February 5, 1637, in the salesroom at the Nieuwe Doelen, a monumental, Renaissance style building. The tulip bulb trade was intertwined with the trade of art, collectibles, and commodities. Merchants but also bakers, brewers, innkeepers, and apothecaries were active participants.[3]

The auction format was known as "in the little o" (in the zero). In Dutch this is called "*in het ootjen*," which nowadays is Dutch slang for "to pull someone's leg." The "little o" referred to the diagram that the auctioneer would draw to keep track of the bidding. The seller, in this case the orphanage, openly offered the bulbs for sale, with bids written on boards. There was a small reward for the highest bidder, *treckgelt* (pulling money), provided by the

© The Author(s), under exclusive license to Springer Nature Switzerland AG 2021
E. van Heck, *Technology Meets Flowers*, https://doi.org/10.1007/978-3-030-69303-9_4

seller as an attempt to attract the interest of potential buyers. The amount would vary depending on the seller's assessment of the value of the bulbs, but it would be somewhere between two and six stuivers—the equivalent of one or two rounds of drinks. Pulling money would be paid whether or not the seller accepted the highest bid. The potential buyers would provide their offers, while the bids were written on the boards. The auction was concluded with a call by the auctioneer: "no one bids? no one? once, no one further, twice, no one? third time, no one? fourth time?" If no one made a higher bid, and the seller was willing to sell at that price, the sale was concluded by the paying of *wijnkoop* (wine money) by the buyer to the seller. This amounted to half a *stuiver* per *guilder* (the Dutch precursor to the euro) of the price (in other words, one-fortieth of the total), with a maximum of three guilders per transaction. If the seller or the buyer decided in the end not to continue with the sale—indicated by wiping out the mark by the price on the board—a small fee known as *rouwkoop* (grieving money) had to be paid. Both *wijnkoop* and *rouwkoop* were a way of maintaining honorable relations when transactions were respectively completed (sealing of a promise) or canceled (restoring of a disturbed relationship).

Although there is no independent confirmation of the results of the Alkmaar auction, some pamphlets were distributed. One pamphlet, written three months before the Alkmaar auction, provided a "vivid impression of what the prices paid for tulip bulbs actually meant to the Dutch of the time. A flower worth three thousand guilders, the writer pointed out, could have been exchanged for a gigantic quantity of goods: eight fat pigs (240 guilders), four fat oxen (480 guilders), twelve fat sheep (120 guilders), twenty-four tons of wheat (448 guilders), forty-eight tons of rye (558 guilders), two hogsheads of wine (70 guilders), four barrels of eight-guilder beer (32 guilders), two tons of butter (192 guilders), a thousand pounds of cheese (120 guilders), a silver drinking cup (60 guilders), a pack of clothes (80 guilders), a bed with mattress and bedding (100 guilders), a ship (500 guilders); a total of 3000 guilders." Within a few days after the Alkmaar auction a one-page pamphlet entitled *List of Some Tulips Sold to the Highest Bidder on February 5th 1637* was printed containing a list of winning prices. Many of these prices "were no more than other prices for bulbs in recent weeks—a Paragon de Man for *f* 260, a Cos for *f* 205, a pound (1000 *asen*) of Max bulbs for *f* 300—and the average price overall for singe bulbs in the main auction was *f* 792.88. But the attention of those reading the broadside was no doubt captured by a few much higher prices: a Viceroy for *f* 4203 and, particularly, an Admirael van Enchuysen with an offset, which reportedly sold for *f* 5200. It was also noted on the printed sheet that the total sold in tulips and other flowers and plants was around *f* 90,000." (the equivalent of €1 million nowadays).[4]

It turned out—much later—that the Alkmaar auction resulted in the highest winning price ever bid for a bulb in history. It is not clear what the purpose of the pamphlet was; it may have been a warning against the craziness of the bulb market or a source of inspiration to attract more potential bidders. These pamphlets were the Twitter and Facebook updates of the seventeenth century.

It is interesting to notice that the Alkmaar auction was held in the middle of the winter. Typically, tulip bulbs were planted in September and remained in the earth until after the next flowering season in April, May, or June. After they blossomed, the bulbs were lifted out of the ground, dried, and stored in a dry place. Only then could the bulbs be physically transferred from the seller to the buyer. Therefore, the outcome of the auction was "precarious and the tulip trade risky," and it ultimately turned out to be problematic for the guardians of Winckel's children. No tulips were available at the time of the auction, no bulbs could be taken away, and none of the high prices were actually paid on the spot. In that sense, these were future contract transactions, a promise to deliver bulbs in the future. Future contracts were officially prohibited in the Dutch economy at that time, but they were common anyway. For example, the trade of Baltic grain and the trade of commodities, such as spices from the Far East shipped by the Dutch East India Company, were sold via future contracts.

William Crowne, passing through Europe in 1636 on a diplomatic mission to the Holy Roman Emperor, took note of a variety of wonders during this trip. In the small town of Vianen, near Utrecht, he noted that "the rarest things in it, are Flowers, for there was a Tulip-roote sold lately for 340 pounds." The Haarlem priest Jodocus Cats wrote his nephew, on February 5, 1637, that like the plague that had been raging since 1635, now "another sickness has arisen. It is the sickness of the *bloemisten* or *floristen*," and "[T]his mania, like a contagious illness, infected the whole Low Countries, & passed in to France," wrote Jean de Parival in his Les Délices de la Holland in 1665. Steven Theunisz van der Lust in Haarlem wrote that everyone "pious and impious, thieves and whores, Haarlemmers and Amsterdammers" was said to be buying and selling tulips. The historian of Haarlem, Theodorus Schrevelius, wrote in 1648 that "I don't know what kind of angry spirit was called up from Hell" and "Our descendants doubtless will laugh at the human insanity of our Age, that in our times the Tulip-flowers have been so revered." Most of the modern-day view of tulip mania is based on Charles Mackay, whose extraordinary *Popular Delusions and the Madness of Crowds*, written in 1841, is still in print and sells well. Mackay's main sources were Johann Beckmann, author of *A History of Inventions, Discoveries and Origin*, written in 1797, and a propaganda pamphlet against the trade by Adrian Roman, *Dialogue between True-mouth and Greedy-goods* of 1637, but both sources were suspect. Nowadays, most people around the world will remember tulip mania as the first major financial bubble with its widespread craziness and bankruptcy.[5] We learned that "thousands were ruined, and the economy of the Netherlands was left in shocked disarray." In the financial and investment world, tulip mania has become a common example of a commodity market that went crazy with juicy details of greed, foolishness, stupidity, hell, or irrational exuberance. A great story, indeed. But there is one problem: most of the story is untrue.

4.2   Tulip Mania Unraveled

Meticulous research in the period 1999–2007 by Anne Goldgar, a professor in Early Modern European History at King's College London, revealed a rather different picture of the tulip trade.[6] She analyzed traders, transactions, transaction documents, letters, and other sources, such as notarial records related to the tulip trade but also other trades such as art (paintings) and other collectible items (shells). Her study showed clearly that there were not so many people involved in the specialized trade of tulips. While some people lost some money, but no one went bankrupt, and the impact on the Dutch economy was very limited. As Goldgar indicates:

> But by looking chiefly at two of the main cities in the trade, Amsterdam and Haarlem (whose estimated populations in 1635 were something more than 120,000 and 42,000, respectively), and one somewhat smaller town, Enkhuizen (whose estimated population in 1622 was 22,000), we are able to get a good picture of the trade in the 1630s. The question is who, in these cities, was actually involved. I have identified approximately 285 in Haarlem—at the time recognized as the center of the trade—who bought and sold flowers, around 60 in Amsterdam, and about 25 in Enkhuizen.

It turned out that "as for Amsterdam, practically everyone we can identify with tulips was at least a middle-level merchant, and even in Haarlem and Enkhuizen the numbers of merchants, wealthy manufacturers, professionals, and artists and high-level artisans made up a sizeable proportion of those who bought and sold tulips." Trade took place with relatives or friends (called *vrienden* in Dutch) and within religious groups: "Mennonites appear in disproportionately large numbers among the bloemisten, and, more than other groups, they seem to have been particularly interested in selling to each other," and "a whole host of Mennonite bloemisten was spread through Haarlem, Amsterdam, Rotterdam, and Utrecht—all connected, and almost always by ties of blood." Also, proximity played a role. Sometimes clusters of traders lived close to each other or owned gardens close to each other, for example, at residences with large gardens at Keizersgracht and Herengracht in Amsterdam, or around Zeedijk and the Geldersekade, or the Grote Markt and Nobelstraat in Haarlem with a cluster of traders that owned houses on the northwest side of Haarlem, near the Kruispoort, and gardens on the southeast side, a district called Rosenprieel. And there is also the proximity of interests: "Of the 167 bloemisten, whose profession could be identified, by far the largest single grouping—forty-six—were merchants involved in the cloth trade." Other professions were bakers, brewers, innkeepers (at inns trade could take place), and apothecaries. And most were organized in professional guilds and had intensive social interactions. However, they did not trade only to their cluster; they traded to anyone: "They might not have sold to each other—but they probably talked to each other." Clusters of bloemisten probably talked and shared information and tulip mania depended on the flow of information.

Innkeepers were "right in the middle of the network of information about tulips." They could observe the negotiations and price levels in their inns; they could identify disputes about prices, the quality, or the promised quantity of bulbs. Other nodes of the information network were gardens where bulbs were planted, reviewed, and handed over from the seller to the buyer (with other traders as witness), around the family dinner table, or even on the street corner. Also, shopkeepers, doctors and surgeons, and notaries played an active role in exchanging the latest information about tulips. Interestingly, wealthy merchants and professionals, such as doctors and lawyers, were also forming art collections: "The collecting of art seemed to go with the collecting of tulips." Transactions were seen where bulbs were exchanged for a number of paintings or other collectibles such as shells and other "rarities." Building up a collection began among aristocrats, but it became a popular activity among citizens as a way to gain social status. "In the mid-seventeenth century in Delft, around two-thirds of the population owned paintings of some kind, and it is estimated that average ownership of paintings at this time among the burghers of the Holland towns ranged between five and eleven simple pictures." This mixed portfolio also reduced the risks of losing all money; paintings or other "rarities" did not show the drastic price rise and price drop that tulips eventually did. Another surprising aspect was that trading took place with buyers and sellers who tried to set up an honest reputation, to deliver what was promised, and to be paid what was agreed upon. It was not always easy because when the negotiations took place, for example, in the winter, the final transaction—after the bulbs were grown and could be harvested—could take place in August or September. A high level of trust was needed from both the buyer and the seller. It was also clear there were many disputes, but self-regulation with the help of experts that acted as arbiters was widely used. Expert committees, so-called *collegie*, "who appear to have made rulings on the trade," were formed in several of the Dutch cities and villages. The claim that many people were able to trade expensive bulbs was not validated: "Only 37 people could be identified who spend more than 300 guilders on bulbs." Very expensive bulbs were traded among a very small group of very wealthy merchants. The claim that bulbs were traded hundreds of times could not be validated: "The longest chain I have found in 1636–1637 is five people, and we know that it must have begun no later than July 1636, because the first member of the chain (in whose garden the bulbs remained) is Volckert Coornhart, who was buried on August 4, 1636."

Although there were some difficult economic times, such as in the early 1620s and 1626–1631, these could not be attributed to the tulip mania. The Dutch economy continued to grow in the seventeenth century. The cause of tulip mania in February 1637 is still debated. A strong argument is that over-supply of bulbs (more heavy bulbs with a larger number of offsets) could generate, in a not very liquid market, a strong effect on price levels. The plague in the summer of 1636 could have generated, as in the Winckel case, an extra stimulus to the supply of bulbs on the market. It could also be attributed to an oversupply of future contracts (promissory notes), which were difficult to audit (and were officially prohibited). It was not easy to verify that each bulb in the ground was related to one promissory note. Sellers could default on their promises. However, the impact of the Alkmaar auction results was less dramatic; most transactions were canceled in the summer of 1637; several disputes at courts were seen, but no bankruptcies were reported that could be attributed to tulip mania.

Tulip mania was the first reported of a series of many economic bubbles—just to name a few: the South Sea Bubble of 1720 (South Sea Company stocks, 1711–1720), the Railway Mania in the UK, Ireland, US (railway stocks, 1840–1846), the Wallstreet Crash of 1929 (stocks, 1921–1929), the Dotcom Bubble (Internet company stocks, 1995–2000), and the Cryptocurrency Bubble (bitcoins and other cryptocurrencies, 2011–2017). However, bubbles are rare and not very common. Every bubble has its specific context and a complex mix of causes. There is no "one-size-fits-all" explanation. Usually, it is a cocktail of a new intriguing phenomena (tulip bulbs, railways, Internet, blockchain), a high uncertainty about the future value or usefulness of the product at hand, a "greedy" interest to make money and a willingness to obtain ownership, enough investment money to buy ownership, and a relaxed market regulation with low entry barriers.

4.3   Social Construction of Value

On October 5, 2018, an excited audience of potential buyers crowded into the salesroom at Sotheby's in London for an evening auction of contemporary art. Established in 1744, Sotheby's is a well-known auction house, dealing in art, wine, and collectibles. It has ten salesrooms, including in London, Paris, New York, and Hong Kong. Sotheby's Bid Now program allows visitors to view all auctions live online and place bids from anywhere around the world. On this particular evening in London, lot 67 was a unique painting entitled "Girl with balloon" created by Banksy, an anonymous street artist.[7] The painting was made with spray and acrylic on canvas and had a large golden frame. The owner of the painting, who was also anonymous, had acquired it directly from the artist in 2006, and the painting was valued at £200,000–£300,000. Sotheby's auctioneer, Oliver Barker, opened bidding at £100,000; bids came in quickly. The price was driven higher and higher as people in the room, and those participating via telephone or online, indicated their bids. The atmosphere in the room became very intense and the auctioneer raised his voice to match the energy of the crowd as bidding progressed: "I hear 600,000; 650,000, excellent, 700,000; 750,000; 800,00; 850,000, last chance on 850,000,"—but then a new bid came in at 860,000, and the auctioneer slammed his hand on his desk—"fair warning, I am selling now, 860,000, last chance, and so be it, 860,000"—the auctioneer hammered on the desk, made a note in his book, and looked up. A beep was heard in the room and just at that moment the Banksy painting was drawn into its golden frame as a mechanical shredder concealed in it whirred to action. Participants looked on in disbelief; some shrieked; some pointed, while others laughed as the canvas spooled into the shredder—they thought it was a joke. Then the machine stopped as abruptly as it started with the half-shredded painting dangling from the frame—incredulity passed over the auctioneer's face for a heartbeat, but he otherwise took in the scene with a stiff upper lip. After the auction Banksy posted an image of the shredding on Instagram with the words "Going, going, gone ….," a phrase often used by auctioneers prior to hammering down the final bid and price for an object.

The Sotheby's case illustrates two essential points. Firstly, it shows the working of an English auction with ascending prices. The auctioneer begins with a reserve price and either increases the price in regular increments, such as 10% of the previous bid, or he or she allows bidders to increase the price by whatever increment they like; the last bid of the Sotheby's auction of the Banksy painting was £10,000, contrasted with the incremental increases of £50,000 prior to the final bid. In an English auction, the price successively raises until only one bidder remains, and that bidder wins the object at the final price or the so-called "hammer price" (the auctioneer uses a small hammer and slams it on desk to confirm that the last bid was indeed the last bid). In the Sotheby's case the hammer price for the Banksy painting was £860,000, but the buyer, an anonymous European art collector, had to pay £1,042,000 ($1.4 million), including the buyer's premium of 20% of the hammer price and other expenses. The payment to the seller is based on the hammer price (£860,000) less a commission and any agreed-upon expenses.

Secondly, auctions are *explicitly* concerned with social context as a means to determine value, known as the "social construction of value," a term coined by the eminent sociologist Charles W. Smith.[8] Smith had observed many auctions in action. He concluded that "The true power of the auction is that its attribution of value represents the collective judgement of the auction community", and we will return to him later.[9] Banksy's partial shredding of "Girl with balloon"—some newspapers called it a prank, and one newspaper declared it "quite possibly the biggest prank in art history"—was designed for the social context of the art world and the art industry. Banksy's act—namely the public shredding of his painting—can be seen as a critique of the international art and art auction scene, where substantial money is made by buyers (eventually), sellers, dealers, art galleries, and auctioneers, but not by artists. The artist had criticized the art industry and its social context many times prior to the auction at Sotheby's, including through paintings such as "Morons (white and gold)" created in 2006, with the quote "I can't believe you morons actually buy this shit," and a documentary film entitled "Exit Through the Gift Shop" in 2010. Others view Banksy as cunning and shrewd, using his deep knowledge of the inner workings of the art industry and its social context for his own advantage. The anonymous buyer of the partially shredded painting asked Pest Control, a handling service on behalf of Banksy, to authenticate it, and the painting was renamed "Love is in the bin." On October 11, 2018, Sotheby's issued a statement on the events as follows: "in the auction at Sotheby's last week, history was made: it marked the first time a piece of live performance art had been sold at auction" and Sotheby's put "Love is in the bin" on display that same week. The value of the painting—due to worldwide news coverage—was estimated at more than £2 million. The spectacle Banksy created at the auction renewed worldwide interest in his art, which will cause the price of his works to rise further, which is good news for Banksy, for the owners of his art, and also for the dealers, gallerists, and auctioneers.

4.4   English Auctions

Have you ever visited an art auction? On a rainy May afternoon in 2019, my wife and I made our way to an impressive building at Rockefeller Plaza in New York City. Inside were large rooms where paintings, sculptures, and jewelry were on display, not unlike a museum. But these items were going to be auctioned and the impressive building was no museum, but the New York salesroom of the auction house, Christie's. James Christie established the company in 1766 and held his first sale in his permanent salesroom in Pall Mall, London.[10] Nowadays, Christie's is an international auction house with a global presence in forty-six countries with ten salesrooms around the world, offering around three hundred fifty auction events annually in over eighty categories, including fine and decorative arts, jewelry, photographs, collectibles, wine, and more. On the day of our visit, Christie's held a sale of Impressionist and Modern art, with masterpieces painted by the likes of Claude Monet, Marc Chagall, Edgar Degas, Bernard Buffet, Gustave Loiseau, and more.

Upon arriving at Christie's, we registered to join the auction and our credentials and creditworthiness were checked. We received a paddle with a bidder number—ours was 438—and we entered the large salesroom. The room had seating for up to two hundred fifty bidders, but participation in the auction was not limited to those onsite. Telephone operators, an online bidding platform, and live streaming of the auction enabled people around the world to participate in the bidding process. We entered the room at the west side. At the north side, the auctioneer's desk was positioned on a platform. Above the auctioneer, a screen displayed a picture of the object at auction, its lot number, the name of the object and the name of the artist, and the current bid price (in dollars and several other currencies). Adjacent to the auctioneer, there was a desk for administrators and auditors. To the auctioneer's left, the paintings on auction were displayed via a rotating wall and there were five telephone operators at a desk; see Fig. 4.1.

Another twenty telephone operators sat not far away, and above them were displays of paintings and sculptures that would be auctioned later that week. On the opposite side of the room from the auctioneer, there were computer screens where the auctioneer could view the incoming online bids—the screens showed the bid price and location (e.g., Singapore and Germany) of the last bidder. That afternoon, the auctioneer was a very friendly gentlemen with a light French accent. He opened the bidding and, as the first item had a reserve price, he prompted the bidders to surpass the reserve.

Fig. 4.1 The auctioneer and telephone operators at work at Christie's auction house in New York City. Author's own image

The auctioneer's commentary was something like the following: "We start at 25,000; 30,000, 35,000; thank you, it is with me in the book; 35,000; an online bid from Singapore at 40,000; 40,000; it is still with me, and an absentee bid of 45,000; and a last chance at the telephones"—and rapidly—"50,000; 55,000, 60,000"—one of the telephone operators indicated she needed some time to consult with the bidder and the auctioneer waited a moment –"would you go for 63,000? Sure. Last chance, it is still with me"—the telephone operator signals by waiving—"63,000; thanks, Zumiko (calling the telephone operator by name), yes, a new bid online, 65,000; thank you, Singapore; anyone in the room; OK, last chance; 65,000"—the auctioneer hammered on his desk, and announced the price and the bidder number of the winner—"65,000 to bidder number: 337." He then continued to the next lot.

There were around one hundred people in the room that day, including private bidders, professional art dealers, and tourists, but only ten of them participated in bidding. The atmosphere in the room was serene. Some of the people knew each other and chatted amiably. Some people came and left during the sale, and it was not clear how many people were connected via telephone or the Internet. But there was a mix of on-site, telephone, and online bidders for almost every auction lot. For example, in the room an elderly man and woman bid on two paintings; two men (one appeared to be the real bidder and the other appeared to be his helper) bid on an expensive painting. The helper raised the paddle after the other man nodded slightly; every nod was another $50,000. One man in the front—wearing a baseball cap—indicated a price of $47,000, although the bid price was already $50,000. The auctioneer said, "Sorry, I can move only in one direction," and the audience laughed. Throughout the auction we had to control the impulse to raise our paddle. But we managed fine, the visit went very well, and we enjoyed our afternoon at Christie's.

On the evening of that same day in New York, "Meules," painted by Claude Monet in 1890, was auctioned off a few blocks away at Sotheby's.[11] The bidding started at $45 million and lasted just eight minutes. Six bidders fought hard, but only one could be the winner. "Meules" had been in private ownership nearly a century when it first came to auction in 1986, and at that time it sold for a relatively modest $2.5 million. But on this May evening, the six bidders pushed the price ever higher. Ultimately, the winning bid was $97 million, for a total $111,747,000, including the buyer's premium, or more than forty-four times what the work fetched in the 1980s. It was a staggering sum.[12]

Most people (including Claude Monnet himself) would have thought that the bidders were crazy, and the winner craziest of all. The winner had been caught in the phenomenon of the *winner's curse*. The winner is cursed because no one else in the world was willing to buy the painting at that price. The bidder—because he was so eager to win—paid too much. As we will see later, the winner's curse is not completely irrational, and it is a fairly common occurrence in auctions.[13]

4.5 Dutch Auctions

Before 1887 most trading was done via direct negotiations between a seller and a buyer, or indirectly via a trader (a broker) that negotiated with the seller and later with the buyer. Sometimes it was done via the English auction format. The rules were clear and defined, and both buyers and sellers were accustomed to the simple structure of these negotiations. However, there was one problem. For perishable products it was way too slow.

In the nineteenth century, the population and cities in the Netherlands, such as Amsterdam, Utrecht, Rotterdam, the Hague, Leiden, and Haarlem started to grow. There were more people to feed, and therefore there was more demand for fresh products. More demand stimulated more supply and more products were distributed from the farmlands to cities nearby, and so more roads and railroads were built, although constructing this infrastructure was challenging, given the need for bridges in swampy areas of the Dutch lowlands.[14] The first railroad between Haarlem and Amsterdam was established in 1839, but it was not until 1860 that a denser transportation network of roads and railroads had been established. Thus, the distribution of fresh products, like vegetables, fruits, and flowers, from farmlands to cities was done via small barges on waterways and canals. In rural villages fresh products were traded directly by the grower to a shipper. Sometimes the grower was represented by the shipper, saving time for the grower, but also making the grower vulnerable to unscrupulous shippers who took advantage of such arrangements. Potential buyers stood at the edge of the canal or on small bridges over the canal. As the barges passed by, negotiations took place between the seller (grower or shipper) and buyers (traders/shippers). This process was cumbersome and very slow.

Friday July 29, 1887, was a relatively cold day for the summertime.[15] The weekend was approaching and there was a limited supply of fresh products. In those days, cauliflowers were scarce, and demand and prices had been driven upward by a previous dry period and a strong eastern wind. Dirk Jongerling—a grower from the small village Zuid-Scharwoude—came to the "Bakkersbrug" (as the bridge was called in Dutch) in the village of Broek op Langedijk, and he wanted an excellent price for his cauliflower. Many shippers responded to his call. Shipper Jan Dirkmaat suggested to auction off the product to the highest bidder. On that day, the descending auction or Dutch auction was invented. Dirk Jongerling started with a very high price and gradually lowered the price until a shipper shouted "mine," and at that price the cauliflower was sold. Instead of many bids in an English auction, there was only one bid, which decreased the time growers and shippers spent in negotiations. In the beginning, Dutch auctions were executed verbally. Soon, it was not the grower, but a trusted third party, the auctioneer, who announced the starting price. For example the auctioneer would announce 24 cents per cauliflower and then gradually reduce the price: 23.5, 23, 22.5, 22, 21.5, 21, 20.5, 20, 19.5, 19, until a buyer shouted "mine," and for 19 cents per cauliflower the whole lot (usually enough to fill an entire barge) was sold.

In case two bidders shouted "mine" at the same time the auctioneer had to decide in a split second which bidder shouted first. Such conflict could easily lead to anger or to frustration, so another invention was needed. This new invention was electrical, and first two prototypes were created by the P.J. Kipp & Zn Company in Delft and installed in two auction centers, in Broek op Langedijk and Enkhuizen, respectively.[16] The system consisted of a screen with 30 numbered fall valves with corresponding electronic buttons that caused the valve to fall when pressed. The screen was placed on top of a bridge over a canal where barges with the fresh products passed by. The numbered buttons were installed on desks with benches adjacent to the canal. For each sale, the auctioneer began by announcing a high price and then gradually lowering it until the first buyer pushed the button, causing the corresponding valve to fall. The number of the valve was shown to the audience and the buyer's identity was known to the audience (this element is important and we will come back to it later). Therefore, it was immediately clear who the first (and winning) bidder was. The button also triggered a bell to ring out and the machine simultaneously blocked all other buttons until it was reset for another auction round. The auctioneer noted the price and the name of the bidder and reset the machine to be used again.

This solved some problems, but not all of them. There were still disagreements about the price at the time that the button was pushed, for example, the auctioneer may have lowered the price too quickly or might not have paid attention to the ringing bell. Disputes were time-consuming and therefore costly for all participants and did not create a great trading atmosphere. Therefore, another invention was needed. In 1902, the P.J. Kipp & Zn. Company transferred their prototype design to the L. van der Hoorn Electro-Technisch Bureau Company in Utrecht, which created another innovative extension: the electrical clock system. The clock system was constructed with a round glass plate. It had a diameter of one meter divided in one hundred parts (like minutes on a clock). One clock hand was set on a high price (such as 24) and gradually descended. When a bidder pushed the button of the prototype it triggered four events: (1) it stopped the clock and the clock hand indicated the price; (2) a bell rang; (3) one valve fell to reveal the buyer's identification number; and (4) the other buttons were blocked such that each auction would have only one bid—the winning bid. The name of the combined valve and clock system was the electric auctioneer (in Dutch: *elektrisch afmijntoestel*); see Fig. 4.2.

In 1903, seven prototypes of the electric auctioneer were installed in different auction sites in the Netherlands. Although there were some hiccups, it worked well. Adjustments were made for specific types of products. For example, for cut flowers and potted plants a wider range of prices was needed, so clocks were developed with a larger diameter of two meters with three circles. In the first circle, prices were indicated with guilders, the middle circle indicated quarters and ten cents, and the inner circle five cents or cents. The prototypes had to be reliable. In 1908, the auction site in North Holland conducted between 1000 and 1500 transactions per day in busy periods, with annual sales amounting to 1 million guilders (the equivalent of €12 million nowadays). The nickname for the electric auctioneer was "the Peacemaker."[17] It prevented disputes between the auctioneer and the buyers, "two buyers never were able to push the button at the same time," and it settled the matter of identifying the first bidder and the winning price.[18] With advanced electrical technologies, the machine indicated the right allocation to the first bidder and at the right price. It was the start of a glorious journey for the Peacemaker.

Fig. 4.2 The electric auctioneer at the flower auction of Rijnsburg in 1914 http://www.canonvankatwijk.nl/onderwijs/bloemen-uit-rijnsburg/. With permission by Royal FloraHolland

4.6 Grower Cooperatives

The Peacemaker attracted many more sellers and buyers. It turned out that the electrification of the auctioneer stimulated an urgent need to professionalize the other tasks at hand, such as to determine the sequence of the auctioned lots, to handle the electric auctioneer, to judge in case of disputes over the quality of delivered products, and to handle the payment between the buyer and the seller. Most growers preferred to concentrate on the production of flowers; the shippers were too busy with transport and reaching the cities to sell the produce to retailers and local markets. Buyers were not fully trusted to handle the auction process. In short, a new invention was needed. After some debate in the local pubs, a new institution was created: the grower cooperative. Growers usually became members of and investors in the grower cooperative, and each local village formed a cooperative that included its growers. Members were obliged to send their products to the cooperative for sale, and each member received a voting right to steer the strategy and investments of the cooperative. The cooperative was held responsible for the marketing and sales of flowers (and later also plants).[19] In December 1911, the first auction cooperative called "Bloemenlust" was founded and "the auction of export flowers took place in Café Welcome." Not long after, the Central Aalsmeer

Auction was launched on January 5, 1912. Five days later, in the "Drie Kolommen" pub, flowers were auctioned using the auction clock. The sales of both Aalsmeer auctions increased every year. In 1918, the Central Aalsmeer Auction achieved—for the first time—annual sales of 1 million guilders (the equivalent of €6.8 million nowadays). Several other local flower auction cooperatives started in different regions of the Netherlands: in Rijnsburg (west) in 1914, in Blerick (south) in 1915, in Poeldijk (west) in 1923, in Eelde (north) in 1927, and in Berkel en Rodenrijs, near Rotterdam (west) in 1929.

The cooperative in Poeldijk, called "Centrale Westlandsche Snijbloemenveiling," was initiated by the association of bulb growers in that region. The cooperative grew gradually and moved, in 1931, to a new auction complex at the Dijkweg in Honselersdijk. Not all members were happy about the move, especially the Poeldijk growers. In 1932, they split and formed their own cooperative called "Bloemenveiling Het Westland."[20] However, the cooperative struggled and dissolved in 1970.

After the recovery from the Second World War, the demand for flowers and plants began to gradually grow. A crucial development for Dutch floriculture was the initiative of the Frenchman, Jean Monnet, to form the European Economic Community in 1957, twelve years after the end of the Second World War. The community consisted of six countries: Belgium, France, Germany, Italy, Luxembourg, and the Netherlands. The decision was made to create a tariff-free zone and many export barriers were reduced. On July 1, 1968, a European free market for flowers and plants was established. The system of cultivation permits was abolished in 1969, leading to lower barriers to entry to start as a grower or exporter. The economic results were spectacular. Exports from the Netherlands to other European countries increased threefold and the Dutch began to expand exports beyond adjacent countries like Belgium, Germany, and Luxemburg to reach France and Italy. The increased demand for flowers and plants, and for more varieties, led to further consolidation of local cooperatives. For example, in Aalsmeer two local cooperatives had grower members that were located in different geographical areas. When more and different members joined, the members were much more distributed all over the village or sometimes outside of the village. A merger was needed and took effect in March 1968 as the United Flower Auction Aalsmeer. The Aalsmeer auction was setting the trend for further expansion. In 1972, a new auction complex was build, and it was subsequently expanded in 1999 and 2009. Nowadays, the auction complex is the largest indoor market building in the world. Other milestones include the introduction of brokerage in 1973, as a second, demand-driven, sales channel, and the decision in 2006 to allow international membership for non-Dutch companies located in countries outside the European Union. Companies from within the European Union were already allowed to become members. In Naaldwijk, flowers produced outside the Netherlands were sold via the auction for the first time in 1971. Naaldwijk merged with the cooperative in Bleiswijk in 1990 and the auction complex was expanded with the Fleur Center. It expanded again around 2000 in Trade Parc Westland. Another merger with the cooperative in Rijnsburg and Eelde was established in 2002. On January 1, 2008, the existing auction cooperatives merged into one, large cooperative: Royal FloraHolland. It has locations in Aalsmeer, Naaldwijk, Rijnsburg, and Eelde. A joint venture between Royal FloraHolland and Landgard was set up in 2010 and as a result a new auction center, Veiling Rhein-Maas, was established in Herongen (Germany).

4.7   Bidding in Dutch Auctions

It is always very exciting to visit the Dutch flower auctions. I have visited many, many times for project meetings, to interview auctioneers and other employees, and to discuss and present my research. Tourists can visit the Dutch flower auctions in Aalsmeer. Tours for individuals or groups are fun, and if you go, you will learn a lot. To see the real action, you need to be there early, around 7 AM. If you follow the signs, it is easy to find the tourist entrance of the largest indoor market building of the world—you need to climb up three flights of stairs and make a turn to the left. At that moment you will be shocked; you will view the enormous distribution hall below you, where stacking carts are driven like little distribution trains. At the front of the train, a dispatcher steers the carts from their origin, usually the warehouse, to their destination in the buyer sections, also called the buyer boxes, at the end of the distribution hall. It is a very colorful scene. The flowers are loaded on the trains and many varieties, shapes, sizes, and colors can be seen. You will follow a walkway passing above the activity on the distribution center floor where the trains come and go. Your next stop is the auction hall where you can observe the auction action from behind windows. You will notice the auction clock screens and nowadays in Aalsmeer there is only one auction trading room left where buyers will be physically present. In this room, buyers can connect digitally to all auction clocks.[21]

Information about the auctioned product and other information cues are indicated on the screen. Information cues are presented, including the number and type of upcoming batches, number of batches of the same type of products that will be auctioned on the same day, supplier information of the current batch and the upcoming batches, and information about the flower products (stem length, quality grade, and quality remarks). (Spoiler alert, the role and impact of the winner identity disclosure will be discussed in Chap. 7.)

The auction clock does not have a clock hand any more. The price per flower stem is indicated by the red dot, and at the beginning of the auction the red dot is positioned at the highest possible price. When the auction begins, the red dot travels counterclockwise from far above the highest price to progressively lower prices. When the first bidder pushes the button at the bidder's desk in the auction hall (or the spacebar on a computer if the bidder is participating online), the clock stops, and the red light indicates the winning price; see Fig. 4.3.

For example, the winning price is 14 cents per stem by the first (and therefore winning) bidder 854, at the second auction clock from the left, in Fig. 4.3. The monetary unit is, in this case, one cent, but can be changed to five cents, ten cents, €1, or €5, to cater to more expensive varieties. The auction lot—supplied by one grower—holds a single type of flower or bouquet and, from a logistical point of view, is called a batch. For example, the auction lot or batch has two trolleys, and each has 27 containers for a total of 54 containers. There are 80 pieces (in this case, flower stems) in one container. So, the total number of flowers in this batch is 54 × 80 = 4320 flowers. Any time a bidder stops the clock (thus winning the auction), the bidder will indicate how many containers he or she will purchase at that price. The minimum number of

Fig. 4.3 Bidders in the auction hall at Rijnsburg https://www.royalfloraholland.com/en/about-floraholland/media-centre/actual-photos. With permission by Royal FloraHolland

containers that the bidder must buy is indicated on the screen under "minimum to be purchased," and this is important to remember. The minimum purchased quantity is set by the auctioneer, and we will come back to this point later. In this case, the minimum purchase is 3, and the buyer purchased the remaining 13 containers. The crux of the Dutch auction mechanism is that the remaining containers will be auctioned again in the next round. The auctioneer will reset the auction clock to a high price, but not as high as the first auction round, because the auctioneer understood from the first round how the buyers value the auction lot. For every sub-batch, the price might change. It is micro auctioning at its best. Every two to three seconds there will be a transaction. One lot can be auctioned all at once, or there could be 50 transactions per lot. In total, there are around 100,000 transactions per day at Royal FloraHolland.

The distribution of trolleys with their containers is very complex. Suppose that the auctioned lot of 54 containers was bought by five buyers: the first bought 1 container, the second bought 12 containers, the third bought 22 containers, the fourth bought 8 containers, and fifth bought the remaining 11 containers. The batch of the 54 containers will be moved to the distribution area and split into the five sub-batches. A single buyer may have bought parts of different auction lots, and if so they will be gathered and coupled into one distribution train and delivered to the buyer boxes at the end of the distribution hall.

The buyer boxes are rented spaces where the buyer will receive the flower products, check if the right products were sent, and process the flower products further. The buyer can decide to repack the flowers or bundle different flowers in a new flower arrangement. The flowers are transported to the next buyer in the supply chain, e.g., a buyer that will export the flowers can send them via Schiphol Airport to the United States, or the flowers can go by truck for export to Germany, or they can be sold to retailers for the local Dutch markets.

Local retailers can purchase their flowers directly from the Dutch flower auctions. However, the auctioneer has to realize the highest price with the lowest distribution costs—and the actions and decisions of the auctioneer will be explored in more detail in Chap. 6. A higher price could be obtained with a lower minimum purchase amount, but that would increase the distribution costs, given the higher number of sub-batches with, on average, a lower number of containers per sub-batch. The auctioneer, acting as the orchestrator of the auction market, has to have a sharp eye to judge both the commercial and the distribution options. This is no easy task.

4.8   Digitizing Flower Auctions

The electric auctioneer—the Peacemaker—has evolved into the current, modern digitized design of the auction clock system and many changes were made over the past one hundred twenty years. Let us explore these changes and focus on the role of information that was presented to the buyers.

With the electric auctioneer, accurate information about the price and about the winning bidder were concealed. Until the 1960s, the auction clock was positioned at the front side of the salesroom. It had one clock hand and looked very similar to the original design. The clock hand indicated the price. On the display of the clock, bidder identification numbers of respective bidders were shown. A light illuminated the number of the winning bidder. On the adjacent side of the room the auctioneer was positioned on a sort of balcony with two administrators sitting nearby. The administration was done with pen and paper. On the opposite side of the room the buyers were sitting at benches with buttons in a setting like a theater. The flowers were laid horizontally on rolling rectangular tables around hundred and eighty inches in length and around sixty inches deep, which was large enough for long-stemmed flowers. The tables had four wheels and were rolled from the east side under the auctioneer's balcony to the west side, passing under the clock. The tables halted by the demonstrator who took some flowers from the table and showed the sample to the audience, sometimes providing comments about the quality. The auctioneer could also provide extra information via a microphone and loudspeaker system in the room. The tables were then rolled to the distribution hall and the flowers were delivered to the different buyer boxes. The flowers on these tables did not get any water and therefore this method shortened their life cycle. There was also no air-cooling system in the distribution hall.

In the 1980s, the auction clock was computerized. Some information was presented at the auction front via digital displays, but the clock still had its one arm. Enormous progress was made in logistics with the development of a standard trolley with three levels. Flowers were positioned vertically in buckets—instead of horizontally as they had been in the decades before—and a computer was linked to the auction clock. The computer stored auction prices and bidder data in a database. This was a more reliable method of data storage, and it could be used to send paper invoices to the identified buyers of the flower products.

In the 1990s, additional new technologies were applied to the flower auctions.[22] Royal FloraHolland recognized that the physical limitations of their auction facilities constrained their growth. Experiments with digital pictures representing the auctioned flowers or plants were carried out. One of the initiatives was the Vidifleur project. In this experiment, the auction clock and the auctioned products were shown on a vidi-wall consisting of 36 digital screens.

The idea behind the Vidifleur auction initiative was to allow buyers to trade from outside the auction hall, thereby uncoupling valuation and logistics. When the flowers or plants arrived at the auction hall in Naaldwijk, a photograph was taken, digitized, and stored in auction computers. The computer transferred the picture for display to the vidi-wall at the auction hall, where buyers could bid based on the image of the product. Buyers were also able to see and bid for products via computer screens in their private offices; they could even see a synchronized representation of the official auction clock. For the sellers and the auction house, these steps seemed logical and represented progress, but buyers did not agree. They complained about the poor quality of the digital images. Moreover, the system provided no efficiencies for the buyers—in fact, off-site buyers missed out on information that had been shared in the auction hall, such as market gossip and buyer's reactions during the auction process. Information asymmetries were created between those in the auction hall and those participating remotely. The buyer's dissatisfaction led to the failure of the Vidifleur auction.

Another initiative was the the Sample-based auction of potted plants in Aalsmeer, in Dutch called *Info-veilen*. In this case, growers sent a sample of the product to the auction house, along with information on the available inventory, packaging alternatives, and delivery constraints. During the auction, the sample represented the entire inventory available to buyers. All of the information was exchanged with the grower through electronic data interchange (EDI), at that time a new way to standardize electronic messages. By reducing the number of times plants were handled, sample-based auctioning was designed to reduce the costs due to transportation, packaging, and damage. The participants expected a number of benefits. First, by uncoupling logistics and price determination, the auction house and the growers expected to increase the number of transactions per hour. In reality, however, the number of transactions per hour decreased because buyers had to specify the terms of delivery. Second, although the auction house expected 45% of the supply to be sold via the sample-based auction, the actual figure was only 10%. Thus, sample-based auctioning did not effectively reduce storage requirements. Third, buyers indicated that the sample was not actually representative of the entire inventory, and they questioned the growers' sample selection process.

The result was a lower price level, because bidders took into account a risk premium for lower quality. After nine months, sample-based auctioning was discontinued in late 1994.

In 1994, the Dutch growers, who were members of the grower cooperative and therefore the owners of the flower auction house, implemented restrictions on imported flowers, because they felt threatened by increasing foreign imports of flowers and their negative effect on prices. In response, the East African Flower (EAF) group created the Tele Flower Auction (TFA). In March 1995, it launched TFA with two growers and seventy buyers. The TFA allowed buyers to bid, Dutch auction style, through personal computers. Logistics and price discovery were uncoupled and decentralized. The flowers were not visible to the buyers and the buyers were not physically present in the auction room. Growers sent the flowers to the East African Flowers group, which organized all transport from Nairobi to the Netherlands as well as distribution, payment, and settlement. Given their experience with Vidifleur, most Dutch growers were very skeptical about TFA and did not consider it as a serious auction market alternative, but that turned out to be a mistake. TFA became very successful. It created compelling value for buyers by facilitating convenient access to East African flowers. It built buyer confidence by establishing stringent quality controls, overseen by the TFA's quality inspectors at the grower's location, and distribution nexus in Nairobi, and at the TFA center in Aalsmeer. The difference between Vidifleur and TFA was that, in TFA, all buyers had to bid online and had the same information disadvantages. No buyer was able to inspect the flowers physically. More foreign growers joined, and by 2001 TFA traded flowers from 60 growers, mostly African, and 125 buyers.

What was the reaction of Royal FloraHolland? After some debate, they decided to implement an online variant called Buying at a Distance (in Dutch Kopen op Afstand (KOA)). Buyers could bid in the auction hall or bid online via KOA. Some buyers were already used to bidding online with TFA, and therefore, the transition was easier for them. International cooperative membership for non-European growers was established in 2006 and a separate channel for African products was no longer needed. In March 2010, TFA was sold to Royal FloraHolland. The success of TFA was a tipping point in the flower industry. It proved that online auctioning could work. Although the video-based and sample-based auctions provided a compelling value proposition to the auctioneer, neither provided significant advantages to the buyer and supplier, and TFA succeeded where prior attempts at online flower markets had failed.

4.9   Other Auction Designs

So far, we have seen two types of auctions. The first auction format is the English auction or ascending auction that was used in the bulb auction in Alkmaar or at Sotheby's to sell the Banksy painting and at Christie's to auction off the Monet painting. In the English auction, there are many bids, and the bidders—when they are in the salesroom—can be identified. Bidders who prefer to remain anonymous may bid via a telephone operator. Revealing the identity of a wealthy or well-known bidder could increase the bidding competition and therefore the price. The process in an English auction is relatively slow because the number of bids can be high, although the auction can be executed in minutes. There is a lower risk of getting a very low price due to the fact that prices will only get higher once the auction begins.

The second auction format is the Dutch auction or descending auction that was invented to auction fresh flowers and plants. In the Dutch auction, the first bid wins. When they are present in the salesroom, all bidders can look to each other, but there will be little or no information revealed about the other bidder's willingness to bid. Every second that a bidder waits, the price will be lower, but the probability to win the auction will also be lower. Thus, there is an advantage to waiting, but only to a certain extent. As the price is progressively lowered, the buyer may get the goods at a lower price or lose if another bidder stops the clock first. Therefore, the Dutch auction is very fast; transactions can happen in seconds. It is an ideal auction type for fresh products, where speed counts.

The Dutch auction has much broader appeal, however. Most retail sales markets for goods, such as apparel, electronics, and books, can be viewed as protracted Dutch auction markets. For example, a new shirt design hits the retail market on March 1with a $110 price tag. Some shirts are sold, but not all, and the price is lowered at the end of the Spring season to $90. Another batch of shirts are sold at that price, and the retailer offers an additional discount on weekdays, bringing the price to $70. More shirts are sold, but some remain and by June the shirts are available with an extra summer sales discount, and the price is now only $35 when purchased by the happy buyer. These are typical features of retail sales: a descending price over a longer time period and many bids to clear off the inventory of products.

There are many other auctions types.[23] Six auction types will be explored in more detail: (1) the combined English–Dutch auction; (2) the sealed-bid auction; (3) the reverse auction; (4) the double auction; (5) the multi-attribute auction; and (6) the combinatorial auction.

An interesting auction form is the combination of English and Dutch auction. This form is used, for example, at the First Amsterdam Property Auction that is a public auction that started in 1860 and continues to this day on Monday evenings. It usually attracts a crowd of around thirty people from different walks of life (property owners, brokers, investors, and tourists), and people can also participate online. Bidding takes place in two phases. To explain how it works, consider the example of an auction of an apartment located in the city center of Amsterdam. In the first phase, the auctioneer would announce the minimum price and increase the price with an increment of, for example, € 5000. Bidders would raise their hands to bid in person or place a bid online. The auctioneer would stop when no one was willing to place a higher bid. Suppose that the highest bid price in the first phase was € 210,000. The highest bidder in the first phase would receive a premium to stimulate bidding, comparable with *treckgelt* (pulling money) in the bulb auction event in 1637. In the second phase, the auctioneer would start with a much higher price, for example, € 400,000, and gradually lower the price: 390,000, 380,000, 370,000, etc. Bidders would indicate their bid by shouting "mine" or bidding online, which would stop the auction. The final price is determined by the first bid in the second phase. Suppose the first bid in the second phase was € 280,000, which is greater than the highest bid in the first phase (€ 210,000). Therefore, € 280,000 would be the winning bid and the apartment would be sold for that price if the seller accepts. If the seller does not accept, a compensation fee must be paid to the highest bidder. If the second phase price is lower than or equal to the first phase price, the seller would decline the offered price and no transaction would take place.

The next auction format is the sealed bid auction. Bidders can hand in their bid in a sealed envelope (or via a private, online message). The auctioneer opens all envelopes or messages and determines the highest bidder. Sealed-bid auctions are used in property auctions, especially where there is a lot of demand and many high bids are expected. A variant of the sealed-bid auction is the second-price sealed-bid auction or *Vickrey auction* named after William Vickrey (1914–1996).[24] In a Vickrey auction, the winner is the one with the highest bid, but the winner will only pay the amount of the second-highest bid. The elegance of the Vickrey auction is that "truth telling"—bidding the true value of the auctioned product—is the best bidding strategy. In academia the Vickrey auction is well understood and appreciated, but in practice it was rarely used until Google decided to use the Vickrey auction format for their advertisement and keyword auctions. The Google AdWords Auctions began on October 23, 2000. The Vickrey auction is now the central mechanism of Google's business model, and in 2018, it generated around $116 billion in advertising revenue for Google (out of a market total of $136 billion), but how does it work?

To find content online related to flowers, for example, one must only type the word "flowers" into a Google search engine and it will generate two lists of web sites: the first list features advertisements and the second list features non-advertisements or so-called organic search results. First, I will guide you through the advertisements (or "ads"). Advertisers compete for the first spot in the ad results, and the highest bidder will get the first spot. The first spot will attract the attention of more customers (although it is an interesting question if customers indeed will opt for the ad in the first spot). As of this writing, a Google search for flowers generated the following ads in the following order: (1) 1800flowers.com; (2) ftd.com; and (3) teleflora.com. Why is 1800flowers.com listed first? The answer is in the Vickrey generalized second price auction. Suppose 1800flowers.com had the highest bid of 30 cents, ftd.com bid 20 cents, Teleflora.com bid 18 cents. As the winner, 1800flowers.com will have to pay to Google the second-highest bid plus one cent (in this case 21 cents). The second-highest bidder will pay the third-highest bid plus one cent, and so on. This example is very stylized and simple, but in practice it is much more complicated. One needs to have advanced knowledge to understand the crucial details of the auction design. Indeed, as the saying goes, "the devil is in the details." The ad position is determined by the ad rank, which is calculated by a Google algorithm (the algorithm is secret, similar to the recipe for Coca-Cola). The bid amount is only one variable, and other algorithm variables include keyword relevancy (of the ad, the search query, and the landing page), the expected clickthrough rate, and the context of the person's search (location, time of search, device). The term "clickthrough rate" (CTR) might be intriguing for you. It is the ratio showing how often people who see an ad actually click on it. A high CTR is an indication that users find the ad helpful and relevant. However, a high CTR might indicate that the content, such as news, is cascading and providing propaganda or misinformation. It can have (and has already had) disastrous social consequences when these tools are put to use to exploit the unsuspecting user.[25] So, every time a user clicks on the 1800flowers.com ad, 21 cents will be transferred from the 1800flowers.com account to Google. Another click, another 21 cents. Please, make sure that you pay more attention next time you do a web search. Google helps advertisers to optimize their bidding strategy and use machine learning and other artificial intelligence (AI) tools to improve the ad performance and Google's revenue stream. Widespread use of Internet search engines, especially Google, gave rise to an industry that helps companies to optimize their search engine marketing and includes both the sponsored search and the organic search.

The specialization to improve a website's results in organic listings is called search engine optimization (SEO). In Chap. 6, the use and impact of artificial intelligence (AI) algorithms will be discussed.

The second list below the ads provides the organic search results ranked according to relevance and usefulness. If you search for "flowers," you probably like to view web sites that are relevant and useful for "flowers." Google determines relevance and usefulness with the help of a ranking algorithm (also secret) that takes more than 200 variables into account, such as keyword usage, site speed, time spent on the site, number of links, and many more. At the time of writing, proflowers.com had the top spot in the organic search listing on Google.

A new application of the Vickrey auction for electricity storage is developed by Konstantina Valogianni and coauthors.[26] A challenge for grid operators and electricity providers is to provide a balanced market of supply and demand of electricity. Electricity supply, based on renewable energy sources, such as solar and wind energy, is not that stable—the sun does not always shine and the wind does not always blow. Demand is also not stable and shows peak load behavior. Most people, for example, travel to work at the same time and they demand electricity at the same time. Electric vehicles can be connected to a smart electricity grid and the batteries of electric vehicles can form a "virtual power plant," a combined storage facility, which can provide electricity during high demand or when there is no sunshine or wind. The Vickery auction market algorithm will allocate charging requests and schedules electric vehicle charging, both in terms of prices and capacity, to the individual electric vehicle drivers.

English, Dutch, combined English–Dutch, and sealed-bid auction formats are used for "forward" auctions, but they can also be run as "reverse" auctions. In reverse auctions, the buyer is the bid taker and the seller is the bidder. Most procurement auctions run in the reverse format.

Another auction format is the double auction. In a double auction, the auctioneer receives bids from buyers and sellers stating both a price and a desired quantity. The auctioneer matches the sellers' offers (starting with the lowest price and then going up) to the buyers' (starting with the highest price and then going down) until all the quantities offered for sale are sold. This type of auction works only for items that are traded in large quantities and are of a known quality, such as securities or commodities.

In multi-attribute auctions, buyers searching and bidding for products specify different prices they are willing to pay for products with various combinations of attributes. Attributes may include product quality, such as stem length, bud diameter, and freshness for flowers, or the delivery time. Likewise, sellers offer their products with multiple-attribute specifications. With a multi-attri-bute auction algorithm, one tries to find the best matches. Nowadays, this type of auction is popular in procurement situations where the quality or delivery time of the product or service is as important as the price.

Combinatorial auctions, in which combinations of items (rather that indi-vidual items) are traded, solve a different kind of resource allocation problem. The goal of combinatorial bidding is to achieve higher value through the com-bination. This auction format is used in the transportation sector. For exam-ple, a transportation carrier may wish to win bids on a group of continuous lanes (a lane is a unique origin–destination pair requiring a specific type of service and equipment). Another application is the auctioning of bandwidth rights, so-called spectrum auctions. Governments allocate the rights to trans-mit signals over specific bands of the electromagnetic spectrum, such as fre-quencies for mobile phone signals, radio signals, or television signals. New auction mechanisms, such as the simultaneous multiple-round auctions, were designed for a better allocation process.[27]

Many auction formats can be applied to specific business situations. To determine the right auction design, for sellers, auctioneers, and buyers, a detailed analysis should be made about the trade-offs among various types of auctions and how details can influence the outcome of the markets. For an overview of auction types with examples, see Table 4.1. Details matter a great deal in auctions.

4.10   Lessons Learned

Returning to the Dutch flower auctions, what did we learn?

First, auctions are an excellent way to determine the value (for how much?) and the allocation (to whom?) of products or services. Value and winner are the key outcome dimensions that an auction can provide.[28] The value is deter-mined by the winning bid and the product or service will be handed over to the winning bidder. Compared to bilateral bargaining (between one seller and one buyer), in an auction many bidders participate, and more information will be exchanged about the other bidders' willingness to pay. Bids reflect "a collective judgement regarding the value of an item at that moment … and is the product of a collective decision-making process that unfolds within the auction itself." In the Dutch flower auction, there are thousands of sellers (growers) and buyers (wholesalers and retailers) involved in this collective decision-making process. Every seller's product will get its moment at center stage, and every buyer can bid on thousands of different flowers. It is the

Table 4.1 Overview auction types with examples

Auction type	Price discovery and winning bid	Number of sellers and buyers	Offline versus online	Examples
English	Increasing bids, highest bid wins, many bids	One seller, many buyers	Offline and online	Art, coffee
Dutch	Decreasing bids, highest bid wins, only one bid	One seller, many buyers	Offline and online	Flowers and plants, fish
Combined English-Dutch	Two rounds with increasing bids and decreasing bids, highest bid wins, many bids	One seller, many buyers	Offline and online	Real estate
First price sealed-bid	Each bidder one bid; highest bid wins	One seller, many buyers	Offline and online	Real estate, procurement
Second price sealed-bid	Each bidder one bid, second highest bid wins	One seller, many buyers	Online	Key words, digital advertisements
Reverse	Increasing or decreasing bids, or one bid. Lowest bid wins	Many sellers, one buyer	Offline and online	Procurement
Double	Both sellers and buyers provide bids; clearing price	Many sellers, many buyers	Online	Stock markets
Multi-attribute	One or many multi-attribute bids; best quality–price ratio bid wins	Many sellers, one buyer	Online	Procurement where product quality is important
Combinatorial	Bids on the combination of offers; highest combination bid wins	One seller, many bidders	Online	Mobile telephone licenses (G3/G4/G5), radio frequencies

largest portfolio of flowers in the world that a bidder can chose from. The Dutch auction format is able to handle this large number of products, sellers, and buyers at a relatively fast pace.

Second, auctions are a good show, a staged event with drama and emotions, both for the winner and the losers. The auctioneer, like a modern maestro of an orchestra, maintains the rhythm, controls the sequence of events, and sets the pace when announcing each new bid or adjusting the peacemaker clock. He or she breaks silence in between and makes jokes to lighten the mood.

A good auctioneer can electrify the audience, build enthusiasm, and win higher prices. Online bidders, whether in Sotheby's, Christie's, or the Dutch flower auctions, surely miss some of the thrill.

Third, research has shown that Dutch auctions win better prices for sellers under the condition that the auction is well designed and the information about the quality of the product is reliable.

Fourth, the digital transformation of the Dutch flower auctions was very challenging.[29] Digital product representation, decoupling logistics from price discovery, and a reliable digital infrastructure were hurdles that had to be overcome. Online auctions expanded the sellers' reach and enabled more bidders to connect to the auction. The result was more transactions and sometimes higher prices.

Fifth, the design of information and information asymmetries, e.g., the quality and distribution of information about products and market transactions among sellers and buyers, is crucial for the success of online auction markets. One does not only auction off flowers, but information about flowers, and this difference makes all the difference.

We have seen how the Dutch became involved in selling flowers with auctions and how the auction methods changed over time. The Dutch auction format has a lot of positive connotations, and indeed, it was a great invention. However, it has one challenging limitation. It is a forward auction driven by existing supply. If a bidder should want a specific product that is not offered by any of the growers, the bidder can only wait, and the product may never appear. To overcome that limitation, a new invention is needed.

Notes

1. The bulb auction of Alkmaar is described in Dash M (1999). With quotes: "more than" (p. 148), Footnote aces (p. 118), "in het ootjen" and "to pull someone's leg" (pp. 143 and 144), "vivid impression" (p. 159).
2. Aces (in Dutch: *asen*) are tiny units of measurement borrowed from goldsmiths. One ace was equal to rather less than two-thousandths of an ounce – one-twentieth of a gram – and mature tulip bulbs might weigh anything from fifty aces to more than a thousand, depending on the variety (Dash 1999, p. 118).
3. Detailed research was executed and presented in Goldgar A (2007).
   Her research is accurate and based on detailed research of different records. For example, Anne Goldgar explains that no actual bulbs were present at the Alkmaar auction and indeed prices of some bulbs were extremely high, but the impact of the Alkmaar auction was modest. With quotes: "The auction"

(pp. 203 and 204), "Both *wijnkoop and rouwkoop*" (p. 210), "a broadside was printed" (p. 203), "were no more" (p. 203), "precarious" (p. 217), "the rarest things" (p. 3), "another sickness" (p. 3). "… [T]his mania" (p. 134), "pious and impious" (p. 134), "I don't know" and "Oure descendants" (p. 3), "Most of the modern-day view" (pp. 5–6), "thousands were ruined" (p. 5).

4. To determine the value of the guilder versus euro in one year compared to another year, the conversion tool developed by the International Institute of Social History is used. The bulb priced in 1637 at *f* 5200 has a purchasing power in 2018 of € 61,739.70 and the total sum of *f* 90,000 has a purchasing power of *one million euro*, or more specific € 1,068,571.76 in 2018. International Institute of Social History. https://iisg.amsterdam/en/research/projects/hpw/calculate.php Accessed 4 Sept.

5. Many sources exaggerate the seventeenth-century tulip mania, like Sooke A. (2016, May 3).

    Many sources in the field of finance and investments discuss tulip mania in a very inaccurate way; see, for example, Malkiel B (2019) and Dennin T (2019).

6. Based on Goldgar A (2007), with quotes from her book: "But by looking" (pp. 136/137), "as for Amsterdam" (p. 147), "Mennonites" (p. 149), "a whole host" (p. 151), "Proximity" (pp. 153, 156, 157), "Of the 167 bloemisten" (p. 166), "They might not" (p. 169), "right in the middle" (p. 176), "The collecting" (p. 67), "rarities" (p. 68), "In the mid-seventeenth century in Delft" (p. 69), "collegie," "who appear" (p. 191), "The longest chain" (p. 228) and Goldgar, A. (2018, February 12). With the quote: "Only 37 people."

7. Sources for the story of the Banksy's shredded painting include Sotheby's (2018, October 5).

    Christian N (2018, October 7).

    Reyburn S (2018, October 11).

8. The "social construction of value" argument is in Smith CW (1989).

9. Quote from Charles W. Smith in Smith CW (1989).

10. His first sale is described in Christie's (2019).

11. The Claude Monet auction is described in Loft H (2019, May 14).

12. On the day of our visit a shiny, stainless steel sculpture created by Jeff Koons in 1986 was on display. It was inspired by a child's inflatable toy. The sculpture was sold the next evening for $91.1 million with fees, breaking the record at auction for a work by a living artist, which had previously been set in November 2018 in the auction of a work by David Hockney, in Reyburn S. (2019, May 15).

13. The winner's curse concept is, for example, discussed in the context of IT outsourcing. In this outsourcing case, the bid taker will outsource IT functions to the lowest bidder, e.g., the specialist that will insource and take care

of the IT functions. In the so-called reverse auction, the bid taker will accept the lowest bid; see Kern T, Willcocks LP, Van Heck E (2002).

14. The development of roads, railroads, and canals in the Netherlands in the nineteenth century is in Sipman MA (1873).
15. The first Dutch auction event is described in Oneindig Noord-Holland (2019, Oct 30).

    One can visit the "Bakkersbrug" where the first Dutch auction was executed. It is now Museum BroekerVeiling in Broek op Langedijk.
16. The development of the electrical auctioneer (in Dutch: het electrisch afmijn-toestel) is based on Bouman ZP (1908).
17. "The Peacemaker" (in Dutch: "De Vredestichter") in Bouman ZP (1908).
18. The quote "two buyers never were able to push the button at the same time" (in Dutch: "nooit twee kooplustigen tegelijk kunnen afdrukken") in Van Stuijvenberg JH (1961).
19. The development of grower cooperatives in Kralt P (2011).
20. Splitting into separate groups is not uncommon in the Netherlands. For example, political parties in the parliament commonly split into smaller sections. In Dutch literature, the book *The Psalms Uproar* (in Dutch: *Het Psalmenoproer*) by Maarten 't Hart tells of a religious group in Maassluis that split in 1776, due to a dispute about the rhyme and speed of psalm singing.
21. The Dutch auction system is in Kambil A, Van Heck E (2002).

    Details of the Dutch flower auction system in Lu Y, Gupta A, Ketter W, Van Heck E (2016).
22. The redesign of the Dutch flower auctions in the 1990s in Kambil A, Van Heck E (1998).
23. Other auction mechanisms including a framework to design online auction markets and exchanges are in Kambil A, Van Heck E (2002).
24. He was awarded the 1996 Sveriges Riksbank Prize in Economic Sciences in Memory of Alfred Nobel with James Mirrlees for their research into the economic theory of incentives under asymmetric information.
25. Twitter research by Vosoughi S, Roy D, Aral S (2018, March 9), has shown that "Falsehood diffused significantly farther, faster, deeper, and more broadly than the truth in all categories of information, and the effects were more pronounced for false political news than for false news about terrorism, natural disasters, science, urban legends, or financial information," and "We found that false news was more novel than true news, which suggests that people were more likely to share novel information." Contrary to conventional wisdom, "robots accelerated the spread of true and false news at the same rate, implying that false news spreads more than the truth because humans, not robots, are more likely to spread it."
26. The electric vehicle charging auction market design in Valogianni K, Gupta A, Ketter W, Sen S, Van Heck E (2019).

27. For advanced work on spectrum and other auctions, see Paul Milgrom, Beyond the Vickrey Auction: Practical Design for a High-Stakes Auction, Key Note, Workshop on Information Systems and Economics (WISE) and Workshop on Information Technologies and Systems (WITS), December 18, 2019, Munich. The 2020 Sveriges Riksbank Prize in Economic Sciences in Memory of Alfred Nobel has been awarded to Paul Milgrom and Robert Wilson for improvements to auction theory and inventions of new auction formats.
28. The line of thinking is based on my inaugural address, Van Heck E (2002).
   Auctions and their social construction of value are based on Smith CW (1989), with the quote "a collective judgement" (p. 77).
29. More competition is discussed in The Economist (2007).
   Schuetze CF (2014).
   Karabell S (2016).

References

Bouman ZP (1908) Het electrisch afmijntoestel. In: De Natuur: Natuurkundige Wetenschappen en haar Toepassingen. J.G. Broese, Utrecht (in Dutch)

Christian N (2018, October 7) Street artist Banksy releases video showing auction shredding prank was years in the making. The West Australian. https://thewest.com.au/news/offbeat/street-artist-banksy-releases-video-showing-auction-shredding-prank-was-years-in-the-making-ng-b88983688z Accessed 4 Sept 2020

Christie's (2019) The history of Christie's auction house. In: Christie's. https://www.christies.com/auctions/the-history-of-christies-auction-house Accessed 4 Sept 2020

Dash M (1999) Tulipomania: the story of the World's Most coveted flower and the extraordinary passions it aroused. Three River Press, New York City

Dennin T (2019) From tulips to Bitcoins: a history of fortunes made and lost in commodity markets. River Grove Books, Austin

Goldgar A (2007) Tulipmania: money, honor, and knowledge in the Dutch Golden age. The University of Chicago Press, Chicago

Goldgar A (2018, February 12) Tulip mania: the classic story of a Dutch financial bubble is mostly wrong. The conversation. https://theconversation.com/tulip-mania-the-classic-story-of-a-dutch-financial-bubble-is-mostly-wrong-91413 Accessed 7 Sept 2020

Kambil A, Van Heck E (1998) Re-engineering the Dutch flower auctions: a framework for analyzing exchange organizations. Infor Sys Res 9:1–19

Kambil A, Van Heck E (2002) Making markets: how firms can design and profit from online auctions and exchanges. Harvard Business School Press, Boston

Karabell S (2016) Royal Flora Holland: Holland's wall street for flowers. Forbes. https://www.forbes.com/sites/shelliekarabell/2016/04/30/royal-floraholland-hollands-wall-street-for-flowers/#360211c0423c Accessed 5 Sept 2020.

Kern T, Willcocks LP, Van Heck E (2002) The Winner's curse in IT outsourcing: strategies for avoiding relational trauma. California Management Review 44(2):47–69

Kralt P (2011) Bijzondere verhalen van mensen achter de coöperatieve bloemenveiling 1911–2011. In: 100 Jaar Kleur. Royal Flora Holland, Aalsmeer

Loft H (2019, May 14) Record-breaking $110.7 million Monet leads impressionist & modern art evening Sale. In: Sotheby's press release. https://www.sothebys.com/en/articles/record-breaking-110-7-million-monet-shatters-records-at-impressionist-modern-art-evening-sale Accessed 4 Sept 2020.

Lu Y, Gupta A, Ketter W, Van Heck E (2016) Exploring bidder heterogeneity in multi-channel sequential B2B auctions. MIS Quarterly 40(3): 645–662. https://aisel.aisnet.org/misq/vol40/iss3/8/ Accessed 15 Sept 2020.

Malkiel B (2019) A random walk down Wall street: the time-tested strategy for successful investing, 2nd edn. W.W. Norton & Company, New York

Oneindig Noord-Holland (2019, Oct 30) De eerste veiling per afslag. https://onh.nl/verhaal/eerste-veiling-per-afslag Accessed 12 Sept 2020.

Reyburn S (2018, October 11) Winning bidder for shredded Banksy painting says she'll keep it. New York Times. https://www.nytimes.com/2018/10/11/arts/design/winning-bidder-for-shredded-banksy-painting-says-shell-keep-it.html Accessed 4 Sept 2020

Reyburn S (2019, May 15) Jeff Koons 'rabbit' sets auction record for Most expensive work by living artist. New York Times. https://www.nytimes.com/2019/05/15/arts/jeff-koons-rabbit-auction.html Accessed 7 Sept 2020

Schuetze CF (2014) Dutch flower auction, long industry's heart, is facing competition. New York Times, p A10, https://www.nytimes.com/2014/12/17/world/europe/dutch-flower-auction-long-industrys-heart-is-facing-competition-.html Accessed 5 Sept 2020

Sipman MA (1873) De Reuzen Werken van Onzen Tijd. J. van Egmond Jr. & J. Heuvelink, Arnhem.

Smith CW (1989) Auctions: the social construction of value. University of California Press, Berkeley

Sooke A (2016, May 3) Tulip mania: the flowers that cost more than houses. https://www.bbc.com/culture/article/20160419-tulip-mania-the-flowers-that-cost-more-than-houses Accessed 7 Sept 2020.

Sotheby's (2018, October 5) Sotheby's gets Banksy'ed at contemporary art auction in London. In: Sotheby's press release. https://www.sothebys.com/en/articles/sothebys-gets-banksyed-at-contemporary-art-auction-in-london   Accessed 7 Sept 2020

The Economist (2007) Petal power: competition is transforming the buying and selling of flowers. The Economist. https://www.economist.com/business/2007/05/10/petal-power Accessed 5 Sept 2020

Valogianni K, Gupta A, Ketter W, Sen S, Van Heck E (2019) Multiple Vickrey auctions for sustainable electric vehicle charging. Paper presented at the 40th international conference on information systems, international congress center Munich, Munich, 15–18 December 2019

Van Heck E (2002) Waarde en Winnaar: over het ontwerpen van elektronische veilingen. Erasmus University Rotterdam.

Van Stuijvenberg JH (1961) Het veilingwezen. In: De bloemisterij in Nederland. Chapter IV. Vereniging De Nederlandse Bloemisterij, 's-Gravenhage.

Vosoughi S, Roy D, Aral S (2018, March 9) The spread of true and false news online. Science 359:1146–1151

5

Flower Bouquets and Ecosystems

5.1   Kenyan Roses

Kenya has several well-known lakes, such as Lake Victoria in the east, shared with Uganda and Tanzania, and covering around 59,947 square kilometers. In the north, Lake Turkana, shared with Ethiopia, covers 6405 square kilometers and is considered the cradle of mankind. Evidence of hominids, some of the earliest human ancestors, has been found at the shore of Lake Turkana, dating back to 4.2 million years. And, in the Rift Valley at an elevation of 1884 meters, Lake Naivasha covers 139 square kilometers. Its name is derived from the local Maasai name, *Nai'posha*, meaning rough water because of the sudden storms that can arise. The lake is fed by the Malewa and Gilgil rivers, and it attracts our attention because 50% of Kenyan flower production takes place on its shores.

The landscape around the village of Naivasha is mainly flat, accentuated by sedimentary hills and volcanic rock formations. A freshwater lake is always an important treasure in a dry and thirsty country, and the people depend on it to survive. Sunlight warms the greenhouses of the Nini Flower Farm bordering Lake Naivasha, where the average temperatures are around 15 °C early in the morning throughout the year.[1] Near the equator, Kenya has plenty of sunshine, and this makes it possible to grow flowers 365 days a year without the need for expensive, energy-intensive greenhouses. Lake Naivasha supplies sufficient water, the sun heats the plastic greenhouses by day, and temperatures fall by night owing to the high altitude.

Early in the morning, employees of Nini Flower Farm walk through the greenhouses, picking and cutting roses that are ready to be transported to the flower markets of Europe and Japan. The employees walk along small paths between high stretches of rose plants. Every individual rose is observed and evaluated meticulously for bud diameter, stem length, and ripeness. When a rose meets all specifications, it is cut with rose scissors at the right stem length for its variety, between 40 and 70 centimeters. The roses are bundled in a sturdy green perforated plastic sheet and a small truck transports the bundles vertically in buckets to the cool storage center. Here the roses are kept at a low temperature awaiting further processing. Nini Flower Farm has a total workforce of 600 employees with 100 people working at post-harvest operations, each with an individual working space, to carry out the next stage of preparing the roses for sale (Fig. 5.1).

They remove the reusable plastic sheets, inspect each rose, remove some leaves, and cut the stems at the same height. The roses are grouped into smaller bundles, the stems are wrapped, and the rose buds are encased in ribbed cardboard. Several bundles of roses are put in long cardboard boxes and sealed with strips. These boxes will be transported horizontally to preserve maximum freshness, delay blooming, and extend the life of the rose at the final destination.

A small insulated and refrigerated truck keeps the roses below a temperature of 4 °C and transports the long cardboard boxes to Jomo Kenyatta International Airport in Nairobi. The narrow and dusty road to Nairobi is crowded with trucks, scooters, and bikes. Many people walk along the road as well, even without an official sidewalk. Vehicles kick up dust and dry sand.

Fig. 5.1 Nini Flower Farm employees prepare and bundle Kenyan roses for transport https://www.youtube.com/watch?v=BhtVWCBntCA. With permission by Nina Flower Farm

The maximum outside temperature reaches between 25 and 30 °C and the small truck arrives at one of the air-transport decks in Nairobi. Border control employees inspect the truck driver and co-driver, and airport employees help to transfer the cardboard boxes into the security center where the temperature is kept constant at around 7 °C. There are further inspections to prepare for export. Border control employees check the status of the flower transport via air and facilitate the export documents. They check the phytosanitary conditions of the roses to ensure no plant diseases, insects, or other animals are transported with the roses to destination countries. After they are cleared for export, the cardboard boxes are weighted and loaded on special air cargo pallets and covered with thermo blankets.

It is very impressive sight when the nose of the Boeing 747–400 cargo airplane is opened.[2] These planes carry cargo only and can take 112,000 kilograms cargo at once. A giant rolling floor stretches all the way to the back of airplane. The pallets of roses are rolled into the cargo hold and fixed in place to prevent the boxes from shifting. The weight of all cargo must be distributed evenly throughout the plane. The specialized air-freight business of Air France KLM Group, Martinair Cargo, departs from Nairobi at 10:30 PM (flight MP8372) and arrives around 5:45 AM at Schiphol International Airport in Amsterdam.[3] Airport employees unload the cargo, and border control employees check the phytosanitary conditions of the roses and the transport documents.[4]

After passing these inspections, the roses are handed over to the importing company, an international wholesaler headquartered in Aalsmeer near the Dutch flower auctions. The wholesaler combines the Kenyan roses with peonies purchased from Israel, gardenias directly bought from a Dutch grower, and white gypsophelia purchased the same morning at the Dutch flower auctions. The wholesaler combines these flower modules into very elegant bouquets and sells them online. A flower retailer in Munich buys a bouquet and it is sent by truck carrier, arriving the next day in Munich for a wedding the day after. The journey from cutting the roses in Nairobi, one module of the final flower bouquet, to the wedding in Munich took four days.

5.2   Fashion and Flowers

Paris is considered the fashion capital of the world and Paris Fashion Week is among the most important events of the global fashion calendar. During Fashion Week, invited guests, including an eclectic mix of celebrities, social media influencers, journalists, and fashion house clients, watch for the latest trends and designs from the most powerful and celebrated designers. Fashion houses, such as Chanel, Dior, Saint Laurent, Stella McCartney, and Valentino, understand the role of Fashion Week in setting the stage for new fashion trends, and they know the power of fashion shows to influence what people will buy and wear. The décor at Fashion Week events is crafted as meticulously as the clothing on the runway to communicate the vision, attitude, and atmosphere of the fashion house. In this way, fashion and flowers are intertwined.

At the intersection of fashion and flowers in Europe is a startup company called Flowerbx that decorated the Blamin post-show party and the Sonia Rykiel showroom at Paris Fashion Week in 2019.[5] Let me explain more.

The founder of Flowerbx, Whitney Bromberg Hawkings, worked as communications director at Tom Ford and as personal assistant at Gucci in Paris where she learned the importance of flowers in communicating the fashion "message" to the world. The shapes and colors of floral arrangements were synchronized with the shapes and colors of the fashion designs. She also noticed that fashion designers preferred bouquets based on a single variety, reflecting his or her taste, rather than old-fashioned mixed flower arrangements. She believed there was a clear market for modern, cool, and more affordable flower bouquets, and she wanted to cater to the tastes of Europe's elite fashion houses.

In the traditional flower supply chain, flowers were cut by the growers, sold via the Dutch flower auctions to wholesalers, and sold again at the wholesale markets. "Usually, flowers go to a wholesale market like Covent Garden, where they sit for three or four days, then to a florist, where they sit a few more days." Hawkings said.[6] At each step in the supply chain, the price will increase, and so Flowerbx took a different approach. The customer orders a flower bouquet online and Flowerbx cuts the flowers on the customer's behalf in the Netherlands and delivers them within 24 hours. "You buy the flowers before we buy them, so it's a negative capital business. We offer fresher flowers at a better value. And we have no waste."

5.3 Disruption

Other companies were also eager to disrupt the traditional flower supply chains. Bloomon was established in November 2014 by three Dutch entrepreneurs, Patrick Hurenkamp, Koen Thijssen, and Bart Troost.[7] They began with in-depth research on the experiences of setting up online ventures such as

Hellofresh (fresh food), MS Mode (fashion), Payleven (mobile payment), Sapph (lingerie), and Westwing (interior design). Hurenkamp and Troost worked as consultants at the Boston Consulting Group and Thijssen worked for Rocket Internet. They combined critical components of online customer behavior, fashion trends, fast delivery and logistics, and mobile payments, and applied those components to the flower business. They were inspired by the fact that the traditional supply chain was supply oriented (what is in a name). It meant that the grower sold—via the auctioneer—flower products to the wholesaler. The wholesaler sold it to the retailer and the retailer sold these flowers (sometimes bundled in bouquets) to the end customer. From an information perspective, this was a one-way street. No information went back from the end customer to the grower. Actually, the grower will not know at all where their flower products will be "consumed." They do not know who their customers are or if they are satisfied. Bloomon aimed to close the loop by feeding back to the grower detailed customer satisfaction data. A shorter demand chain with less parties involved would speed up transactions and would lead to fresher products and more "tulip time."

In the opinion of the three Bloomon entrepreneurs the flower bouquet also needed a drastic makeover—fresher, lighter, with different types of flowers instead of the traditional bouquets that included commodity types of flowers (chrysanthemums, gerberas, and roses) and lots of green fillings (like leather fern, lemon leaf, and gyp). Bloomon wanted to create a "look and feel" of flower bouquets that was different and therefore modern. With the creation of a new type of flower bouquet Bloomon could create a new type of brand name in the global flower markets driven by consumer needs instead of grower supply. Branding, marketing, and consumer satisfaction were all concepts that inspired Bloomon based on the examples set by modern digital companies, such as Netflix and Spotify. Or as one of the headlines in the news quipped: "How Dutch startup Bloomon became the Netflix of flowers."

Netflix was established in August 1997 in Scotts Valley, California, by Reed Hastings and Marc Randolph.[8] Since then it has become a media service provider and movie and television production company. Movies such as *Bird Box*, *Murder Mystery*, and *Triple Frontier* are very popular worldwide, and TV series such as *Stranger Things* and the *Umbrella Academy* are watched by millions. Netflix started to produce their so-called Netflix originals—a strategy to control both production and distribution of digital content—and therefore gain competitive advantage in a very crowded market. Netflix originals have high production costs, such as *The Crown*, at a whopping $130 million per season, or House of Cards, at $60 million per season. Netflix established a user base of 148 million paid users in 190 countries with 5400 employees. Total revenue over the year 2018 was $15.8 billion and net income was $1.2 billion.

Spotify was established in April 2006 in Stockholm, Sweden, by Daniel Ek and Martin Lorentzon and provides an audio streaming platform with music and podcasts from record labels and media companies. Currently, around 4100 employees work at Spotify, serving 232 million listeners, including 108 million users that pay for the service. The total revenue over the year 2018 was $6 billion with net income of $89 million. Both Netflix and Spotify provide digital products and services (music, movies). Bloomon has an even more challenging task; it provides digital services with perishable, fresh non-digital products.[9]

From startup to scale-up is always a turbulent period. Between 2014 and 2018, Bloomon was able to double its number of employees and its revenue every year. Bloomon is headquartered in Amsterdam, with offices in Aalsmeer, near the Dutch flower growers, for flower bouquet design and distribution. Every week a new flower bouquet is designed and offered to customers. Also, offices were established in Berlin and Paris for the German and France flower markets. In the four-year time period between 2014 and 2018, around 250,000 bouquets were delivered to customers in Europe. These results are impressive for a startup. However, the next step to scale up operations and customer relations in Europe is even more challenging. The existing companies, such as Fleurop, Euroflorist, or 1800flowers, are very keen to strike back. They established critical mass and have a solid customer base. They might be able to mimic the strategy that Bloomon developed with carefully selected and designed flower bouquets every week. To create sustainable customer value in a digitizing world is not easy to do.

5.4   Flowers by Parcel Post

Mail delivery is heavily impacted by digitization. Who is still writing letters to their loved ones? We communicate nowadays via e-mail and social media messages. The delivery of post mail is rapidly declining and physical mail is distributed less frequently. My grand-father-in-law, born in 1896, was a postman for his entire working life and delivered letters and mail every day by foot covering a wide area around Boxtel, a village in the southern part of the Netherlands. If he were still alive, he would be surprised to see the rapidly declining mail delivery and at the same time the exceptional growth of parcel post. The increase in the number of packages initiated by online ordering and e-commerce is astounding.

In Europe, PostNL is a market leader.[10] Established in 1799, PostNL has seen a dramatic decrease of mail delivery by 50% in five years. However, parcel post is growing by 20% per year and reached 800,000 parcels per day in 2018. PostNL delivers to customers in the Netherlands and Belgium and can accommodate so-called XL products that customers order online, such as mattresses, garden furniture, or dishwashers. Food suppliers deliver meal boxes, groceries, and other fresh products to customers. Companies in pharmaceuticals and health care require temperature-controlled shipments of medicines and medical equipment. And the latest trend is that 40 e-retailers are using the PostNL service called Flora@Home to deliver fresh flowers and potted plants (up to 130 cm high and a maximum pot diameter of 30 cm) within seven countries in Europe.

Flora@Home links consumer to growers logistically and digitally. What is the business concept? A customer starts to order flowers online via an e-retailer. PostNL receives the order and sends it to a specific grower. The grower sends its products to the Royal FloraHolland distribution complex in Aalsmeer where PostNL has a dedicated fulfillment location. Perishable products are transported in specialized cardboard packaging. Potted plants are included with soil, and pots are wrapped in plastic foil to keep the soil from spilling over. The potted plant is packaged vertically in a cardboard box with a clear "This Side Up" logo, while flower bouquets are wrapped in plastic foil and packaged in a special cardboard box. No water will be included to avoid leakages. Finally, PostNL delivers the packages to the address specified by the customer.

There are two different value propositions for flowers and plants. They can be the primary value proposition and may include extra products and services, such as a different type of pot or a special type of nutrition. The other value proposition is that flowers and plants are complementary to the value proposition of other, primary, products such as home design, lingerie, or wine. In that case, flowers provide a higher order value including a higher customer retention and satisfaction level.

PostNL distinguished three types of business clients for its Flora@Home service. The freemium client—usually the website of a smaller flower shop—needs a standard assortment and standard distribution solutions. The premium client—a larger retailer chain for example in home improvement—needs exclusivity in both assortment offers and distribution service. The platform client—a large digital platform provider—needs customer service and marketing. Amazon is a platform provider and the number one e-retailer in several larger European countries. The second-place platforms include providers such as Otto (Germany), Cdiscount (France), Argos (United Kingdom), Zalando (Italy), and Elcorteingles (Spain). Business clients like to be connected to the digital platform of PostNL and its logistical network. Its digital platform is connected directly into the client's platform, and this entails lower risks for the client and less investment in setting up these capital-intensive logistical networks. The end customer receives fresher products because they are sent directly from the growers. PostNL delivers the products and invoices the business client (the e-retailer) for the cost of fulfillment after the end customer has received the delivery. Because the end customers paid the e-retailer when the order was initiated, business clients have already received the payment. The business client pays PostNL after the end customer's order has been fulfilled.

5.5   Digital Business Design

It is impressive to land at Logan Airport in Boston and have a bird's-eye view over the Boston area with its prestigious academic institutes such as Harvard University and Massachusetts Institute of Technology (MIT). The area between these two universities—on the north side of the Charles River and therefore in the municipality of Cambridge, Massachusetts—is packed with university research centers, laboratories that are co-financed by universities and many companies, and startup centers with hundreds of companies working on the newest business ideas. I took a taxi across the Charles river to First Street, at the edge of the Boston innovation cluster. Situated on the fifteenth floor of a slack building is the MIT Center for Information Systems Research (CISR). MIT CISR was established in 1974. The eminent and amiable Jack Rockart (1931–2014) cofounded MIT CISR and became the first director. Successors over the years include Peter Weill, Jeanne Ross, and Leslie Owens. MIT CISR helps executives to meet the challenges of leading dynamic, global, and information-intensive organizations with advice that is grounded in the MIT tradition of rigorous field-based research. Through research, teaching, and events, the center stimulates interaction among scholars, students, and practitioners. More than 90 firms sponsor MIT CISR's work and participate in their consortium. The basic research question of MIT CISR is: What is the relationship between digital technologies and firm performance?

The latest research results are presented by Jeanne Ross, Cynthia Beath, and Martin Mocker in their book *Designed for Digital: How to Architect Your Business for Sustained Success*.[11] They identified challenges for "big, old" companies that want to adopt new digital technologies such as smart mobile technologies, robotics, blockchain, 3D printing, and Internet of Things (IoT), to name a few. Based on their research they identified that "big, old companies are simply not designed for digital." Business leaders are "less likely to own responsibility for designing the interactions among their people, processes, and technology to ensure their companies can execute new digital strategies. They must design their companies for digital success." Ross, Beath, and Mocker define digital business design as "the holistic organizational configuration of people (roles, accountabilities, structures, skills), processes (workflows, routines, procedures), and technology (infrastructure, applications) to define value propositions and deliver offerings made possible by the capabilities of digital technologies."

Five building blocks are identified by Ross, Beath, and Mocker that help companies to succeed digitally. These five building blocks are:

1. Shared customer insights. Organizational learning about what customers will pay for and how digital technologies can deliver their demands.
2. Operational backbone. A coherent set of standardized, integrated systems, processes, and data supporting the company's core operations.
3. Digital platform. Repository of business, data, and infrastructure components used to rapidly configure digital offerings.
4. Accountability framework. Distribution of responsibilities for digital offerings and components that balances autonomy and alignment.
5. External developer platform. Repository of digital components open to external parties.

These five building blocks will help companies that were not born digital to transform incrementally into digital companies by developing three interacting elements: *people* who understand what needs to be done and how to do it, *processes* that guide a company from idea through delivery to support digital offerings, and *technology* that supports both efficient organizational processes and innovative digital offerings. Research by Ross, Beath, and Mocker has not found the optimal digital design or a specific order for developing the five building blocks. However, research made clear that large companies cannot simultaneously address all the building blocks at once. Leaders have to decide which building block(s) they will focus on and a transformation roadmap can help leaders to sequence the development of the building blocks.

Royal FloraHolland (RFH) is a clear example of a big, old company in the flower industry that has overcome several challenges in the ongoing transformation to a digital company. Actually, there are two transformations for most of the traditional companies. One that *digitizes* the company (i.e., uses digital technologies to enhance operational efficiencies) and one that pursues new *digital* value propositions (i.e., uses digital technology to rapidly innovate new digital offerings).[12] RFH works, in my opinion, both on the digitizing transformation and on the digital transformation as follows:

- To digitize the operational processes in the company to provide operational efficiencies (better or faster commercial, logistical, or financial processes). For example, to experiment with offering the pre-sales digital channel that will enable faster auction and distribution processes. Research by Huong May Truong, Erasmus University Rotterdam, Alok Gupta, University of Minnesota, and Wolf Ketter and myself revealed a positive signaling effect of flower products offered at the pre-sales channel.[13]
- To add digital value to existing products and services to enhance end-customer experience. For example, one could introduce a QR code, i.e., a two-dimensional barcode, that enables end customers to share data via a digital channel that includes intuitive and convenient apps. For example, customer satisfaction (or dissatisfaction) data can be shared with the producer of the flowers.
- To add digital value to existing products and services by introducing new features such as AI-driven tools that will help the auctioneer to make better decisions with the specification of the minimum transaction amount for each auction lot. We will discuss some of these AI-driven tools in Chap. 6.
- To offer fundamentally new customer value propositions such as a pre-sales digital channel where growers can offer part of an auction lot ahead of time. Customers can digitally order part of the lot and the products are distributed to the buyer.

It is clear that a fundamental digital transformation will be a long journey. Changing a traditional industry to a new way of working is not easy. Perceptions, uncertainty about the outcome, lack of digital knowledge, and leadership are some of the factors that will play a role. It might be that in the near future young customers would like to buy and receive digital flowers, instead of the real "analog" flowers, and if so, RFH will have to transform further to provide digital flower product offerings on a global scale. While it is unlikely that customers would like to purchase digital flowers—they love real flowers after all—but in case they do, the industry would have to make an even more drastic digital transformation.

5.6   Platform Ecosystems

Although big, old companies may see themselves at the center of the world, multisided platforms and platform ecosystems are becoming the dominant way of creating value for customers and a more dominant way of doing business.[14] One can argue that the flower industry—particularly the invention of the Dutch auction clock in the beginning of the twentieth century—was the first advanced two-sided platform ecosystem. A platform provides the infrastructure and rules for a marketplace that brings together sellers and buyers. In the beginning of the twentieth century, the fast and structured Dutch auction mechanism acted as a trusted third party or "peacemaker" and contributed to a feeling of trust between the sellers (growers) and the buyers (wholesalers, retailers). Gradually, more sellers and buyers were attracted to the village marketplace—each village had its own. Over a period of more than one hundred years, local markets and cooperatives merged into larger and larger units and this process eventually resulted in the establishment of RFH. This large cooperative orchestrates a two-sided platform that connects around 5406 suppliers and 2458 buyer. In 2019, the cooperative had 3894 members with a total turnover of €4.8 billion with €2.1 billion from auctioning and €2.7 billion from direct sales. The turnover of €4.8 billion represents €2.6 billion in cut flowers, €1.8 billion in house plants, and €0.4 billion in garden plants.

There are ten trends that matter in the upcoming transformation of the platform ecosystem for trading flowers and plants. These ten trends will have an impact on the strategies and design of the businesses for seed suppliers, growers, market makers, transporters, wholesalers, retailers, and consumers. These ten trends are as follows.

1. Consumers want excellent service both in terms of the ease of using the online ordering tools and the services that are provided with the flowers or plants, such as receiving detailed information about the producer, the production process, instructions to keep produce as fresh as possible, and having the opportunity to provide feedback to the producer.
2. Consumers expect that the production and distribution of flowers and plants will be done in a sustainable way with low levels of carbon output.
3. The direct sales channel will become more important—based on increasing online consumer power—and will lead to order-driven smaller batches that will create a different transport and distribution process compared with the auction channel.

4. Based on the fact that consumers order more in terms of quantity and orders are more personalized online—retailers and wholesalers will also order their products online via e-retailers because they can consolidate the individual personalized customer orders into larger order transactions.

5. There will be a further concentration of the online auction process to bring more online buyers to fewer auction clocks. It will lead to more product availability, a better match between supply and demand, and it will probably lead to higher average prices at the auction.

6. In the auction channel, transport and distribution of products will be decoupled from the auction process, i.e., the products can be distributed in different ways: directly from the grower to the buyer, via a regional distribution center, or even forward distribution before the product is purchased. Forward distribution is based on advanced prediction models that will predict who the potential buyer of these products will be and where the products need to be delivered.

7. The financial processes will start to be redesigned. For example, by introducing new technologies like blockchain or by creating new community currencies.

8. Data sharing, in the commercial, logistical, and financial processes of the platform ecosystem, will become a dominant strategy. By sharing data in the flower platform ecosystem, companies will be able to improve their efficiency, effectiveness, and innovativeness.

9. Consumer data in Europe belongs to the customer—in other parts of the world data belong to either companies or the government—leading to new ways to handle and process data and create new types of business models.

10. Data monetization will lead to new business models for some companies that gather an enormous amount of data and would like to sell data to other companies that can use the data for better predictions. Customers will also explore the option of data monetization and sell their data to companies.

Each of these ten trends will have an impact on the functioning of the flower business. However, there is uncertainty about how fast and how deep the impact will be for each of the stakeholders. There is also uncertainty about the interaction effects among the different trends. Do some of the trends complement each other or will some trends substitute other trends, i.e., decrease or increase the potential impact of other trends? Are we missing important trends? These are the crucial questions for board members of the companies in the flower industry to discuss and answer. We do know that the digital transformation of multi-sided platforms is a tedious task but crucial for the performance of the companies that do business with each other. Let us explore the different strategic decisions that shape the design of these platforms.[15] Here the focus will be on RFH as the focal company. However, one could decide to focus on other potential companies that could fill in the future platform orchestrator role, such as companies within the industry, for example, the wholesale company, Dutch Flower Group, or the retail company, Fleurop. Even outsiders, such as the online retailers Amazon or Alibaba, could become the dominant platform orchestrator. Both Amazon and Alibaba have in-depth experience in orchestrating advanced platform ecosystems, and it would be interesting to see if they would be able to move into the flower industry.

But let us explore the strategic decisions for RFH. Actually, these decisions deal with the number of sides to bring on board, the design of the platform, the pricing structures of its products and services, and the governance rules.[16]

Number of Sides The typical feature of most multisided platforms is that the value to customers on one side of a platform increases with the number of participating customers on the other side, also known as the "cross-side network effects." Sellers derive more value from the platform when there are more buyers and vice versa. However, cross-side network effects are also a double-edged sword because they can create high barriers to entry for new platforms that would like to enter the flower industry. No side will join a new platform without the other side, also called the chicken-and-egg problem. High switching costs, i.e., the costs to switch to another platform or high costs to belong to more than one platform, are incentives for both sellers and buyers to stay on the current platform. For example, growers are usually members of the cooperative RFH and therefore they have to trade their products via RFH's platform and will incur switching costs when moving to another platform. One can opt for two-sided platforms such as Alibaba and eBay (with sellers and buyers), Airbnb (dwelling owners and renters), Booking (accommodation providers and travelers), Uber (professional drivers and passengers), and Ticketmaster (event venues and consumers), or three-sided platforms such as LinkedIn (individual professionals, recruiters, and advertisers), or Microsoft (users, third-party application developers, and third-party hardware manufacturers). More sides could lead to larger cross-side network effects, larger economies of scale, and a diversity of income sources. However, fewer sides have the advantage that the platform could be more economically viable, complexity could be managed, and conflict of interests could be avoided. For RFH the challenge is to explore the notion of moving from the traditional one-way (supply driven), two-sided market (with sellers and buyers) to a two-way (supply and direct), two-sided market. Actually, a three-way (supply, direct, futures), three-sided market (sellers, buyers, and transporters) could be envisioned. Here the three types of participants transact on one platform and interact with both supply and direct, spot transactions and future transactions. In a spot market trades occur after the transaction agreement has been made. In a future market, the flower products can be bought and sold at some agreed-upon date in the future at a price fixed at the time of the deal.

Platform Design Platforms have to provide functionalities and features that reduce transaction costs or increase transaction revenues of the basic trade processes such as search, pricing, logistics, payment and settlement, and authentication. Both sellers and buyers would like to use the basic trade processes to trade in an effective and efficient way. The platform should also be designed to cater to trade context processes such as product representation, legitimation, influence, and dispute resolution. Mostly these functionalities and features are software related and therefore platform orchestrators are or will become software companies to provide state-of-the art software that will help their customers to execute transactions over the platform. Software companies are characterized by their intense customer orientation, the focus on software details, teamwork with the agile way of working, the advanced way of software testing including A/B testing, and with the organized and regular release of new software versions.

Chapter 4 provided several examples of flawed two-side market designs, such as the video-based and sample-based auction designs, to illustrate the case that buyers and sellers will not get significant advantages, such as lower transaction costs or higher transaction revenues. For the video-based auction, online buyers had less information about market transactions, and in the sample-based auction, buyers questioned the grower's sample selection process. The result was a lower price level that resulted in less trade and fewer sellers and buyers with a death spiral as a result. When buyers or sellers are not better off, the transition to a new platform design will not happen. It is obvious that sellers and buyers have different interests, but they have a coherent view on how to overcome conflicts of interest and serve all sides of the platform not only in the short term but also in the longer term. For example, buyers would like to have more up-to-date information about the supply side of the market. Even they would like to have the opportunity to sell products before these will be auctioned and suggested a pre-sales channel that was implemented in 2013. Before the implementation, a careful design and experimentation of the pre-sales channel was executed. Based on the data in 2015, a detailed analysis of the pre-sales channel was done and revealed some unintended consequences. One was that when the seller decided to put part of the lot in the pre-sales channel and nothing was sold, still it had a positive impact on the subsequent auction price of the lot. The seller's willingness to sell with the indicated price was a signal to potential buyers to bid higher. Actually, the design of information exchange over platforms is the most crucial design feature nowadays. One does not trade flowers so much as information about the flower trade. In general, one favored the paradigm that more digitized information is better for all sellers and buyers involved. However, in Chap. 7 a field experiment in the flower markets will be described that revealed the impact of *less* information on the behavior of sellers and buyers. The results of this experiment led to the redesign of the platform's information architecture.

Pricing Structures Multisided platforms serve different types of customers and they have multiple revenues and profit sources. Some platforms offer services for free or at subsidized prices to attract customers to one side of the platform that will generate profit on the other side of the platform. In case of RFH, the initial platform is designed to sell the products of the growers, who are the owners of RFH. The purpose of the platform is to sell the products for the highest price to the buyers. However, RFH is not a cooperative for profit-making, but it is in the interest of the growers to make a profit. The buyers are attracted to the platform due to the year-round availability of a broad range of products. Actually, there is no platform in the world with a similar product range year round. Services are priced either as a flat fee for buyers (wholesalers and retailers) or based on the number of transactions or the volume that buyers purchase on the platform.

Some pricing principles are useful to explore. The price sensitivity for each group using the platform will differ and the platform operator can increase the price of the service if price sensitivity is low. A lower price sensitivity means that participants are not sensitive to a price decrease or increase and are willing to continue using the offered service. In case of a higher level of price sensitivity, the participants start to move away from the service when the price changes. The price sensitivity will be lower when there are not many alternatives or when the switching costs to other alternatives are high, and therefore, the bargaining power of the platform orchestrator is high. In case there is a priced transaction between two sides, it could be helpful to charge more on the side that will extract more value from the other side. Actually, in case of RFH's platform, the supply-driven auction channel RFH would like to attract as many buyers to raise auction prices and could provide lower fees for potential buyers. After buying flower products, buyers could incur a specific level of fee discount for less frequent, but larger transactions. The argument could be made that a few large transactions will incur lower logistical costs compared with many small transactions. In the demand-driven direct channel, where the buyer will initiate the transaction, RFH would like to stimulate many growers to fulfill the transaction and, therefore, once the transaction has been secured, provide discount fees for handling larger, less frequent transactions. In case of a non-priced transaction one has to review the extracted value for each of the platform sides and charge more to the side that can extract more value from the other side.

Governance Rules The governance rules are decisions that the platform orchestrator has to make with regard to access and interactions on the platform, such as authentication, product representation, legitimization, and dispute resolution. The decision to provide access to all or to restrict access for some participants is not an easy one. In 1996, the members of the cooperative, mostly Dutch growers, were not happy about the rising supply of African flower products causing downward pressure on flower prices. A ban for African growers was initiated. The result was that the first online flower auction, Tele Flower Auction (TFA), was successfully established, as explained in Chap. 4, and later RFH had to reopen the platform to African growers. Access can be denied to companies that do not follow international rules about corruption, child labor, minimum wages, tax evasion, and environmental pollution. RFH will require suppliers to have an environmental certificate by 2021. The certificate is based on the Floriculture Sustainability Initiative (FSI) and will stimulate growers to do business in a sustainable way. Tighter rules give the advantage to quality over quantity. The effect of cross-side network effects is determined by the number of participants and the number of interactions that they are engaged in, but also by their quality. The decision to establish standardization rules is complex. Crucial standards in the RFH platform concern auction trolleys and Danish trolleys (also called CC containers) with standardized labels and radio frequency identification (RFID) chips. The standardized trolley is a great way to speed up logistics, similar to the intermodal container for transport via ship, rail, and truck.

Even digital networks, such as the Internet, operate with standardized modules. Data sent over the Internet is modularized, i.e., encapsulated in packets and transmitted via the packet-switching method. For example, the e-mail that you will send to your friend will be chopped into packages and each of these packages will travel individually over the Internet via different trajectories. At the receiver's destination the packages will be combined into your e-mail that can be read by your friend. The Internet's data modularization approach led to two advantages. The first advantage is that computers that process packets are not able to read your e-mail because packages follow different routes. The second advantage is that data communication is very fast because there is almost no data traffic congestion—packets can always find routes with no data congestion. Even with the exponential growth of Internet traffic congestion is very rare.

Actually, the modular approach for both products and processes will lead to better outcomes for both sellers and buyers. Standard interfaces of the modules will lead to lower redesign costs and higher usage benefits. Other standards include the standardized electronic data interchange (EDI) messages that are used to communicate among the computers of sellers and buyers. The benefits of higher quality have to be weighed against the costs of implementing more tight governance rules. There are three market failures that should be avoided. The first failure has to do with the product and service quality and its digital representation. Insufficient information and transparency with respect to the quality of the flowers and services may lead to a "lemons market failure," i.e., low-quality suppliers drive out high-quality ones and the market collapses. Inspectors at the flower auctions assess the quality of the flower products, but quality levels are broadly defined. A refined quality grading system will create the opportunity for higher quality products to become visible in the market. The second failure results from a concentration of competition on one side of the market. This can reduce the incentive to invest in high-quality products and services. For example, in recent years many growers in the Netherlands switched to produce chrysanthemums and an oversupply was created. Some growers reacted with a cost-cutting strategy and reduced their investments in improving the quality of products or production processes. The third type of failure is that some strict forms of governance will result in less investment in other sides of the platform and therefore positive spillover effects to other platform sides will not be realized. For example, RFH requires growers to become FSI certified by 2021. This strict rule might cause some growers to end their RFH membership and to stop trading over RFH's platform. A continuous assessment by RFH is needed on the resistance to change of the different platform stakeholders, the changes of stakeholders' business models, and the disruptive potential of new upcoming platforms and technologies.

To become the dominant player in the global flower business it took a lot of focus, leadership, and the willingness to make difficult decisions. To stay the dominant player, even more stamina is needed. At MIT CISR, Peter Weill and Stephanie Woerner identified four pathways that companies can take to become top performers in the digital economy.[17] These pathways are based on surveys of several hundreds of enterprises in 2015 and 2017. The first pathway is "standardize first" and its focus on application programing interfaces (APIs) enabled business services with internal and external stakeholders.[18] The second pathway is "improve customer experiences" and it focuses on increasing customer satisfaction dramatically by introducing new digital offerings with mobile and web site applications and by empowering employees to serve customers in a better way. The third pathway is "take stair steps" to improve customer satisfaction and operational efficiencies. The fourth pathway is "create a new organization." The advantage is that a new organization can build its own customer base, people, culture, processes, and systems from scratch to be future-ready. The most logical pathway for RFH is in my opinion the third pathway. Taking stair steps requires in-depth coordination among the different stakeholders inside and outside RFH. It also requires RFH to develop deep customer orientation, to act as a software company, and to break down internal silos.

5.7   Direct Flow Distribution

As you approach the auction and distribution centers of RFH, in Aalsmeer, Rijnsburg, Naaldwijk, or Eelde, you will notice the intensive flow of trucks that drive to and from the centers. Insiders recognize two main logistical streams of flower products. The first stream is the auction flow, and it serves the auction channel. In the evening and early in the morning, trucks deliver flower products from the grower's greenhouses to the auction centers. Early in the morning the products are auctioned and distributed with standardized trolleys to the buyer's boxes in the distribution centers; see Fig. 5.2.

At these buyer's boxes wholesalers or retailers bundle flowers into flower bouquets, package the bundled products, and deliver these to retailers and local markets around the world. Some transporters distribute products to Schiphol Airport for export to the United States or other further destinations. Some depart for long drives over European highways to the bigger cities and to Germany, while others take a ferry to cross the North Sea with destinations in the United Kingdom. The second stream is the direct flow from the grower's greenhouse to the buyer's distribution center. It is interesting to notice that a lot of distribution activities take place in both flows, but keep in mind that around 25% of these trucks are driven rather empty. There are significant

Fig. 5.2 Standardized trolleys speed up logistics. https://www.royalfloraholland.com/en/about-floraholland/media-centre/actual-photos. With permission by Royal FloraHolland

waiting times because trucks arrive too early or too late. There are traffic jams on the Dutch highways nearby Schiphol Airport or the Rotterdam or IJmuiden seaports that cause these delays. And there is fierce competition among the 80 logistic service providers (LSPs) who act selfishly and do not yet share data with their competitors. Both the supply chains (the auction flow) and the demand chains (the direct flow) are designed and executed in a sub-optimal way. Each player will optimize its part of the chain for themselves, but nobody is taking care for the overall end-to-end optimization of the chain network. The chain is a path in a business network executed by several network participants (grower, transporter, wholesaler, transporter, retailer, transporter, end consumer). All players are smart especially for themselves, but is the overall chain network smart enough to serve the customers?

Let us focus on the second distribution stream, the direct flow, which is around 57% of the distribution portfolio of RFH. Quoc Viet Nguyen, supervised by Jacqueline Bloemhof and Behzad Behdani at Wageningen University & Research, concentrated on how to improve logistics decisions with the use of advanced big data, including data with a higher level of variety, velocity, volume, and veracity, in the floriculture chain network.[19] In the direct flow the customer order is the starting point of the logistics process. The customer orders from the supplier via the online trading platform. Suppliers are required to send an electronic delivery form (EDF) for each order, in advance of trolley arrivals, stating supplier information, product quantity, and delivery destination. Since 2016, RFID-enabled tracking and tracing systems have been implemented and pilot projects have been rolled out. The Chapter Notes include an overview of the different positions of the RFID scanners in the supply chain network. Suppliers and customers have access to these systems to trace product location at the trolley level. Trolley scans take place at the greenhouse indicating the departure of the trolleys (the farmer/greenhouse departure scan), at the entrance of the RFH cross-docking warehouse (the warehouse receiving scan), at the buffer (the buffer processing scan), and at the departure of the customer clusters (the cluster departure scan). RFH is responsible for deploying the trolleys from the receiving point at the inbound docks to customers within one hour. From the buffer, trolleys move to the different customer clusters and are transported by tractors to the customer boxes. Data on the direct flows include historic and real-time EDF data, and the scan data at all stages in the supply chain network. The advanced scanning technology will increase the volume, variety, and velocity dimensions of the data based on the increasing number of daily transactions between suppliers and customers. For suppliers there are several challenges, such as increasingly smaller order quantities with a more diverse product portfolio leading to less-than-full trolleys. Also 4-hour order lead times are becoming the "new" normal and LSPs have to load and dispatch their trucks as soon as possible without enough time to consolidate multiple less-than-truckload orders. The LSPs have to schedule trucks to pick up multiple less-than-truckload loads under severe time constraints resulting in a lower truck utilization level and a higher number of truck movements in the areas of the Glass City and the distribution centers of RFH. For suppliers, challenges arise to establish better in-time delivery combined with higher truck utilization to reduce transportation costs and transport-related carbon dioxide production. It is challenging for cross-docking operators to schedule the appropriate number of workers at each distribution stage for each time period. Uncertainty about the volume and timing of inbound arrivals and a broad range of operating hours complicates the workforce scheduling task. The estimated time of arrival (ETA) of trucks is not available in the EDF,s and therefore, there is a high uncertainty about inbound flows and the needed workforce. In research by Quoc Viet Nguyen and colleagues at Wageningen University & Research investigated four data analytics applications to support logistics decisions in the floriculture chain network (Fig. 5.3).[20] Two decisions are at the individual-firm level and the other two decisions are at the supply chain level. The four decisions with their data analytics solutions are as follows.

- The first decision deals with the real-time workforce adjustment at the cross-docking facilities. Based on the historical time scan data and the historical and the real-time EDF data, the inbound volume can be predicted at a smaller, hourly, time horizon. The predicted inbound volume will be used to forecast the needed workforce in the hours to come.
- The second decision has to do with the design of storage and fulfillment services at the cross-docking. RFH would like to provide new services to their suppliers and customers. A new, innovative service is anticipatory shipping, i.e., to ship flowers to customers *before* they place an order.[21] Indeed, this is a very counterintuitive strategy: you ship flowers before the customer buys them.[22] You expect—based on previous orders and other customer data—that these customers will buy specific flowers again and you distribute them toward these customers before they order. The anticipatory shipping algorithm is discussed in more detail in Chap. 6.
- The third decision is about delivery postponement in real-time process coordination. The decision has to do with facilitating coordination and

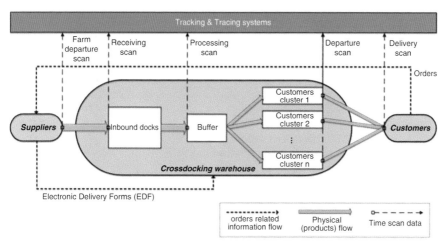

Fig. 5.3 Physical and information flows in the logistics processes of direct flows Nguyen QV (2019, September 6) Value of Information in Agro-food Logistics Management, A Case of the Dutch Floriculture Supply Chain Network. Dissertation, Wageningen University & Research. Figure 5.3, page 88. With permission by Quoc Viet Nguyen

collaboration among the suppliers, the cross-docking facility, and the customers. Between the suppliers and the cross-docking facility data from the farmer/greenhouse departure scan can help to predict when the products will arrive at the cross-docking station to help improve inbound scheduling. Cross-docking aims to distribute trolleys within 1 hour. However, customers might not have the required storage capacity or the required workers to handle the incoming trolleys. Cross-docking can postpone the delivery of trolleys when the customer boxes are too busy. Therefore, a long queue of trolleys before the customer boxes will be avoided. A simulation model was built and showed that timely postponement signals from a large number of customers to the cross-docking operator are crucial to gain more benefit for this type of coordination and could serve the customers and reduce the total cross-docking workload.

- The fourth decision focuses on the strategic partner selection in horizontal collaboration. The historical time scan data provide details about arrival times at the cross-docking for products from all the different suppliers. Using the scan data, a frequent pattern-mining algorithm is developed to determine patterns, e.g., a set of suppliers that arrive frequently at the time at the RFH inbound docks. There are a substantial number of supplier sets (suppliers that arrive at the same time) that potentially could lead to a discussion among these suppliers to share truck capacity and therefore lower the transportation costs and the carbon output.

All four examples show the value of information for supply chain decisions with the help of advanced big data analytics.

5.8 Payments and Currencies

As the orders move from the end consumers to the retailer and the wholesaler, and finally to the growers (the direct flow), the physical flower products move in the opposite direction: from the supplier to the wholesaler and retailer to the end consumer (the logistical flow). But there is an important third flow that is usually taken for granted but is getting more and more attention. Indeed, it is the money flow. Once the end consumer orders online, a payment is made. Every time a retailer orders, a payment is made. Every time a wholesaler orders, a payment is made. The rhythm of payments is synchronized with the rhythm of moving flower products and the rhythm of orders. If you know the rhythm of orders, you could predict the rhythm of the moving flower products and the rhythm of the money. Traditionally, when you, as end consumer, bought a flower bouquet at the local flower shop, products were moved via the suppliers and wholesalers to the local retailer and payments were made between these supply chain partners. You got the flower bouquet and do the payment: first the flower and then the money. Nowadays, you order flowers online from an e-retailer and pay, i.e., the order flow and the money flow start already to move in the direction to the suppliers. The flower bouquet flow is initiated and will arrive within a couple of hours or within a day: first the money and then the flower.

Payments are at the core of economic activities. Digital payments are crucial for the success of the digital transformation of any business. There are many examples of digital payments: bank apps on mobile phones, such as the ING app, other apps, such as Apple Pay, or payments via WhatsApp using a digital payment service like "Tikkie" in the Netherlands where payments can be ordered from accounts at different banks, in addition to new digital currencies such as the *Libra* initiated by Facebook and a consortium of companies.[23] The last option is a very exciting one that will be explored.

Libra is a global currency and financial infrastructure that might empower billions of people. People that have a Facebook account, but not a bank account, will be able to buy and sell products and services and participate in the digital economy. Libra has three parts that will work together: (1) it is built on secure, scalable, and reliable blockchain, (2) it is backed by a reserve of assets designed to provide intrinsic value, and (3) it is governed by the independent Libra association tasked with evolving the ecosystem.[24]

The payment infrastructure of RFH is very advanced. Buyers can bid via the auction system or can order products directly via the RFH Floriday platform. As explained, the products can be delivered within a couple of hours. The logistics are fast, as are the payments. Within 24 hours, payments are made from the buyers to the growers. Most business-to-business transaction payments in other industries take much longer. Within Europe there is the Single Euro Payments Area (SEPA) that speed up the payment between a payer's bank and the payee's bank. However, payer companies tend to be slow and payments, after the goods or services were received, could take weeks or sometimes months. Indeed, RFH cleared the market very quickly and therefore transaction risks for both sellers and buyers will be lower and the liquidity of companies was not jeopardized. However, higher transaction risks are often associated with currency volatility. The currency fluctuations of both the flower-producing country as well as the flower-consuming country are a source of transaction risks for both exporting growers as well as importing and exporting wholesalers, and also importing retailers around the world.

Consider, for example, two scenarios involving a supplier of roses from Kenya, with the Kenyan Shilling (KES) as local currency, exporting to the Netherlands (with the Euro as the local currency) where the roses are auctioned and bought by an exporting wholesaler who in turn sells the roses in Russia (with the Russian ruble (RUB) as currency). The first scenario is as follows. It begins with an exchange rate of 11,000 KES to €100. Suppose that the value of the Kenyan Shilling unexpectedly *decreased* by 10%, and the depreciation of the currency changed the exchange rate to 11,000 KES to €90 (€100 minus €10 (10%)). A depreciation of the currency, in general, means that the exports of flower products from Kenya to the outside world are cheaper and demand will increase. Meanwhile, imports to Kenya—for example, imported greenhouse technology from Europe—will be more expensive and could lead, in the long run, to higher production costs for growers in Kenya. Looking at Russia, there might be an exchange rate of 7000 RUB to €100. Suppose that the value of the Russian ruble suddenly *increased* by 10%, and the appreciation of the currency changed the exchange rate to 7000 RUB to €110 (€100 plus €10 (10%)). The appreciation of the currency, in general, means that imports of flower products to Russia will become cheaper and will increase. At the same time, exports from Russia—for example exported energy such as natural gas to Europe—will be more expensive. In this first scenario, one can expect more flower trade to flow from Kenya, via the Netherlands, to Russia. The second scenario is the reverse: 10% appreciation in Kenya and 10% depreciation in Russia will lead to the effect that demand in Russia for Kenyan flowers will decrease, and fewer will be sold. One has to keep in mind that the different central banks—the Central Bank of Kenya, the European Central Bank (ECB), and the Russian Central Bank—will take into account many different factors in their decision to depreciate or appreciate currencies.

In general, for growers, wholesalers, and retailers in the global flower industry, price stability is desirable for doing business. Actually, it is interesting to explore the options for RFH to design not only the commercial and logistical components of the business but also the financial component. One strategy that RFH could explore is the introduction of the *FloraCoin* (FC). The FloraCoin concept is inspired by my research with Eduardo Diniz and Erica Siqueira, at the business school Fundação Getulio Vargas, and Edgar Kampers, founder of Qoin Foundation.[25] The FloraCoin currency could be a global currency used for the transactions that run over RFH's digital platforms. Growers, wholesalers, and retailers will trade in FloraCoins to avoid volatile currency fluctuations within the chain networks of the floriculture industry. At the borders of the industry, such as the inputs (seed material, labor, energy, greenhouse technology) for growers or the outputs (flower bouquets) to end consumers, local currencies will remain. Even at these borders, however, the end consumers could be given an incentive if they purchase flowers with FloraCoins. As research has shown, community currencies have the potential to strengthen local regions and economies. They keep the money within the community. When linked to global currencies, local community currencies may exert a stabilizing influence on the world economy and shrink the widening income gap between the rich and the poor.

5.9   Web Redesign and Data Ownership

What is next? Well, reader, before this question can be answered, from a technology perspective, we have to go back in history. The World Wide Web (WWW) was invented in March 1989 by Sir Tim Berners-Lee, of the United Kingdom, who was working as a fellow in Geneva at Conseil Européen pour la Recherche Nucléaire (CERN, the European Council for Nuclear Research).[26] CERN hosts the world's largest particle physics laboratory. Scientists and researchers from around the world use the specialized equipment at CERN to expand the horizons of human understanding of the universe, and there are many research projects going on all the time. Managing the records of those experiments and sharing the knowledge they produced had become a challenge. In response to this challenge, Berners-Lee's wrote a 20-page document called "Information Management: A Proposal," in which he proposed an innovative approach to storing and retrieving information from the thousands of projects at CERN. These projects run different experiments, with different people, concepts, software, and hardware. He recognized that "the method of storage must not place its own restrains on the information." In the proposal Berners-Lee connected three elements. The first element was developed by himself and was called *hypertext*, i.e., the text displayed on a computer or electronic device with references (called hyperlinks) to other files that the reader can immediately access by "clicking" the hyperlink. The second element was the use of the Transmission Control Protocol (TCP). The protocol provides a reliable, ordered, and error-checked delivery of a stream of bytes between applications running on hosts communicating via an Internet Protocol (IP) network.[27] The third element was the Domain Name System (DNS), a hierarchical and decentralized naming system for computers, services, and other resources connected to the Internet. Domain names, such as www.nytimes.com, are linked to numerical addresses needed for locating and identifying computer services and devices. The World Wide Web, with the underlying Internet architecture, TCP/IP protocol, and domain name system, continues to flourish, and around 55% of all people in the world use it.

The 30-year anniversary in 2019 was a moment of reflection on the use and societal impact of the World Wide Web, and three crucial issues were discussed.

The first issue was about the design of the technical infrastructure. Originally, the TCP/IP protocol was meant as a network of networks.[28] It was a protocol to connect reliable networks with each other. However, the design is now used in a very different way; the connected networks are not reliable at all and as such a tool is used with a different purpose, i.e., to connect unreliable networks with each other. Kees Neggers, one of the Dutch Internet pioneers, called the Internet a "splendid accident," splendid because it is so widely used nowadays, but an accident because in terms of security, reliability, and scalability the design no longer fits the current usage.

The second issue was that it is very difficult to assess the quality of the information that is presented on the web. In general, anyone can put anything online or distribute information over the web and the impact of "fake" news has already had a dramatic impact on how people think and make decisions.

The third issue has to do with the control of the data. The world is going in three diverging directions. The first direction takes the position that data belong to companies. For example, many technology companies based in the United States, such as Facebook, Amazon, Apple, Microsoft, and Google (FAAMG), want access to all consumer data. The advanced technology companies process and analyze individual customer data and are able to target individual customers with a personalized web page or with personalized advertisements. Their algorithms absorb all the data they can get from their customers such as the visited web pages and locations, the searched keywords, the exchanged messages, the interaction with friends and family, the traveled routes, the ordered products, and the payments that were made. Those companies profit from using that data for their business or marketing that data to advertisers. Take, for example, the advertising model, Google's main business model. Users can use Google search for free and will try to get an answer on anything. If someone will search for flowers Google will show on the web pages two parts that will help the user to find the relevant information related to the searched keyword. The first part of the search results is called organic search and it provides a list of web sites that is determined by the number of web links from other web sites to a specific web site. More links indicated a higher relevance related to the keyword and therefore a higher rank in the ranking of web sites. The second part of the search results is called advertisements (Ads) where companies can bid, via Google Ads, on keywords that are searched by users. The highest bidder will get the highest place for its Ads ranking. Companies will get more sales through targeted advertisements. The fees by the companies are paid to web site publishers. These publishers will use these fees to generate quality content, via Google AdSense. The quality content is provided for free to the Google users. Chapter 6 will pay attention to advertisement auction algorithms and the impact on consumer behavior. The second direction takes the position that data belong to governments. In several countries, governments are quickly building a surveillance society where data are used to monitor and control the behavior of citizens.

The third direction takes the position that individuals owns the data about themselves. The European Union has chosen the third direction with the introduction of the General Data Protection Regulation, a regulation on data protection and privacy in the European Union (EU) and the European Economic Area (EEA).

Based on these technological infrastructure issues and to mark the thirtieth anniversary of the World Wide Web, Sir Tim Berners-Lee launched a campaign to redesign and decentralize the web (Dweb), and aimed to persuade governments, companies, and citizens to commit to uphold nine principles of a free and open Internet.[29] At the announcement of these nine principles—as the contract for the Web, he stated "The power of the web to transform people's lives, enrich society and reduce inequality is one of the defining opportunities of our time. But if we don't act now—and act together—to prevent the web being misused by those who want to exploit, divide and undermine, we are at risk of squandering that potential."

Several startups developed applications that used the so-called Solid standards, these are concrete design rules inspired by the nine principles. The Solid standards were designed by Berners-Lee and his team to give users more control over their personal data, let users decide where their data will go and who is allowed to access certain data elements, and which apps are allowed to see that data.[30] They developed products and services, including the following: Beaker Browser, a new independent browser to explore the peer-to-peer web; DTube, a YouTube alternative; Graphite Docs, a Google document alternative; Matrix, providing a WhatsApp alternative; OpenBazaar, a decentralized marketplace; and Textile Photos, an Instagram alternative for storing, managing, and sharing photos. Actually, the first initiatives are taken to develop decentralized web solutions that are compliant with the strict GDPR rules. For example, flower transporters can start to share data using the uniform set of agreements or schemes that give each other access to their data. The uniform set of agreements were developed by iSHARE, an initiative of the Neutral Logistics Information Platform (NLIP), which is the leading platform promoting data exchange in the transport and logistics sector.[31]

A pioneering group of leading logistics companies and their customers inspire other companies to follow in their footsteps and begin sharing data among companies. As we have seen with the research of Viet Nguyen of Wageningen University & Research, data sharing in the flower chain networks can create business opportunities and business value.

Companies can also monetize data, i.e., combine and aggregate data into information-based products or services. These information-based products or services are sold to clients and need to be "rare, hard to replicate, and difficult to substitute." RFH could execute several data monetization strategies, for its growers (probably for free) and for its clients (wholesalers and retailers) with a price tag. *"Selling information about flowers next to selling flowers"* is my favorite slogan to explain the upcoming business models in the flower industry. These unique business models can draw upon the sources of value.

Research at MIT CISR identified six sources of value[32]:

- *Data.* For RFH all data related to transactions of both sellers and buyers in the auction market is a unique dataset that will create value for both sellers and buyers. For example, one can identify bidding strategies based on in-depth analysis of transaction data. Buyers, the auctioneers, and sellers can learn from these data analytics research endeavors.
- *Data architecture.* The architecture to deal with real-time transactions in fast-paced markets will be a source of value in itself. The large datasets and how to handle these in real time can be used by other companies. RFH could create a value proposition for other companies that could use the logic of RFH's data architecture.
- *Data science.* With the help of data science specialists, RFH established a department on Data Science and Business Intelligence. One of the information-based services, called *Insights*, is offered to growers at the RFH Floriday platform.[33] Member suppliers pay €50 per month, and non-member suppliers €70 per month. With the help of advanced analytics, growers will get insights related to questions like: What will tomorrow's price be? Which auction location is best for the products you are selling? And, how does your performance compare with other growers like you?
- *Domain leadership.* Information sellers often understand the business domain better than their clients. Deep domain knowledge can enable them to provide advisory service for their clients. RFH, given its deep knowledge of the different flower product groups, could provide consultancy service to the wholesalers and retailers about flower product portfolios and logistical optimization strategies.

- *Commitment to client action.* Information sellers "recognize that their clients must act upon the seller's information products and service in such a way that it will generate business value, otherwise the seller's business model is not sustainable." Therefore, sellers pay a lot of attention to how their clients use their products and services and help their clients to improve its usage. Actually, RFH could detect how *Insights* information impacted a client's decision outcomes and measure these impacts in more detail.
- *Process mastery.* Information sellers "become masters of the business processes that their offerings inform." RFH has deep insights about the transport and logistics processes among growers and RFH's distribution centers. Actually, the research by Quoc Viet Nguyen and colleagues of Wageningen University & Research showed that RFH could help to improve the collaboration among the different transportation companies and optimize the loading of their trucks.

In Chap. 6, *Blooming Algorithms,* several detailed examples of AI-driven algorithms with data monetization strategies will be presented and discussed.

Notes

1. Insights about the Nini Flower Group, including Lamorna Flowers and Nini Flowers, and the flower industry in Kenya are in Nini Flowers (2020).
2. Holland Flower Alliance and Amsterdam Logistics (2019, Feb 14).
3. Fresh (2019, June 19).
   YouTube (2016, Sept 13).
4. In De Vries E (2018).
5. Insights about Flowerbx are in Thomas D (2019, February 27).
6. Quotes in Thomas D (2019, February 27). Quotes "Usually, flowers go to" and "You buy the flowers".
7. The story of Bloomon is in Bloomon (2014, November 20).
   Top of Minds (2018).
   De Graaff A (2019, March 20).
   InkefCapital (2018).
   Banis D (2018, January 4).
8. Netflix data are based on Koblin J (2019, October 17).
   Spangler T (2019, Jan 18).
   Regalado M (2018, April 30).
9. A digital hologram of a flower bouquet, including digital floral scent, could be the ultimate digital flower product. In such a case these digital flowers will be provided over a digital platform such as digital movies over Netflix or digital music over Spotify.

10. The PostNL case is based on Van Dam B (2018, November 30).
11. The MIT CISR research is based on Ross J, Beath C, Mocker M (2019). With quotes: "big, old companies," "less likely to own responsibility" (p. 9), "the holistic organizational configuration" (p. 5).

    Mocker M, Ross J, Van Heck E (2014, February 27). For an overview of MIT CISR research have a look at https://cisr.mit.edu/. Accessed 7 Sept 2020.
12. Many companies transform toward digital. However, as Jeanne Ross (MIT CISR) concludes one needs to distinguish between digitization and digital. As she indicates: "Digitization involves standardizing business processes. It is associated with cost cutting and operational excellence. But "becoming digital" is a totally different exercise from digitizing. Although digitization is an important enabler of digital—and digital technologies can certainly support operational excellence—all the digitization in the world won't on its own make a business a digital company. Becoming digital involves a very different kind of transformation. Digital refers to a customer-centric value proposition." in Ross J (2017, Sept 29) and Ross J, Beath C, Sebastian I (2017, October 19). We will return to the important distinction between digitization and digital in Chap. 7.
13. The pre-sales channel analysis is in Truong HM, Gupta A, Ketter W, Van Heck E (2019).
14. In 1935, the British botanist Arthur Tansley introduced the *ecosystem* concept into biology. It is described as a community of organisms interacting with each other and the elements of their environments, such as air, water, and earth. In order to thrive, these organisms compete and collaborate with each other to divide available resources, and they co-evolve and jointly adapt to external disruptions. Tansley AG (1935).

    See for a historical review Willis AJ (1997).

    In 1993, James Moore, president of a management consultancy firm, introduced the *business ecosystem* concept in the field of business strategy and implementation, where a company is viewed "not as a member of a single industry but as part of a *business ecosystem* that crosses a variety of industries. In a business ecosystem, companies evolve capabilities around a new innovation: they work cooperatively and competitively to support new products, satisfy customer needs, and eventually incorporate the next round of innovations." Moore JF (1993, May/June).

    According to Amrit Tiwana a platform-based ecosystem consists of two major elements—a platform and complementary apps and the alignment between platform ecosystem architecture and governance is a necessary condition for success. See Tiwana A (2014).
15. Ajit Kambil and myself researched the design of electronic markets in our book *Making Markets* that was inspired by the redesign of the Dutch flower markets at that time.

Peter Vervest and myself initiated in 2005—in collaboration with academic colleagues and business executives—the Smart Business Network Initiative (SBNI) and developed the concept of smart business networks with a focus on business network orchestration, network structure and processes, and the underlying digital infrastructure.

Several academic colleagues active in the Workshop of Information Systems and Economics (WISE) community developed the notion of platform ecosystems such as Marshall van Alstyne, Erik Brynjolfsson, Geoffrey Parker, Amrit Tiwana, and D.J. Wu.

Strategic decisions about the design of electronic markets, smart business networks, or platform ecosystems are based on:

Kambil A, Van Heck E (2002).

Van Heck E, Vervest P (2007).

Hagiu A (2014).

16. Details of the flower platform ecosystem design are based on Van Heck E (2018, November 30) And Van der Zwet C (2018).

17. The company readiness research with the four paths is based on Weill P, Woerner S (2018).

18. Application programming interfaces (APIs) are a set of routines, protocols, and tools for building software applications. An API specifies how software modules should interact. Companies that are born digital use APIs to design and implement software for all their products, services, and processes.

19. The value of information and data sharing in floriculture logistics in Nguyen QV (2019, September 6).

20. The four decisions and data analytics applications are based on Nguyen QV (2019, September 6). It is also published in Nguyen QV, Behdani B, Bloemhof J, Hoberg K (2020).

For an overview of the physical and information flows in the logistical processes of the direct flows from the suppliers (growers) to the customers (wholesalers or retailers) in the floriculture chain, see Fig. 5.3.

21. Anticipatory shipping was invented by Amazon Technologies Inc. and the patent was granted in December 2013 (Patent US8615473B2).

22. Amazon's anticipatory shipping is Kopalle P (2014, January 28).

Bensinger G (2014, January 17).

Spiegel JR, McKenna MT, Lakshman GS, Nordstrom PG (2013, Dec 24).

23. About Libra in Libra Association Members (2019, June 16).

24. A blockchain is a growing list of records, called blocks, which are linked using cryptography. Each block contains a cryptographic hash of the previous block, a timestamp, and transaction data. By design, a blockchain is resistant to modification of the data.

25. In a paper by Diniz E, Kampers E, Van Heck E (2017), ten key questions were identified that are helpful in the design and implementation of digital community currencies and can be used in the design of the FloraCoin as the flower community currency.

These ten key questions are:

- "Key Question 1: what are the objectives and purpose of the currency platform?"

   The objective of FloraCoin is to create currency stability for the floriculture community and to minimize currency fluctuation risks.

- "Key Question 2: what is the adopted business model for the currency platform?"

   The business model of FloraCoin is that participants will get lower currency fluctuation risks and that there will be a more stable price level for flower products and services for the producers, wholesalers, and retailers of flowers. Sources of income could be via grants and donations, fees (membership, transaction, and exchange), or advertising.

- "Key Question 3: what is the governance model for the currency platform?"

   Governance broadly refers to who decides what in any platform's ecosystem. Although there are other levels of decision (e.g., strategic and operational), one way to understand the governance of a community currency is to evaluate how centralized or shared is the decision-making process about rules for issuance for a particular project, given that this is central to the process of managing a currency. With Royal FloraHolland as grower cooperative a shared governance model of FloraCoin with their clients (wholesalers and retailers) is foreseen.

- "Key Question 4: what is the architecture model for the currency platform?"

   The level of openness of the architecture in a given platform can be considered at three levels—provider, technology, and user level. The provider level recognizes the strategic involvement of key stakeholders that provide a platform. The technology level is concerned with the interoperability of a platform across different technologies. The user level relates to what extent a platform discriminates different segments of the customer base. The FloraCoin architecture will be closed in nature and membership will be members and clients of the RFH cooperation.

- "Key Question 5: what is the regional scope for the currency platform?"

   A community currency can be designed to be used only under certain geographical limits or being global by definition. FloraCoin will be a global currency given the global nature of the flower industry.

- "Key Question 6: what is the backing system for the currency platform?"

   Backing is a design feature of a currency which guarantees the long-term purchasing power of a currency. This means that the issuer of a currency guarantees the exchange of a currency for either another currency or a commodity. The backing principle can be used to limit the issuance of a currency as well as to infuse trust in project that does not have government endorsement. Backing of the FloraCoin will be provided by the flower business community.

- "Key Question 7: on which pegging system (parity) the currency platform is based?"

  Community currencies can be pegged in units that allow them to be compared with other value systems, i.e., when one unit of a community currency is equal to one unit of any official currency. The FloraCoin parity with the Euro currency is a logical choice given the dominance of flower trading in the European Union.

- "Key Question 8: what are the categories of transactionality performed by the currency platform?"

  Transactionality refers to the types of transactions that can be performed by the distinct groups of users that the platform brings together varying from single to multiple profiles. With FloraCoin we can distinguish among growers, transporters, logistic service providers, wholesalers, and retailers as the main group of users.

- "Key Question 9: does the currency platform allow convertibility?"

  Convertibility to the official currency provides the "sensory connection" needed to ensure the "real value" of a community currency, thus making it more amenable to adoption. Thus, in terms of convertibility to official currencies, a community currency can be convertible, offer limited convertibility, or not be convertible. In case of FloraCoin a limited convertability to the Euro will be foreseen.

- "Key Question 10: what is the level of virtuality offered by the currency platform?"

  Virtuality is related to the physical closeness between two agents operating a payment transaction. The face-to-face transactions improve "knowledge acquisition, trust and friendship" since buying physically in local shops offer opportunities for sociable interactions in local communities, reinforcing the community feelings often desired for a community currency. Payments made by inserting cards in a Point-of-Sales (POS) machine or with Near Field Communication (NFC) technologies are examples of transactions where physical presence is demanded. For FloraCoin digital payments are foreseen given its advanced payment system.

The taxonomy is developed in Diniz E, Siqueira E, Van Heck E (2019).
The concise summary of the research results is in Diniz E, Van Heck E (2018, Nov 6) and Van Heck E, Diniz E (2019, Jan 17).

26. The invention of the World Wide Web in Berners-Lee T (1989, March).
27. On October 29, 1969, three months after Neil Armstrong and Edwin "Buzz" Aldrin landed on the moon with the Apollo 11, for the first time a message was delivered between two computers. These two computers were at the University of California in Los Angeles and the Stanford Research Institute in Menlo Park, California. The message text was meant to be the word "login," but only the L and O were transmitted before the system crashed. The

Internet, at that time called ARPANET, and its underlying TCP/IP protocol were born.

28. The development of TCP/IP in Mols B (2019, Oct 29).
    Neggers K (2019, Nov 8).
29. The redesign of the Internet is in Berners-Lee T (2019, March 12).
    Contract for the web defines "nine principles and indicates that principles 1 to 3 are for governments, 4 to 6 are for companies, and 7 to 9 are for citizens":

    1. "Ensure everyone can connect to the internet."
    2. "Keep all of the internet available, all of the time."
    3. "Respect and protect people's fundamental online privacy and data rights."
    4. "Make the internet affordable and accessible to everyone."
    5. "Respect and protect people's privacy and personal data to build online trust."
    6. "Develop technologies that support the best in humanity and challenge the worst."
    7. "Be creators and collaborators on the Web."
    8. "Build strong communities that respect civil discourse and human dignity."
    9. "Fight for the Web."

    The contract for the web and its nine principles are in: https://contract-fortheweb.org/
    Accessed 7 Sept 2020.
30. Solid-based startups are in Corbyn Z (2018, September 8).
31. iShare is based on principles developed and explained in Liezenberg C, Lycklama D, Nijland S (2019).
32. Data monetization strategies are based on work by Wixom B, Buff A, Tallon P (2015, January). Buff A, Wixom B, Tallon P (2015, August). With quotes: "that are rare, hard to replicate, and difficult to substitute." (p. 2), "recognize that their clients" (p. 2), and "become masters" (p. 2).
33. The Insights example is from Royal FloraHolland (2020).

References

Banis D (2018, January 4) How Dutch startup Bloomon became the Netflix of flowers. The Next Web – Insider. https://thenextweb.com/insider/2018/01/04/dutch-startup-bloomon-became-netflix-flowers/ Accessed 7 Sept 2020

Bensinger G (2014, January 17) Amazon wants to ship your package before you buy it. Wall Street Journal

Berners-Lee T (1989, March) Information management: a proposal. In: CERN. https://www.w3.org/History/1989/proposal.html. Accessed 7 Sept 2020

Berners-Lee T (2019, March 12) 30 years on, what's next #ForTheWeb? In: Web Foundation. https://webfoundation.org/2019/03/web-birthday-30/. Accessed 7 Sept 2020

Bloomon (2014, November 20) Bloomon zorgt voor revolutie in traditionele bloemensector. In: Press Release Bloomon

Buff A, Wixom B, Tallon P (2015, August) Foundations for data monetization. MIT Center for Information Systems Research (CISR), CISR WP No. 402 and MIT Sloan WP No. 5213-15

Corbyn Z (2018, September 8) Decentralisation: the next big step for the World Wide Web. The Guardian. https://www.theguardian.com/technology/2018/sep/08/decentralisation-next-big-step-for-the-world-wide-web-dweb-data-internet-censorship-brewster-kahle. Accessed 7 Sept 2020

De Graaff A (2019, March 20) Forse verliezen bij bloemenbezorger Bloomon leiden tot ontslagronde. In: QuoteNet. https://www.quotenet.nl/zakelijk/a219701/forse-verliezen-bij-bloemenbezorger-bloomon-leiden-tot-ontslagronde-219701/. Accessed 11 Sept 2020

De Vries E (2018). Kenyan flowers keep blossoming despite challenges. Floribusiness, Edition 1. https://digital.floribusiness.com/floribusiness-edition-1-2018/kenyan-flowers-keep-blossoming-despite-challenges/. Accessed 7 Sept 2020

Diniz E, Van Heck E (2018, November 6) Digital community currencies and global challenges. In: RSM Discovery. https://discovery.rsm.nl/articles/368-digital-community-currencies-for-global-challenges/. Accessed 12 Sept 2020

Diniz E, Kampers E, Van Heck E (2017) Integral typology of digital community currencies. Paper presented at IV International Conference on Social and Complementary Currencies: Money, Consciousness, and Values for Social Change, Universitat Oberta de Catalunya, Barcelona, 10–14 May 2017

Diniz E, Siqueira E, Van Heck E (2019) Taxonomy of digital community currency platforms. Inf Technol Dev 25(1):69–91

Fresh (2019, June 19) Air France KLM Martinair Cargo's flower flow from Kenya now FlowerWatch approved. Press Release Air France KLM, https://www.afklcargo.com/WW/en/common/news/flower_watch_Kenya.jsp.   Accessed 7 Sept 2020

Hagiu A (2014) Strategic decisions for multisided platforms. MIT Sloan Manag Rev 55(2):71–80

Holland Flower Alliance and Amsterdam Logistics (2019, February 14) Watch our video on optimizing the floral logistics chain. https://hollandfloweralliance.com/watch-our-video-on-optimizing-the-floral-logistics-chain/. Accessed 7 Sept 2020

InkefCapital (2018), INKEF empowers us with the information we need to build our business into the global brand we want to become. https://www.inkefcapital.com/portfolio/bloomon/. Accessed 11 Sept 2020

Innovative Fresh (2017, July 6) Quality insights. Fiona Coulson: Nini Flowers. https://innovativefresh.com/en/Article/Fiona-Coulson-Nini-Flowers   Accessed 7 Sept 2020

Kambil A, Van Heck E (2002) Making markets: how firms can design and profit from online auctions and exchanges. Harvard Business School Press, Boston, MA

Koblin J (2019, October 17). Netflix's top 10 original movies and TV shows, according to Netflix. New York Times. https://www.nytimes.com/2019/10/17/business/media/netflix-top-ten-movies-tv-shows.html Accessed 7 Sept 2020

Kopalle P (2014, January 28) Why Amazon's Anticipatory Shipping Is Pure Genius. Forbes. https://www.forbes.com/sites/onmarketing/2014/01/28/why-amazons-anticipatory-shipping-is-pure-genius/#6be8752d4605 Accessed 7 Sept 2020

Libra Association Members (2019, June 16) An Introduction to Libra. White paper. https://libra.org/en-US/wp-content/uploads/sites/23/2019/06/LibraWhitePaper_en_US.pdf. Accessed 12 Sept 2020

Liezenberg C, Lycklama D, Nijland S (2019) Everything is transaction, about data, trust and the unprecedented opportunities of the transactional Internet. Amazon

Mocker M, Ross J, Van Heck E (2014, February 27) Transforming Royal Philips: seeking local relevance while leveraging global scale. In: MIT CISR. MIT Sloan CISR Working Paper 394. https://cisr.mit.edu/publication/MIT_CISR_wp394_Philips_MockerRossVanHeck. Accessed 7 Sept 2020

Mols B (2019, October 29) 50 jaar internet – een schitterend ongeluk. NRC Handelsblad. https://www.nrc.nl/nieuws/2019/10/29/50-jaar-internet-belangrijker-dan-de-maanlanding-a3978376. Accessed 7 Sept 2020

Moore JF (1993, May/June) Predators and prey: a new ecology of competition. Harvard Business Review: 75–86

Neggers K (2019, November 8) Het internet & TCP/IP was 50 jaar geleden een schitterend ongeluk. In: NRC Handelsblad. https://www.vincenteverts.nl/het-internet-tcpip-was-50-jaar-geleden-een-schitterend-ongeluk-kees-neggers-ex-directeur-surfnet/. Accessed 7 Sept 2020

Nguyen QV (2019, September 6) Value of information in agro-food logistics management, a case of the Dutch floriculture supply chain network. Dissertation, Wageningen University & Research

Nguyen QV, Behdani B, Bloemhof J, Hoberg K (2020) Value of data in multi-level supply chain decisions: a case study in the Dutch floriculture sector. Int J Prod Res. https://doi.org/10.1080/00207543.2020.1821116

Nini Flowers (2020) We Are Nini Group. In: Niniflowers. http://niniflowers.com/. Accessed 7 Sept 2020

PostNL (2020) Parcels In: PostNL. https://www.postnl.nl/en/about-postnl/about-us/our-organisation/parcels/. Accessed 7 Sept 2020

Regalado M (2018, April 30) The Most Expensive Netflix Original TV Shows. In: ShowBiz CheatSheet. https://www.cheatsheet.com/entertainment/expensive-netflix-original-tv-shows.html/

Ross J (2017, September 29) Don't confuse digital with digitization. MIT Sloan Management Review

Ross J, Beath C, Sebastian I (2017, October 19) Digital ≠ Digitized, In MIT. CISR. MIT CISR Research Briefing, Vol. 17, No. 10. https://cisr.mit.edu/

publication/2017_1001_DigitizedNotDigital_RossBeathSebastian. Accessed 7 Sept 2020

Ross JW, Beath CM, Mocker M (2019) Designed for digital: how to architect your business for sustained success. The MIT Press, Cambridge

Royal FloraHolland (2020) Insights. https://insights.floriday.com/ Accessed 7 Sept 2020

Spangler T (2019, January 18) Netflix spent $12 billion on content in 2018. In Variety. https://variety.com/2019/digital/news/netflix-content-spending-2019-15-billion-1203112090/ Accessed 7 Sept 2020

Spiegel JR, McKenna MT, Lakshman GS, Nordstrom PG (2013, Dec 24) Method and system for anticipatory package shipping. US patent 8615473B2. https://patents.google.com/patent/US8615473B2/en. Accessed 7 Sept 2020

Tansley AG (1935) The use and abuse of vegetational concepts and terms. Ecology 16:284–307

Thomas D (2019, February 27) The flower disrupter. Fashion's favorite florist learned her trade at Tom Ford, watching all the bouquets go by. New York Times, section D, p 3. https://www.nytimes.com/2019/02/27/fashion/florist-flowerbx-london.html. Accessed 11 Sept 2020

Tiwana A (2014) Platform ecosystems: aligning architecture, governance, and strategy. Morgan Kaufmann, Burlington

Top of Minds (2018) Patrick Hurenkamp, co-founder and CEO of Bloomon. In: Top of minds. https://topofminds.com/founder-patrick-hurenkamp-bloomon/. Accessed 11 Sept 2020

Truong HM, Gupta A, Ketter W, Van Heck E (2019) Understanding B2B buyer behavior in multichannel markets: how posted price channel affect buyers strategic behavior in auctions. Paper presented at the International Conference on Information Systems (ICIS), The International Congress Center Munich, Munich, 15–18 December 2019

Van Dam B (2018, November 30) De invloed van ecommerce op de sierteeltsector. Digitaliseringsbijeenkomst Sierteelt, Aalsmeer

Van der Zwet C (2018) Eric van Heck op een bijeenkomst digitalisering: 'Een groot platform is het meest wenselijk'. Vakblad voor de Bloemisterij 49:12–13

Van Heck E (2018, November 30) Big data, Disruptie en Bedrijfsmodellen. Digitaliseringsbijeenkomst Sierteelt, Aalsmeer

Van Heck E, Diniz E (2019, Jan 17). Who needs banks? Why digital community currencies are becoming so popular and how to make one work. Forbes. https://www.forbes.com/sites/rsmdiscovery/2019/01/17/who-needs-banks-why-digital-community-currencies-are-becoming-so-popular-and-how-to-make-one-work/#3e0fcb2b19f4. Accessed 7 Sept 2020

Van Heck E, Vervest P (2007) Smart business networks: how the network wins. Commun ACM 50(6):28–37

Weill P, Woerner S (2018) Is your company ready for a digital future? MIT Sloan Manag Rev 59(2):21–25

Willis AJ (1997) The ecosystem: an evolving concept viewed historically. Funct Ecol 11:268–271

Wixom B, Buff A, Tallon P (2015, January) Six sources of value for information business. MIT Center for Information Systems Research (CISR). CISR research briefing, Vol. XV, No. 1

YouTube (2016, Sept 13) Air France KLM Cargo transportation of flowers from Kenia, https://www.youtube.com/watch?v=BhtVWCBntCA. Accessed 7 Sept 2020

6

Blooming Algorithms

6.1 Street Markets

Saturday mornings are an ideal time to stroll through Rotterdam. Station Blaak in the city center is known for its surprising and iconic buildings. On the west side is the Markthal, an indoor marketplace with many small restaurants and shops and a spectacular ceiling depicting the Horn of Plenty.[1] On the east side there are several cube-shaped houses situated like a small grove of trees surrounded by the city. Adjacent to them is a pencil-shaped apartment building, appropriately called the Pencil, which stands next to the Central Library of Rotterdam. The Library façade is dominated by modern balconies and yellow steel tubes that run from the roof downward, and at the top of the building in neon letters is a quote from the Dutch philosopher and humanist, Desidirius Erasmus Roterodamus, known as Erasmus, born in 1466: '*Heel de aarde is je vaderland*' (The whole earth is your homeland).[2] Further to the northwest a statue of Erasmus is situated in front of the Laurenskerk, a church built between 1449 and 1525 and the only remaining late Gothic building in Rotterdam.

The central street market is situated at the Binnenrotte, a large plaza. The view is always spectacular. More than four hundred stalls are set up early in the morning and broken down in the afternoon. The stalls are arranged in long lines with paths to walk in between, and a wide array of products are offered for sale. You will find not only high-quality fresh products, such as flowers, vegetables, fruit, cheese, nuts, bread, and fish, but also clothes, smart phone accessories, vintage goods, fabrics, and souvenirs. The market is typically crowded in the afternoon with thousands of locals and tourists.

© The Author(s), under exclusive license to Springer Nature Switzerland AG 2021   **149**
E. van Heck, *Technology Meets Flowers*, https://doi.org/10.1007/978-3-030-69303-9_6

The regular visitors are loyal to their favorite vendors, while rookie visitors are likely to explore and try out new products from various vendors.

Market vendors must compete for the attention of passersby and convince them to make a purchase. Vendors have different strategies to advertise their products. They create appetizing displays of fresh products, such as cheese and vegetables—usually with the very freshest products in the front row. They may offer samples so potential customers can taste the product. Some attract attention by calling out a sales pitch: "Great codfish, best in town, only three euro." People hear the vendor, look at the codfish, and buy. The atmosphere is lively and exciting. For market vendors, the location of their stall is important. Is it near the entrance to the street market? Is it visible and also easy to access? Is their enough space for customers to queue up? Street vendors in the Binnenrotte or any other street market are keenly aware that it is all about "location, location, location."

But how about the vendors in online markets? Compared to the orderly rows of street market vendors in the Binnenrotte, the online market is like the "Wild West" with intense competition for the best deals. The market size of digital advertising in 2020 is approx. $365 billion with search advertising as the largest segment at 38% and classifieds as the smallest segment at 6%.[3] These markets are complex and not very transparent. Companies advertise their products or services by purchasing advertising space from publishers, such as newspapers (*New York Times*, *Washington Post*), social media platforms (Facebook, Instagram), or search engines (Bing, Google) via advertisement open exchanges (Google Ad Exchange, OpenX) or via private marketplaces (Concert, Vox Media).

The fascinating world of online markets—with online individuals, advertisers, and publishers—may seem very different from the street market at the Binnenrotte, yet many market dimensions remain the same. In fact, just like street markets, online markets are also about "location, location, location."[4] Let me explain.

6.2   Online Markets

Online customers have easy access to information and they can compare potential products, services, and buying options. They can effortlessly order home delivery, or they can locate nearby restaurants or taxis that can take them almost anywhere. Online vendors can reach a much wider range of potential customers with personalized offers, and they can have instant feedback from their customers. Each of these processes use algorithms, which are simply "a sequence of instructions telling a computer what to do."[5] With this in mind, consider the way vendors sell flowers online.

If you want to buy flowers online, the first step is to search for them. Google's search engine is the most popular one in the world. Once you search you have already used an algorithm, i.e., the secret software developed by Google—called Page Ranking Technology—that determines the ranking of all web sites in the indexed internet (this includes everything that can be found through search engines).

When you type in "google.com," an almost empty web site appears with a space to type in the keywords in your search, followed by two button options: "Google search" or "I'm feeling lucky" (when you use a desktop, not your mobile). While a Google search returns a list of pages related to the keywords, "I'm feeling lucky" directly loads one of the web sites from the list.

When I try "I'm feeling lucky" with the keywords "flower bouquet," the browser loads the web site "flowers.nl," which has excellent looking flower bouquets and fast order fulfillment. (Each Google customer will get a personalized suggestion based on the customer's search history and location.) The results of an "I'm feeling lucky" search may save you the time it takes to select an option from the list of "Google search" results. If you place an order following an "I'm feeling lucky" search, Google strengthens its business model.

Unlike the fixed locations of vendors' stalls in the street market that are the same for every visitor to the market, the Google page ranking algorithm dynamically reorganizes vendors' web sites according to what is most relevant to each person searching the web. With each search, Google sorts the vendors and puts the most relevant vendors in the best possible location, saving you the trouble of looking around, and an "I'm feeling lucky" search saves you the trouble of scrolling through the search results.

Algorithms use inputs, including your keywords, to generate outputs—specifically the search results. As you use Google, your search and browsing history are further inputs, not only to the algorithms behind Google search results, but also to the algorithms that determine which advertisements and vendors you see in the online market. You may think of yourself as using a free service offered by Google, but actually you have traded valuable information about your online behavior and purchases for access to Google's search engine. Your information and attention are sold to the advertisers who are Google's paid customers.

As explained in Chap. 4, Google uses two types of rankings. Firstly, Google page ranking algorithms respond to the number of links that a web site received from other web sites (called organic search results). Secondly,

Google-sponsored search ranking algorithms respond to the highest bid level of the vendor's keyword bids (called sponsored search results).

One major way for Google to provide a competitive advantage to flower retailers, flower wholesalers, or flower growers in floriculture, and thereby to differentiate their service from that of other platforms competing for the attention of individuals, is to increase ad relevance through *personalization*. Search advertisement personalization, based on sponsored search results, refers to showing advertisements that are most relevant for an individual with the aim of increasing sales (called "conversion"). Imagine searching for a "bouquet with a combination of orange tulips and red, white, and blue chrysanthemums" and suddenly an ad pops up with exactly that type of flower bouquet offered by a specific flower retailer. The probability that this ad will lead to a sale is larger compared to a generic flower bouquet ad, because it fits the specified search criteria.

There are five ways to achieve personalization of ads: analysis of browsing behavior and actual transactions, social network analysis, explicit targeting, cross-device effects, and the quality of impressions.[6] Each of these five ways of personalization will be explored.

The first way to personalize ads is to look at *actual transactions and browsing behavior* of the individual. Actual behavior is stored in the historic transactions and browsing database of the search engine, the social media platform, and the retailer or wholesaler firm and/or is stored—as cookies—in the browser history on the individual's computer.[7] Based on previous transactions one can predict an individual's potential personal demand. In the past two months, if an individual had ordered orange tulips every Friday, next Friday this order might be expected again. Or one can analyze the individual's actual browsing behavior in real time to predict that the individual would like to purchase a specific product that might fulfill a specific need.

The second way is to look at the behavior of the social network (digital friends or family) of the individual also called *social advertising*. For example, Facebook can determine each individual's social network and their interests. Facebook can sell these social network preferences to retailers or wholesalers. It could be that specific flower preferences of the members of the social network will be the predictor of the flower preference of the individual. Indeed, research has shown that the behavior and preferences of individuals can be predicted based on the behavior and preferences of their social network. If your social network members like orange tulips, there is a higher probability that you like orange tulips. However, the impact of social endorsement differs between product-specific ads and category-specific ads. A large study conducted in Europe found that product-specific ads generally outperform category ads for both clicks and conversion probability. However, the study found that "ads that are more specific and therefore perceived as more unique are harmed more by the inclusion of social endorsements in the ad."

The third is the focus on *explicit targeting*, which makes the advertising personalization explicit to individuals by stating it clearly. A study investigated two types of ad message framing for a product: one based on the utilitarian perspective, representing the functional benefits of the product, and the other based on the hedonistic perspective, representing the affective and experiential benefits of the product. The product was a mobile application that stores consumers' loyalty cards and the study looked at advertising clicking behavior and actual purchase decisions (app installations). The results indicated that the individual's privacy concerns outweighed potential gains in advertising relevance.[8] While utilitarian ad messages reinforced the negative effect of explicit targeting, the use of hedonic ad messages alleviated the negative effect.

Increasing *cross-device effects* is another form of personalization. Individuals are increasingly using mobile phones to inform their purchasing decision, with more than half of their search queries beginning on mobile devices. However, the majority of individuals use multiple devices such as mobile, tablet, or desktop. A study of cross-device effects assessed the impact of an increase in an online electronics retailer's mobile ad bid on observed ad impressions, clicks, and conversions across mobile, tablet, and desktop, compared with periods in which mobile search ad spend was not increased. The findings suggest that "increasing mobile search ad spend has an effect that spills over to tablets and desktops."

The fifth form of personalization looks at *quality of impressions* and the underlying information asymmetries and dynamics of the digital advertising markets. Advertisers and publishers transact impressions via reservation contracts (RCs) or via real-time bidding auctions (RTBs) or a mixture of the two. RCs are bilateral agreements between advertisers and publishers regarding the volume of advertising to serve on the publisher's outlet at a given price. The RTBs match the demand and supply of advertising impressions by first or second price sealed-bid auctions in real time. Initially, all negotiations between advertisers and publishers used RC, but nowadays publishers can opt to diversify and use both transaction methods (RCs and RTBs). Publishers hold private information about the quality of the impressions, i.e., how many customers in the target group actually see the ad, and because there is an information asymmetry between the publisher and the advertiser, there is a risk that publishers will use their information advantage and expose advertisers to potential losses. Research investigated the quality of impressions offered by publishers that used both RCs and RTBs and found that publishers may leverage private information to offer better quality of impressions through RCs, thus altering the average quality of impressions offered in RTBs. By exploiting information asymmetry and strategically allocating impressions across transaction methods, publishers can inflate their profits from the RTB markets. Advertisers as buyers of impressions at the RTB markets get fewer "real" impressions than they pay for. The phenomenon is called the "market for lemons," and it was discovered by George Akerlof in 1970, decades before online ad markets developed.[9]

All five ways to achieve personalization have specific opportunities and risks. Digital advertising markets are complex and flower retailers, wholesalers, and growers have to understand the details of these markets, as do all other industries, such as the perfume, fashion, or consumer electronics industries. Individuals can opt for other products instead of flowers, so it is important to create smart linkages between flower markets and digital advertising markets. New players will introduce new information asymmetries and will create competitive advantages. Online vendors need the best digital "location, location, location" to make sales, like their counterparts in traditional street markets.

6.3   Deep Learning

Nowadays, deep learning is everywhere. Deep learning is used in the automatic translation of text. Shazam, a service that recognizes songs in a couple of seconds, uses deep learning to do it. Deep learning is used to scan the streets to identify crossing bikers, traffic lights, and traffic signs, among other things, for self-driving cars or for video surveillance. Deep learning is used to detect fungal diseases in flowers. Robots will use deep learning to pick fresh fruits and vegetables. Deep learning is used to detect the brightest and most colorful individual flower, both its genotype and its phenotype, out of thousands of seedlings. And deep learning is used to fly drones when they catch moths in glasshouses.

To explore how *deep learning algorithms* work and the role of *pattern recognition*, let us consider the example of Instagram, a photo and video-sharing social network and one of the most used mobile apps.[10] Anyone using the app can upload photos or short videos to share publicly or only with a selected audience. Instagram includes filters and tools for photo editing. Tags and location information can be added, and users can browse public content by tags or locations, and view trending content. As of May 2020, the most followed woman is singer Ariana Grande with over 187 million followers and the most followed man is footballer Christiano Ronaldo with over 220 million followers. Users can create or follow trends via hashtags like #SelfieSunday, with 10 million posts, or #Flowers with 183 million posts. In 2020, over 50 billion photos were uploaded to Instagram.

When you post a picture of tulips on Instagram, you can use the tag "#tulip," but even if you do not, sophisticated algorithms can still identify it as a tulip picture. How does it know that the picture represents "tulips"? The answer has to do with pattern recognition and deep learning algorithms. Deep learning uses big data and massive computer power. Computer power and digital storage capacity have developed exponentially. For example, the computer that was on board Apollo 11 on its voyage to the moon, the Apollo Guidance Computer, had 32,768 bits of random access memory (RAM) and 589,824 bits of read only memory (ROM). In 1969, this computer landed Neil Armstrong and Edwin "Buzz" Aldrin on the moon. Nowadays, smart phones have over *100,000 times* as much processing power.[11]

The first spectacular results based on the increase of processing power were established in the 2010s. For example, in 2012 Google identified cats in pictures with 20,000 distinct items. These were identified by using 16,000 computer processors and 10 million digital images found in YouTube videos.[12]

Deep learning builds on the concept of a neural network, which was developed in the 1980s to cluster and label data.[13] A neural network is derived from the way neurons work together in your brain. Figure 6.1 illustrates a neural network, consisting of the input layer, hidden layers, and the output layer with via artificial neurons (the dots of the layers) and weighted inputs and outputs (the lines between the layers).[14]

The illustration shows the deep learning neural network for a 12-megapixel photo of a tulip. Each of the 12 million pixels is identified as black or white (or as red, green, or blue in case of a color picture) in the input layer.[15] Next, three hidden layers are identified. These layers are called "hidden" because they are not directly observable from the networks input and output. A cluster of pixels—the edges of the flower—is labeled and identified in the first hidden layer. The second hidden layer will cluster and identify combinations of edges and the third layer will cluster and identify features. Examples of features of flowers are the petal of the flower, the pistil (female) or stamen (male), the style, or the stigma, among others. The output layer is where the algorithm will decide, based on the identified combination of features, what is in the picture. In the tulip example, the algorithm has two options: "yes, there is a tulip in the picture" or "no, there is no tulip in the picture."

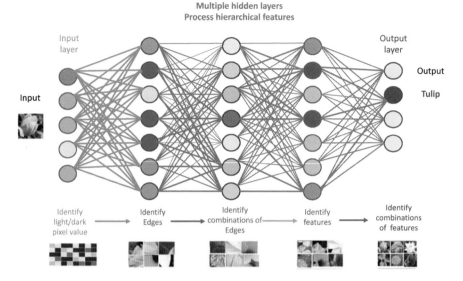

Fig. 6.1 A deep learning neural network to detect tulips in digital pictures. https://www.pnas.org/content/116/4/1074. Adapted from Mitchell Waldrop, "News Feature: What Are the Limits of Deep Learning?", *PNAS*, January 22, 2019, 116 (4), Figure, page 1075

Based on the third layer analysis, the algorithm will detect a combination of three essential features: chalice-shaped petals (yes or no), symmetrical shaped petals (yes or no), and more than two petals (yes or no). Each of these three essential features will be weighted, such as 6 for chalice-shaped petals, 2 for symmetrical shaped petals, and 3 for more than two petals.

Suppose that one picture scores 0 (no) for chalice-shaped petals (0*6), 1 (yes) for symmetrical shaped petals (1*2), and 0 (no) for more than two petals (0*3). The overall weighted value is 0*6 + 1*2 + 0*3 = 2. Suppose we chose 4 as threshold value, and then the prediction, based on (2 < 4), would be "no, there is no tulip in the picture." Suppose that another picture scores 1 (yes) for chalice-shaped petals (1*6), 0 (no) for symmetrical shaped petals (0*2), and 0 (no) for more than two petals (0*3). The overall weighted value is 1*6 + 0*2 + 0*3 = 6. With a threshold value of 4, the prediction, based on (6 > 4), would be "yes, there is a tulip in the picture."

After the algorithm provides an output (either yes or no), the predicted "tulip" value of the algorithm can be compared with the actual "tulip" value of the picture. There are four options.[16] The first option is that the algorithm predicts there is a tulip in the picture and indeed there is. This option is called a true positive (TP). The second option is that the algorithm predicts there is a tulip in the picture, but actually there is not. This second option is called a false positive (FP). The third option is that the algorithm predicts there is no tulip in the picture and indeed there is not. This option is called a true negative (TN). And the fourth option is that the algorithm predicts there is no tulip in the picture, but actually there is. This fourth option is called a false negative (FN). The predictive performance of an algorithm can be measured by analyzing the results in all four categories. More of the true (TP and TN) results indicate a better predictive performance, while more false (FP and FN) results indicate a worse predictive performance.

In the example the algorithm and Fig. 6.1 are reviewed from the input to the output. In deep learning this way of working is called *forward propagation*. An input provides the initiation information that propagates to the artificial neurons of the hidden layers and finally produces the output. The algorithm can also work backward—from the output to the input—which is called *backward propagation*.[17] It starts with the output, propagating and calculating the errors and the updated weights of the different neurons in the hidden layers leading to the input. By doing both forward and backward propagation, the algorithm can be fine-tuned, and the predictive power of the algorithm will increase.

Well reader, now you have a basic understanding of deep learning, the most sophisticated algorithm in the world. However, deep learning is only very strong in pattern recognition based on a large volume of existing pictures. When a new type of flower is discovered, the flower algorithm will not be able to identify the new flower type until there are enough pictures of it to enable deep learning.

6.4 Algorithms for Distribution

Google search, Instagram likes, or influencer recommendations are the new initiators of flower orders from the end consumer to the retailer and the wholesaler, and finally to the growers (the direct flow). The physical flower products move in the opposite direction: from the growers to the wholesaler and retailer to the end consumer (the logistical flow). Flower transport over road, rail, or air is complex and time sensitive. There are many stakeholders involved that take care to bring the flower products, as fast as possible and under the right temperature conditions, to the end consumer with the lowest transportation costs and the lowest carbon dioxide output. Algorithms are able to support or take over decision-making by humans in the field of logistics and distribution. Let us explore three fascinating examples on "last-mile" logistics, anticipatory shipping, and electric vehicles as virtual power plants.

Millions of packages are delivered every day around the world, including flower bouquets or packaged plants, as discussed in Chap. 5. It is a challenge to distribute these packages over the "last mile" to the individual homes of the customers.[18] In many cities and suburbs, small trucks deliver packages from logistics providers or retailers.[19]

One crucial decision for retailers is to schedule time slots in each zip code to fulfill delivery requirement and minimize delivery costs.[20] The following variables play a role:

- Number and location of zip codes
- Number and length of time slots
- Number of vehicles
- Expected demand for each zip code for each time slot
- Vehicle capacity (in terms of the number of orders that can be accommodated)
- Vehicle fixed costs
- Costs per mile for vehicle and driver usage when driving within a zip code and within a time slot
- Cost per mile for vehicle and driver usage when driving between zip codes and consecutive time slots
- Cost per mile for vehicle and driver usage when driving to or from the depot
- Distance between centers of zip codes and dwell time per order

An advanced optimization algorithm was developed for the delivery service of the Dutch supermarket chain, Albert Heijn. The approach provided the best allocation of two-hour timeslots, such as 16:00–18:00, for the expected delivery of the customer's order. It enabled online orders to be assigned a specific delivery time slot using the spare capacity of a truck that was already assigned to deliver to the same zip code. This approach provides better service to customers, makes better use of delivery trucks (resulting in lower carbon emissions), and reduces transportation costs for the retailer.

The next time that you order "Bromelias" online, your order might have been anticipated days earlier, and it may already be on its way to you. *Anticipatory shipping*, as introduced in Chap. 5 with the iFlow research by Quoc Viet Nguyen, Behzad Behdani, and Jacqueline Bloemhof at Wageningen University & Research, means sending flowers *before* they are ordered, because the order is already anticipated. A detailed case study of a large-sized ornamental potted plant company located in Aalsmeer explored the potential value of anticipatory shipping.[21]

Based on historical orders and customer data, future orders and product shipments are predicted before customers place actual orders. Customer-order decoupling points are located closer to the customer, in this case at the cross-docking station.

Two decisions are important. The first is to decide which products and volumes are suitable for anticipatory shipping and to which cross-dockings these products should be sent.

An association rule mining algorithm, i.e., a market basket analysis, is used to determine the products that are purchased with the same frequency and order time. With these mining rules, the size of the order sets and daily volumes for an examined period can be defined at the product level to rule out products that are not frequently ordered and select products with sufficient daily aggregate volume to benefit from anticipatory shipping. Second is the decision on how to redesign production and transportation processes for effective anticipatory shipping. There are two options. The first is the one-time anticipatory shipping (OAS) option, i.e., either at the beginning of the working day, *before* anticipated orders are received, or at the end of working day, *after* all anticipated orders are processed. The second is the distributed anticipatory shipping (DAS) option, where the supplier integrated anticipated orders into the processing of actual orders. For example, anticipated orders can be transported in the same truck, because trucks are not fully loaded.

Both OAS and DAS were explored with a multi-agent simulation for a Dutch supplier. The simulation model included a worker agent responsible for receiving orders, scheduling and executing the production process, and planning the transportation process, and a number of truck agents that execute the transportation. Out of 194 products, 15 were selected for anticipatory shipping, with the aggregate volume of approx. 45% of the total supply. The simulation output showed a trade-off between the delivery service level and operational costs such as driving time, holding costs, and obsolete volumes. The OAS option outperformed the DAS option and provided both an increase of the delivery service level, i.e., the percentage of the total on-time delivery volume among the total delivered volume, by 27.6 % and up to 35.3% and a reduction of the associated costs, i.e., production and transportation costs, from around 3.4% and up to 9.3%.

Algorithms can aid in the transition from vehicles with combustion engines to electric batteries fed by renewable energy sources such as solar panels or wind turbines. Most electric vehicles nowadays are still powered by the traditional and centralized power plants that run on coal, gas, or nuclear energy, but their batteries could be charged by decentralized renewable energy. As the number of electric trucks increases, new challenges will emerge for planning transportation, including the charging frequency and timing, and for grid operators aiming to balance supply and demand for the grid. Algorithms can be created to manage and optimize use of the grid for electric vehicle battery recharging.

Let us consider the following two innovation projects.[22] The first project deals with the optimal allocation algorithm of available charging slots to battery-powered electric buses, by RET as the main public transport operator in Rotterdam. The aim is to minimize the impact on the electricity grid while ensuring continued operation of a predetermined trip schedule and bus network structure. Charging more during off-peak periods would minimize the impact on the grid, and therefore, the dynamic wholesale electricity prices are taken as a proxy for the demand–supply balance of the power grid at each hour during the day. Two optimization algorithms are developed to simulate possible solutions. The first is a discrete time optimization (DTO) solution that will resemble a time-expanded network with one-minute time slots with arrival and departure times communicated via digital displays in minutes. In this case the proposed solution could decide for every minute which bus should use which charger. The second is a discrete event optimization (DEO) solution that will resemble an event-expanded network with time slots based on the arrival and departure events (rather than minutes) in the network. It ensures that there is a driver to plug or unplug the bus from the charger and decide which bus at arrival or departure needs to be charged. The computation showed that DEO had an advantage both in practicality and computation performance. The DTO resulted in lower charging costs and impact on the grid. RET will implement the solution to charges busses at the beginning and end of a bus route during the day and at the garage during the night.

The other innovation project proposed to optimally schedule electric vehicle charging in the Netherlands so that the electricity grid is not overloaded. As the number of electric vehicle users increases, it becomes more urgent that their electrical usage is properly scheduled and managed. The overall goal is to reduce demand during peak periods by allocating the diver's request for charging to different charging speeds to either reduce the cost of charging delays or improve grid revenue. Connecting an electric vehicle to the grid triggers a review of the requested charging availability and speed, and a Multiple Vickrey auction (MVA) mechanism was created to schedule electric vehicle charging, both in terms of prices and capacity, to individual electric vehicle drivers. The Vickrey auction was discussed in Chap. 4. The algorithm used real-world data from the Netherlands, including a year of observations from charging poles, drivers of electric vehicles, and transactions with the grid operator. Using the MVA mechanism leads to reduced demand for electricity during peak periods and provides optimized charging speed.

6.5   Flower Auctioneers

Auctioneers at RFH are early risers.[23] Usually, the first auctions will start at 6 AM; however, there is much to be done even before the auctions begin. In Aalsmeer products are sold via ten flower auction clocks and four plant auction clocks that run simultaneously. This morning, auction clock 1 will begin with roses, and Erik Wassenaar, the auctioneer, arrives around 5 AM to make sure everything is in order. As a representative of the growers, his aim is to sell all of the flowers for the highest price he can get, and he will consider several factors as he prepares for the day.

Firstly, Wassenaar checks on the products that will be auctioned. The evening before, suppliers submitted their lots to RFH to be auctioned, and the price will be determined by supply and demand forces in the market. Prices can be driven down by a high supply in the same product group, a lower product quality, and a relatively poorer reputation of the supplier. The price will be lower today if a high volume of the product was sold the previous day. Conversely, prices will rise if there is a lower supply in the same product group, a lower supply of alternative products, a higher quality, and better reputation of the supplier, and the price will rise if a lower volume of the product was sold on the previous day.

Secondly, the auctioneer checks up on excess supply. It might be that one supplier—or several suppliers—will try to sell a large quantity of similar products. These offered lots are indicated by the suppliers in the supply information system (in Dutch: *Aanbod Informatie Systeem* (AIS)). If there is excess supply, the auctioneer can discuss different options with the supplier and may decide to delay auctioning some of the products. The auctioneer can also talk with auctioneers at other auction sites handling the same products, to discuss how to handle the day's excess supply. Royal FloraHolland has 35 auction clocks in four locations: Aalsmeer, Naaldwijk, Rijnsburg, and Eelde. The auction sequence of products is coordinated so that the same type of product is auctioned at almost the same time at the four different locations.

Thirdly, the auctioneer checks the quality of some of the lots. Quality control managers will have evaluated all of the lots, but some atypical or extreme outcomes need to be verified by the auctioneer.

Fourthly, the auctioneer will check for special events, including specific popular days to buy flowers, such as Valentine Day or Mother's Day and the day of the week (prices are usually higher on Mondays and Fridays). Greater demand for flowers leading up to Mother's Day will result in higher prices, but warm weather usually will have a negative impact on flower demand, and prices will drop.

It is 6 AM and Wassenaar rings the morning bell to signal to all buyers, onsite and online, that the auction has started; see Fig. 6.2. "Ladies and gentleman, good morning. We start today with red Naomi Roses produced by producer Kees van Os. Starting price is 70." To get the highest prices possible in each round of the auction, the auctioneer can adjust several parameters. He monitors how many bidders are connected and how many bidders actually bid within each lot. As you might remember, the first bidder is the winner in a Dutch auction. The bidders that tried to buy, but lost, are not registered. However, this information is very useful for the auctioneer, because it indicates the "willingness to buy" among bidders. The auctioneer can keep that information in mind to adjust the auction parameters to achieve a more profitable balance of supply and demand. Meanwhile, bidders also take into account all types of information, both from the supply side and the demand side, as they decide how much to bid and how many lots to buy.

What auction parameters can the auctioneer control to secure a better sale price for growers?

A very important parameter is the minimum transaction size. In Chap. 4, we saw that auction lots are sold in sub-lots. For example, an auction lot or batch may have two trolleys, each with 27 containers for a total of 54 containers, and within each container are 80 pieces (in this case, flower stems). So, the total number in the auction lot is 54 * 80 = 4320 flower stems. Each time a bidder wins the auction, he or she will choose how many containers to purchase at that price. The auctioneer sets the minimum number of containers that the winning bidder must buy from each auction sub-lot. In this case, the

Fig. 6.2 The auctioneer and onsite buyers in the auction hall at Naaldwijk. https://www.royalfloraholland.com/en/about-floraholland/media-centre/actual-photos. With permission by Royal FloraHolland

minimum transaction size is 1 container. If the winning bidder buys 1 container the auctioneer will reset the auction clock and the 53 containers that remain will be auctioned again in the next round. The auctioneer will adjust the auction clock based on bidder activity in the first round, including information about the willingness to buy of other bidders. More information will be gathered in each subsequent round, and for every sub-lot, the price might change and the minimum transaction size.

Usually, the auctioneer starts with a minimum transaction size of 1 container, and both smaller and larger buyers are able to bid. More potential bidders will lead to higher prices. However, it is more expensive to distribute many small transactions to a large number of buyers, so the auctioneer will gradually increase the minimum purchase quantity based on his or her own reasoning and knowledge of the auction market. Auctioneers are experts, yet the world of big data and algorithms can help them recognize the optimal time to increase the minimum transaction amount and get the highest sale price for the growers. Let me show you how it works.

6.6   Algorithms for Auctioneers

In the Dutch auction market there are hundreds of bidders. By reviewing the auction outcomes, one is able to identify how much each bidder was willing to pay for a type of flower. One can get even more understanding by taking into account two characteristics of the bidding process: bidders have multiple purchase opportunities for the same product, and winning bidders in each round can acquire multiple units of the same product. Using this data, it is possible to identify patterns and forecast the impact of changes to the market parameters.

In 2014, Yixin Lu, nowadays at George Washington University, with Alok Gupta, University of Minnesota, and Wolf Ketter and myself at Erasmus University Rotterdam, created an excellent algorithm, based on real auction and bidding data from the Dutch auction market (Fig. 6.3).[24] Her algorithm predicted bids, both in terms of price and the number of units, that would be made if the auctioneer varied the minimum purchase quantity. The simulated situation could be compared with data from real auctions. Consider the estimated winning bids compared with the observed winning bids on September 1; as an example, see Fig. 6.3. The horizontal axis shows the cumulative bid price of the Red Naomi rose, and the vertical axis shows the likelihood of the cumulative bids. The chart shows the likelihood increased slowly with the price, so slowly it seems constant. Then it started to change faster, then very

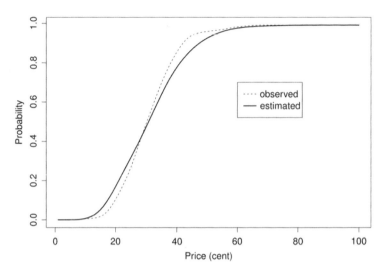

Fig. 6.3 Comparison of cumulative distributions of the estimated and observed winning bids on September 1 https://doi.org/10.1287/mnsc.2018.3118. Reproduced from Lu Y, Gupta A, Ketter W, Van Heck E (2019) Dynamic Decision Making in Sequential Business-to-Business Auctions: A Structural Econometric Approach. Management Science 65(8): Figure 8, page 3867. With permission by Informs

fast, then slower and slower until it becomes almost constant. This curve, which looks like an elongated S, is known as the logistic, sigmoid, or S curve. Pedro Domingos calls it "the Most Important Curve in the World."

Next, she created simulations of five alternative auction designs with different minimum purchase quantities ranging from one lot to nine lots. For each of the alternative designs, the bidders' private valuations were simulated and then their optimal bids were calculated. The minimum purchase quantity was manipulated in each round. Two performance criteria were chosen: revenue (in euros) and turnaround (measured by the total of rounds taken to finish the auctions). The results in Table 6.1 below indicate the performance evaluation of the observed design and the five alternatives.

The first column indicates the total revenue (in Euros) and the second column the total of number of rounds. More rounds mean that the auction process will take more time. Have a look at Table 6.1 and ask yourself which alternative design you would like to implement.

The results indicate that the lowest minimum purchase quantity is expected to yield the highest revenue. Compared with the observed design, the revenue of alternative design 1 is expected to increase by approximately 14.5%. However, such an increase entails many more rounds, as the total number of transactions increased by 38.7%. Given that a tight auction schedule is critical for highly perishable goods, this alternative design would not be suitable.

Table 6.1 Performance evaluation of different auction designs

	Total revenue (in euros)	Number of rounds
Observed design	920,116	5,536
Alternative design 1 (minimum purchase quantity = 1)	1,053,874 (10,518)	7,682 (33)
Alternative design 2 (minimum purchase quantity = 3)	1,004,604 (9,526)	6,296 (34)
Alternative design 3 (minimum purchase quantity = 5)	945,941 (8,925)	5,362 (25)
Alternative design 4 (minimum purchase quantity = 7)	886,203 (11,057)	4,667 (16)
Alternative design 5 (minimum purchase quantity = 9)	820,157 (11,759)	4,158 (16)

Note: The numbers displayed in the parentheses from row 2 to row 6 (Alternative design 1–5) are standard errors of the estimates https://doi.org/10.1287/mnsc.2018.3118. Reproduced from Yixin Lu, Alok Gupta, Wolfgang Ketter, Eric van Heck, "Dynamic Decision Making in Sequential Business-to-Business Auctions: A Structural Econometric Approach," *Management Science*, Vol. 65, No. 8, August 2019, Table 8, p. 3868. With permission by Informs

Similarly, alternative design 2 is undesirable. Alternative design 3, however, seems to be a great option: it generates 3% higher revenue while maintaining a high turnaround rate. Finally, alternative designs 4 and 5 show a drop in the revenue compared with the observed design.

As with the minimum purchase quantity, simulations of other key auction parameters, such as starting price and reserve price, can help predict changes in the bidding dynamics as well as the outcome of auctions. Without the assistance of a simulated model, the auctioneer cannot fully optimize these parameters because it is not possible for the auctioneer to adequately process all the market information while under extreme time pressure. Auctioneers rely on their intuition and experience to set key auction parameters, but simulations like the ones Yixin Lu created can augment the auctioneer's capabilities with high-performance decision support systems. To be useful, these systems must be able to (i) make successful predictions of future states (e.g., the number of bidders, the winning prices, and purchase quantities in the upcoming auctions) and (ii) identify and suggest actions based on the predictions.

6.7   Bidder Behavior

Reader, you have survived a preview into the complexity of algorithms and their importance not only for the flower business but also for other businesses and society at large. Nowadays, algorithms are everywhere including in the floriculture industry. They help transporters predict the fastest route in a distribution network, and they inform retailers about the flower preferences of individual customers. They can predict the growth rate of flowers in greenhouses, they help growers to decide the best time to sell their flower products, and they assist the auctioneers to determine the most profitable minimum purchase quantities. Algorithms can do those things and much more.

The most challenging part of the *Technology Meets Flowers* book is reached. A closer look is taken at the data science of algorithms. Beyond optimizing the parameters of the auction, algorithms can be used to analyze the bidding strategies of buyers in an auction. You might guess that bidding strategies would converge as bidders gain more experience, but you could know for sure if you analyze the data on bidders' behavior. Auctioneers are very interested in the strategies of bidders, because the auctioneer's main objective is to achieve high revenues and a quick turnaround for buyers, since flowers are perishable goods and bidding time is costly. By controlling key auction parameters such as starting prices, minimum purchase quantities, and reserve prices, auctioneers can influence the dynamics of the auctions and increase profits for growers and improve the throughput time for buyers. The answers are in the data, and the answers can be discovered through *unsupervised learning* algorithms and *supervised learning* algorithms.[25] Supervised learning algorithms have a target variable, i.e., the proposed outcome that one would like to explain or predict, such as sales prices. Unsupervised learning algorithms do not have a target variable. Both supervised and unsupervised learning algorithms can be used to explain or to predict. Explanatory algorithms explain business events. The examples of clustering and causal modeling in the Dutch flower auction markets are explanatory algorithms. Prediction algorithms are forward looking and predict what is likely to happen in the future. The example of anticipatory shipping is based on prediction algorithms. In general, prediction models are successful at prediction, but they are not as good at explaining. The reverse is also true: explanatory models are successful at explaining, but not as good at predicting.[26]

Let us look at clustering as an example of unsupervised learning algorithms as an entry point.[27] To analyze bidders' behavior in Dutch flower auctions, one needs to start with an appropriate dataset. A dataset was gathered on auction transactions for the Avalanche Rose because its total transaction amount was the largest among the entire assortment, and it was sold steadily throughout the analyzed auction days. Our dataset included auction transactions in which no actual flowers were shown in the auction hall; instead, the bidders observed a picture of the rose flower from the current lot, together with product information such as product category, characteristics (e.g., stem length), and quality, as well as supplier information.

To analyze the bidder behavior, four variables were created: the time of entry in an auction, the time of entry on a day, the time of exit on a day, and the frequency of bidding on a day. The *time of entry in an auction* records the ranking of the sub-auction where the bidder wins. For instance, if a bidder wins in the second round and the entire auction took ten rounds to finish, the bidder's time of entry is 2/10 (0.2). Bidders often participate in many auctions on a given day. There are multiple auctions for the same product on any given day and the auction schedule is publicly announced, so some bidders may observe the first few auctions to learn about the market conditions, while others bid actively from the beginning of the day. To capture such behavioral differences, the *time of entry on a day* was introduced, which is the ranking of the auction where a bidder has his or her first win of the day. If there were six auctions for the Avalanche Rose on a given day, and a bidder's first winning bid was in the third auction, the time of entry on a day is 3/6 (0.5). The timing is considered when bidders drop out of the competition. Given that most bidders are buying on order, their daily exit timings can reflect as many useful insights about their bidding strategies as their daily entry timings. The *time of exit on a day* is defined as the ranking of the auction where a bidder places his or her last winning bid. The *frequency of bidding on a day* is considered, which is a bidder's total number of winning bids per day. In a Dutch auction, the frequency is closely related to the bidders' potential hedging behavior, that is, some bidders prefer to purchase across multiple auctions, even if they can fulfill their total demand in one auction, and they do this to alleviate the risk of making a single suboptimal bidding decision.

Using these four variables, the clustering algorithm identifies five strategic bidding patterns in the dataset. Based on the bidder's time of entry in an auction, we have *early bidders* who bid early in an auction, *opportunists* who bid late and tend to look for bargains in an auction, and *analyzers* who bid in between the former two scenarios. The bidder's time of entry on a day is also informative. Early entry suggests a high urgency of purchase, whereas later entry indicates a strategic consideration of upcoming auctions. With this in mind, early entries were labeled as *conservatives* and later entries as *forward-looking*. With the exception of the analyzers, conservative bidders all exit the auctions early in the day. Finally, on average, the analyzers had more than twice the number of winning bids per day as others. Given that all bidders in the Dutch flower auctions are professional and have more than sufficient bidding experience, the existence of these distinctive bidding strategies challenges the popular view that bidders' strategies tend to converge as they gain experience. They do not converge, prompting the question of why there are distinctive bidding strategies.

To answer this question, the help of supervised learning algorithms that have a target variable is needed, i.e., the proposed outcome that one would like to predict or improve, such as sales or revenue. Let us look at causal modeling as an example of supervised learning algorithms as an entry point. *Causal modeling* investigates the causal relationship between events or actions. For prediction, correlation is often sufficient, but for interventions/actions, causation is needed.

Three economic factors impacting bidders in Dutch flower auctions are considered: *budget constraint, demand,* and *online channel adoption.* Small family-run florists would bid in later auctions on a day, in the hope that those who already fulfilled their demand or consumed their budget in earlier auctions would have dropped out from the market. The purchase quantity in each round of the Dutch flower auctions has to meet a predetermined minimum amount. Bidders were accustomed to auctioneers setting a low minimum purchase amount at the beginning and gradually increase it as the auction proceeded. As a result, if a bidder with a high budget constraint missed the first few rounds of an auction, the bidder would not be able to afford purchasing that auction any more. Bidders have, in general, a multiunit demand for any given type of flower. Such demand could be order-driven or speculation-based, that is, some bidders are exclusively purchasing on order while others purchase a greater quantity of a certain flower when they foresee a "hot" market for it. When bidders are buying on order, they typically receive a commission of 10–15% of the purchase price. These bidders do not shade their bids or reduce the demand. Actually, they would bid aggressively to make sure they can fulfill the order for their customers. However, when bidders have a large speculation-based demand they are more likely to postpone their bidding in the first few rounds and wait for a bargain. Further, given that there are often multiple auctions with closely substitutable products, they may spread the demand over several auctions to maximize their expected payoff.

Bidders' transaction cost refers to the time and effort invested in gathering information, preparing bids, and participating in an auction. Bidders incur incremental transaction costs if they have to wait in slow Dutch auctions. Given the high complexity and extreme time pressure of Dutch flower auctions, monitoring market dynamics and learning market trends are time-consuming and cognitively challenging. The adoption of the online bidding channel (i.e., KOA—from the Dutch: *Kopen Op Afstand,* buying at a distance) can all but eliminate the opportunity cost of time and transportation associated with physical attendance at the auctions. Further, it allows bidders to easily switch from one auction to another and thereby enhance their ability to monitor the auctions and reduce their search costs.

A causal modeling algorithm was developed as a linear combination of the three economic factors (budget constraint, demand, and channel adoption). Overall, bidders with high budget constraints are more likely to choose an *early bidding* strategy, bidders with large demands have the tendency to choose an *analytical* or *opportunistic* strategy, and the bidders using the online bidding channel are more likely to choose an *opportunistic* strategy.

The impact of bidding strategies on the amount of the winning bid relative to other winning bids is analyzed. Bidders' valuations—the specific value associated with a specific product—are unknown, so the range of winning bids is compared. Loss-of-surplus is the difference between a bidder's winning price in an auction and the lowest winning price within the same auction but in another round. A bidder with the lowest loss of surplus is considered to have extracted the highest surplus among all the bidders in the same auction. Note that bidders in sequential auctions can learn the market dynamics and opponents' profiles from previous rounds—the identity of the winning bidder is shown to all bidders—and they can respond to that information by updating their willingness to pay to maximize their payoff.[28] The clustering results suggest that opportunists tend to be more patient and wait longer in an auction than other bidders. Waiting allowed them to acquire an *informational advantage* in the bidding process. Our results suggest that opportunists outperform both analyzers and early bidders in surplus extraction.

Significant effects of auction design parameters are found. In particular, both lot size and minimum purchase quantity have a negative effect on the winning price, and this effect is moderated by bidding strategies. A higher lot size and a higher minimum purchase quantity lead to lower winning prices. It suggests that early bidders are likely to be more risk averse and they prefer to pay a risk premium at the beginning of an auction to ensure fulfillment of orders. On the contrary, the opportunists take bigger risks in order to acquire the products at the best price; they trade the opportunity to purchase in earlier rounds for more information about market conditions and opponent's profiles.

Currently, the lot sizes are determined by the suppliers, but this is not optimal because, compared to the auctioneer, suppliers have little information about the strategic characteristics of the bidders. Given the significant interaction effect between lot size and bidders' strategies, auctioneers could change the lot size in response to the preferences of the bidders. *Early bidders* and *analyzers* are more sensitive than *opportunists* to an increase in the minimum purchase quantity. Therefore, auctioneers could change other market parameters to speed up the market process. In light of *opportunists'* competitive advantage in surplus extraction and their channel usage patterns, auctioneers could also develop effective information revelation policies across different market channels. Finally, the separation of bidders with conservative strategies from those with forward-looking strategies according to their entering time suggests that there is great potential to customize the daily auction schedule and further improve the total revenue.

Causal modeling is very effective and extremely useful for business. Business leaders must make cost/benefit analyses, where the costs of not knowing are weighed against the benefits of knowing (and the investments needed to obtain the data science-based knowledge). A very fine method to analyze costs and benefits is the *expected value framework* by Foster Provost and Tom Fawcett, see Chapter Notes.[29]

6.8   Predictive Flower Power

As you enter the flower auction and distribution complex in Naaldwijk and turn at the roundabout of the Dijkweg, you will see on your left side a range of dock loading stations and offices for the different Royal FloraHolland (RFH) clients. One of the clients is Zentoo, a cooperative of 14 growers that produce high-quality chrysanthemums. Zentoo has a reputation in the market for high quality rather than "lemons." These 14 growers can produce more varieties together than individually.

As International Women's Day (March 8) approaches and flower demand increases, the market becomes hectic. The distribution center is in full swing; orders need to be finished for clients, including international wholesalers and retailers. The 14 Zentoo cooperative growers are each member of RFH, and their membership obliges them to send their products either to the RFH auction clocks or to Zentoo's web shop, for direct sales, where wholesalers and retailers can buy chrysanthemums year round. The web shop manager has a challenging task every day: what price tag should Zentoo products have? If the price level is too high, clients will choose to buy elsewhere. If the price is too low, the web shop loses profits on those sales. The web shop manager has to choose between Scylla and Charybdis, and it is difficult to know which one is the lesser of the two evils. The question is: could the web shop manager use sophisticated algorithms to make better decisions?

A recent study investigated the web shop manager's prediction of the next day's average auction price and compared it to the prediction made by a predictive algorithm model: human learning versus machine learning.[30] Historical web shop prices were used to create the predictive human model (PHM) to represent the web shop manager's predictions. Historical data were also used to build the predictive algorithm model (PAM). Similar to the human model, PAM predicts the next day's average auction prices. The results indicate that the PAM produced more accurate predictions than the PHMs, with a 2–3% increase in prediction accuracy. Next, the study compared the models on web shop performance, measured in average revenue per product. The PAM was applied as input for the historical web shop prices and the sales outcomes were calculated accordingly. The results show that the web shop performance increased for both products by approximately 2%. One of the main reasons for this improvement is that the PAM underprices (i.e., underpredicts) to a lesser extent. Secondly, in situations of underpricing, it is shown that the PAM performs better on crucial days where web shop sales are highest. The study showed a higher performance increase for products offered by only one supplier (monopolistic competition). Moreover, it showed that different variables had predictive power across different products. The differences in variables confirmed that the suppliers that have a monopoly hold a certain leverage to influence auction prices, whereas suppliers in a condition of perfect competition do not.

6.9   Algorithms for Value

Talking about algorithms is relatively easy, but it is much more difficult to develop algorithms that will create value for customers, companies, and society at large. Many traditional companies, including in floriculture, struggle with these advanced digital technologies. Let me guide you through the steps to create advanced algorithms with business value; see Fig. 6.4.[31]

Fig. 6.4 The development cycle of algorithms to create value for business and society. Author's own figure

Although there is a lot of hype and excitement about algorithms, the question is: will algorithms be able to create business value? Therefore, the first step is to execute a proper business analysis, which will reveal how algorithms can create business value. In essence there are three ways to create business value: to improve business efficiency, to improve business effectivity, and to create new business.

Logically most companies start with the first business goal type, efficiency, learn from it, and move to the second goal type, effectivity. The third type, new business, is the most challenging and most interesting one. Startups are well equipped to invent new business models, but also companies with innovative board members are able to create continuously new business.

Business efficiency has to do with using the least resources (in terms of labor, material, energy, and waste) necessary to achieve the required output of business processes. An example of this is the algorithm for optimal allocation of available charging slots to battery electric buses.

Business effectivity has to do with achieving the intended results. It is usually related to the promised product or service offering to the end customer, in terms of quality, price, and delivery time of the product or service offering. One example is the algorithm that helps to advise the auctioneer to adjust the minimum transaction size during auctioning. As we have seen, the auctioneer has to balance between higher prices (and higher profits) for the grower and faster auctioning (with less time and lower transaction costs) for the buyers. Customized advice for the auctioneer will create a more effective auction process with high prices for the growers and, at the same time, a speedy process for the buyers.

New business is the third and most challenging form. For example, an algorithm was designed to create a new business model for the car sharing company Car2Go. The business model was extended from car rental alone to car rental plus selling to the grid the electricity capacity stored in the batteries of electric cars. The algorithm coordinates and combines a fleet of electric cars as a virtual power plant.

After analyzing the business process and identifying how algorithms can create business value, the second step is to identify digital sensing technologies that will generate the data needed to feed the algorithm. A crucial capability is to have deep knowledge about how sensing technology will create the data and how accurately the data represent the business reality. There are many examples of data sources that feed algorithms, including RFID usage in distribution and logistics, smart meters for energy usage, sensor technologies to measure blood pressure and other health indicators used in mobile health apps, smart temperature meters that help to predict flu and virus waves in communities, new Internet of Things (IoT) technologies that will predict and control flower development, and flower growth in glasshouses or vertical farms. The diverse portfolio of sensing options will increase the volume, variety, velocity, and veracity of used data.

After the digital sensing technologies have been identified, the third step is to properly store data that are characterized by high volume, variety, and velocity. Most companies outsource data storage to specialized cloud service companies such as Amazon Web Services, Google, and Microsoft. If high-speed operations and the fast availability of data are a crucial component of the success or failure of the data-driven business model, the data storage must enable it.

The fourth step is to analyze and understand the advice of the algorithm and respond according to the advice. In this step, responding to the output of the algorithm is a crucial component, i.e., a concrete action to follow up the explanatory or the prediction advice provided by the algorithm. Many algorithms in business practice work, but there is no business response. Warning signals are not taken seriously, and business continues as usual—without responding to the advice.

After responding to the output of the algorithm, the fifth step is learning from the response. If a mobile app connected to sensing technologies that monitor greenhouse conditions signals to the grower that flower growth was too low and the response was to provide more carbon dioxide in the greenhouse, then it is important to ask if that would lead to a faster flower growth. What can be learned about the response and its relation to the desired outcome? Does the algorithm need fine-tuning or are there other factors to adjust? Human learning and machine learning are part of this step. Will the deep learning algorithm learn from its forward and backward propagation steps? And how sure are we humans that learning by the algorithm will take place? We can also consider this the other way around: how sure are algorithms that human learning will take place?

6.10   Challenges

The fast development of algorithms led to a worldwide exploration about their use and potential positive and negative impacts. Actually, companies and industries will face six challenges to create business value with algorithms. The Chapter Notes provide sources for further reading on how companies can deal with these challenges.[32]

The first challenge is that in most companies and industries there is no common digital platform in use. In general, there is a core platform that usually is based on enterprise resource planning (ERP) software. Extensions are made to the digital multi-channels such as mobiles, laptops, desktops, and other devices. Digital platforms—as discussed in Chap. 5—with multiple sides and multiple stakeholders in a networked business setting are rare. However, as will be revealed in Chap. 7, the circular and digital transformation will rapidly reshape companies and industries and create new types of platforms and positions.

The second challenge is that decision rights and governance are a crucial component for digital business success. Digital businesses intertwine business and information technology (IT), but most companies are organized with separate business and IT units, each with their own working culture and preference for their own core competences. It is very challenging to create a collaborative environment where both business and IT people work together at state-of-the-art digital business solutions with advanced algorithms. To overcome this challenge requires a careful design of decision rights to balance autonomy and alignment.

The third challenge for companies is the absorptive capacity of the members of the executive board. Do they understand the newest digital technologies, including topics such as application program interfaces (APIs), deep learning, new digital business models, and their interfaces? Do they discuss these topics during board level meetings, and do they provide a vision about the "what, how, and why" of the digital transformation of their company and industry including the blurring of lines between different industries and the development of new circular business ecosystems.

The fourth challenge is about the ownership of data that feed the algorithms. The world is moving in three directions. The first direction states that data belong to companies. Once you sign a user agreement with Facebook or Google, these companies "own" your data and user data are the central commodity in their business model. The second direction implies that data belong to the government. A detailed analysis of the data of citizens is used for surveillance and control. The third direction favors data ownership by citizens. The European Union and the European Economic Area implemented the General Data Protection Regulation (GDPR) on data protection and privacy, which assert a citizen's data ownership as an essential element of the democratic state. These diverging views will be challenging for multinational companies and industries because they will have to design algorithms that work in different data ownership settings.

The fifth challenge is about who is responsible for the working of algorithms. After a spectacular start and the promise of many positive impacts, it became clear that algorithms could have unintended negative consequences. In terms of pattern recognition algorithms do a pretty good job. However, in other applications some incredible algorithmic failures were reported, such as placing the wrong ad or not placing the right ad, incorrectly labeling someone as a future criminal or labeling someone as not a future criminal, promoting the wrong person or rejecting a good candidate, or categorizing someone as at home when they are not or deciding someone is not at home when they are. The algorithmic failures look stupid to us, and that is because computers see and learn very differently from us. Actually, who is responsible for the potential negative impact of algorithms? Is the designer of the algorithm responsible or the CEO of the company that used the algorithm? Do we need institutes that will evaluate the working of algorithms and provide certificates for proper functioning algorithms—similar to institutes that check the proper working of elevators? New research about algorithm accountability and algorithm fairness will develop rules and approaches and these will be implemented soon.

The sixth challenge is to respond to the potential impact of algorithms on work and jobs. For example, will there be any work and jobs left for taxi drivers when all cars are self-driving? Indeed, more tasks and work will be automated and executed by machines, a development that started in the eighteenth century with the industrial revolution. We can already foresee the need for a continuous redesign of tasks and work, and it will be essential for humans to adapt and move into new and unchartered work territory. The question is about who is in control: the human versus the machine. Will the human have the final say about the predicted output developed by the machine or is it the other way around that the machine has a final say about the predicted output by the human. It is a fascinating discussion that has already taken place in the airline industry. The pilot of a Boeing airplane always has the final say about the instructions suggested by the automatic pilot. In case of an Airbus airplane, it is the automatic pilot that will overrule the human pilot and co-pilot and their instructions. Some but not all humans excel at creating new ideas, designing and implementing new solutions, thinking out of the box, and improvising. These are tasks that most algorithms cannot perform yet.

At the moment most algorithms are "stand-alone" applications. In the flower ecosystem, they focus on a specific task, process, or decision-maker (Table 6.2).[33] However, it is clear that the exponential development of both computer power and big data will continue. Different algorithms will be connected and start to work together as networked algorithms. It could lead, as Pedro Domingos explained, to "the Master Algorithm," the ultimate learning machine that will discover everything, even in floriculture.[34] Indeed, algorithms will bloom.

Table 6.2 Overview of the use of algorithms in the flower chain network

Flower chain network phase	Type of application	Type of algorithm
Flower home delivery	Home delivery	Integer linear programming and multi-agent simulation
Flower advertisement	Ad personalization	Econometrics Difference-in-differences (DiD) Social network analysis
Flower sales	Web shop pricing	Time series forecasting with linear and seasonal autoregressive integrated moving average (SARIMA)
Flower auctioning	Pre-sales channel optimization, Bidder classification, Auctioneer decision support Winner Identification Disclosure	Linear probability models Clustering Causal modeling Multi-nominal logistic regression (MNL) Markov decision process Difference-in-differences (DiD) Social network analysis
Flower distribution	Anticipatory shipping Electric vehicle charging	Multi-agent simulation Multiple Vickrey auctions Mixed integer linear programming (MILP)
Flower processing and packaging	Robotization Automated quality control	Deep learning
Flower producing	Production automation and robotization Use of drones for insect control Vertical farming	Deep learning
Flower breeding	Seed germination and selection automation	Deep learning

Notes

1. The Horn of Plenty, referring to the cornucopia from the ancient Greek mythology, depicts enlarged images of flowers, grapes, fruit, insects, vegetables, sweets, grains, and fish. This colorful masterpiece, created by Iris Roskam and Arno Coenen, was printed on 4500 aluminium plates covering the 11,000 square meter arched interior.

2. Erasmus University Rotterdam is named after Desidirius Erasmus Roterodamus (1466–1536). By the 1530s, the writings of Erasmus accounted for 10–20% of all book sales in Europe.

   One of his best-known works is *Praise of Folly*, a satirical attack on superstitions and other traditions of European society in general and the Western

Church in particular. It was written in 1509 and published in 1511. Revised edition: Erasmus D (1993).

 Erasmus University Rotterdam. https://www.eur.nl/ https://www.erasmus.org/index.cfm?itm_name=500yearspraise-EN. Accessed 8 Sept 2020.

3. Data about the size of the digital advertising markets are in Statista (2020).
4. Thanks to Francesco Balocco for suggesting the location argument and the comparison of street markets and online markets. The discussion of the location details of online advertising markets is in Agarwal A, Hosanagar K, Smith M (2011).
5. Algorithms is in Domingos P (2015).
6. The different personalization strategies are based on several sources: Frick T, Li T (2016). Quote "making the targeting mechanism" (p. 13).

 Tsekouras D, Frick T, Li T (2018).

 Andrews M, Li T, Balocco F (2018). Quote "increasing mobile search" (p. 1).

 Balocco F, Li T (2019). Quote "those impressions sold" (p. 2).

7. The term "cookie" was coined by web-browser programmer Lou Montulli in 1991 and derived from the term "magic cookie," which is a packet of data a program receives and sends back unchanged, used by programmers.
8. On the one hand, consumers are interested in personalization, but on the other hand they desire information privacy. Increased privacy awareness leads to privacy concerns and resistance toward personalized ads. Balancing the benefits of personalization with the consumers' desire for information privacy is called the personalization–privacy paradox.
9. There is the analogy with the flower markets where nowadays growers and buyers can transact via the direct sales channel, with bilateral contracts, and via the Dutch auction market channel with competitive bidding among the buyers. In the flower markets, flowers with lower quality attributes (analogous to "lemons" in used-car markets) might drive out flowers with higher quality attributes. Information asymmetry deals with the study of decision in transactions where one party has more or better information than the other. For example, the grower will have more information about the real quality of the offered flower than the buyer. Adverse selection is the market situation where buyers and sellers have different information, so that a market participant might participate selectively in trades which benefit them the most, at the expense of the other trader: "lemon" flowers can drive out higher quality flowers of the same product group. The "Lemons" principle in markets is in Akerlof GA (1970).
10. After the launch of Instagram in 2010, it gained popularity rapidly, with one million registered users in two months, 10 million in a year, and 1 billion as of May 2019. In April 2012, Facebook acquired Instagram for almost US$1 billion in cash and stock. Instagram introduced image and video ads in 2013 and introduced later "carousel ads," allowing advertisers to display multiple images with options for linking to additional content. In 2016, Instagram

launched Instagram Insights for business accounts. It allowed these business accounts, via the corresponding Facebook page, to view top posts and ad impressions and get demographic data on followers. In November 2018, Instagram enabled business accounts to add product links directing users to a purchase page or to save products to a "shopping list." Instagram added the option to "Checkout on Instagram," so merchants can sell directly through the Instagram app. In 2016, Instagram attracted 200,000 advertisers, and forecasts for 2020 predicted there would be 25 million business profiles, with 2 million monthly advertisers, 500,000 active influencers, and an estimated 75% of US businesses on Instagram. https://www.instagram.com/. Accessed 8 Sept 2020.

11. The comparison of the computer power of a mobile phone with the Apollo 11 computer is in Kendall G (2019, July 2).

12. The use of massive computer power and big data to identify cats by Google is in Markoff J (2012, June 25).

13. The deep learning essentials are inspired by Krohn J (2019) and Krohn J, Beyleveld G, Bassens (2020).

The book provides a great introduction to deep learning including the discovery of how visual information triggered the activation of neurons in the brain of a cat.

In 1959, pioneering research by David Hubel and the Torsten Wiesel at Johns Hopkins University, Baltimore, USA, led to the first insight into how visual information was processed via the primary visual cortex of cats, the first part of the cerebral cortex to receive visual input from the eyes. They showed a cat white or black dots on a screen and measured the activity of individual neurons of the cat. Their discovery was serendipitous, but spectacular. As Hubel and Wiesel explained: "… rather by accident one day we were shining small spots, either white spots or black spots, onto the screen and we found that the black dot seem to be working in a way that first we couldn't understand until we found it was the process of slipping the piece of glass into the projector which swept alike a very faint and precise narrow line across the retina and every time we did that got a response." Quote from the videoclip YouTube (2009, March 29).

Simple neurons in the cat's brain were not activated by the black dot but by the simple, straight edge of the piece of glass. The layered networked structure of the billions of simple and more complex neurons in a cat brain, and later the human brain, was the groundwork for the understanding of the human brain and human intelligence and led to the new field of artificial intelligence, machine learning, and deep learning. Deep learning involves "a network in which artificial neurons— typically thousands, millions, or many more of them—are stacked at least several layers deep. The artificial neurons in the first layer pass information to the second, the second to the third, and so on, until the final layer outputs some values." Quote from the preface of Krohn J, Beyleveld G, Bassens (2020).

14. The tulip deep learning neural network example was inspired by Waldrop M (2019).

15. A pixel—a word invented from "picture element"—is the basic unit of a digital picture. Each pixel consists of 24 bits (3 bytes) for a color image—one byte each for red, green, and blue. The iSight camera in my iPhone 7 is pretty good. It has a six-element lens and a 12-megapixel sensor, meaning each picture will contain 12 million pixels. One digital picture taken with my iPhone camera stores around 2.1 megabytes (equivalent to 2,100,000 bytes) of data.

16. The discussion of the four options of predictive performance is based on the confusion matrix that is presented and discussed in Provost F, Fawcett T (2013).

17. The concepts of forward and backward propagation in deep learning are in Krohn J, Beyleveld G, Bassens A (2020).

18. The total number of trucks on tolled crossings into New York City and within the five boroughs rose about 9.4% in 2018, to an estimated 35.7 million, from 32.6 million in 2013, according to the transit data. From 1990 to 2017, carbon dioxide emissions from automobiles and trucks in the New York City area grew by 27%, making the region the largest contributor of driving-related carbon dioxide emissions in the United States. Data in the footnote about package delivery in New York City is in Haag, M., Hu, W. (2019, October 27).

19. According to the *New York Times*, in 2018 the average number of *daily* deliveries to households in New York City was 1.5 million packages.

20. The examples of algorithm usage in logistics and distribution in Agatz N, Campbell A, Fleischmann M, Savelsbergh M (2011).

21. Based on Nguyen QV, Behdani B, Bloemhof J (2020).

22. Research on electronic vehicle charging in Abdelwahed A, Van den Berg P, Brandt T, Collins J, Ketter W (2020) and in Valogianni K, Gupta A, Ketter W, Sen S, Van Heck E (2019).

23. Wassenaar E (2019, January 8).

24. The algorithm to support the auctioneer is based on Van Heck E, Ketter W, Lu Y, Gupta A, (2017, October 18). And based on Lu Y, Gupta A, Ketter W, Van Heck E (2019).

    Quote from Domingos P (2015).

25. The overview of the supervised and unsupervised learning methods is in Provost F, Fawcett T (2013).

    The unsupervised learning algorithms do not have a target variable and there are four methods: clustering, co-occurrence, similarity matching, and profiling.

- *Clustering* is grouping individuals based on similarity (but no specific goal in mind). It is a form of data reduction, often useful for "getting a feel for the data."
- *Co-occurrence grouping*, also known as market basket analysis, or association-rule mining, this method is transaction-based instead of individual-based to identify that certain items in transactions are associated more often.
- *Similarity matching* identifies similar individuals based on data known about them.
- *Profiling* characterizes the "typical" behavior of individuals, groups, or populations. It is often useful for identifying *atypical* behavior (e.g., fraud).

The supervised learning algorithms do have a target variable and there are four methods: causal modelling, classification, value estimation, and link prediction.

- *Causal modeling* investigates the causal relationship between events or actions. For prediction, correlation is often sufficient; for interventions/actions, causation is needed.
- *Classification* is used to predict for each individual, which set of (mutually exclusive) classes this individual belongs to. Scoring (or class probability estimation) gives a score for each individual representing the probability that the individual belongs to each of the classes.
- *Value estimation* provides a numerical value for each event, action, or individual. Whether something will happen is classification, while how much something will happen is value estimation/regression.
- *Link prediction* estimates connections between data items, e.g., identifying possible new connections in a social network, such as LinkedIn.

26. The discussion of explanatory and predictive models in the Information Systems (IS) field is in Shmueli G, Koppius OR (2011).
27. The clustering example and the causal modeling example results are in Lu Y, Gupta A, Ketter W, Van Heck E (2016).
28. This analysis was executed in a setting with auction clocks that disclosed the winner identity, later research revealed the surprising impact of winner identity disclosure, see Chap. 7.
29. The expected value framework that is presented and discussed in Provost F, Fawcett T (2013).
30. Research to compare human decision-making with algorithmic decision support was executed in the iFlow project by BIM master student Prins R (2019, April 30).
    Other excellent BIM master thesis research helped to shape the iFlow project in: Bouts S (2016, July 22).
    Van Zijl R (2016, July 7).
    Haring R (2017, July 25).
    The iFlow project is presented and discussed in Van Heck E, Ketter W, Lu Y, Gupta A, Truong M (2020, March 12).
31. The algorithm development cycle is inspired by my keynote: Van Heck E (2014, October 3).

32. The challenges are based on my keynotes: Van Heck E (2014, October 3) and Van Heck E (2018, November 30).

     For more in-depth insights about these six challenges:

     Digital Platforms
     McAfee A, Brynjolfsson E (2017).

     Digital Business
     Ross JW, Beath CM, Mocker M (2019).

     Active Board Members
     Kane GC, Philipps AN, Copulsky JR, Andrus GR (2019).

     Data Ownership
     Perzanowski A, Schultz J (2016).

     Algorithm Accountability
     Martin M (2019).
     O'Neil C (2016).

     Potential Impact on Work and Jobs
     The Boeing versus Airbus debate in Slutsken, H. (2019, February 12).
     Davenport T, Kirby J (2016).

33. In Chap. 6, several applications and algorithms in floriculture are discussed. Table 6.2 provides an overview of the applications and algorithms. Laboratory and field experiments (also called A/B testing) are nowadays the dominant research approaches.

34. The ultimate algorithm that discovers everything is presented and discussed in Domingos P (2015). In this excellent book, Pedro Domingos identified five tribes (pp. 51–55) and suggest combining the five perspectives to design the ultimate algorithm. The five tribes are:

- *Symbolists.* All intelligence is about manipulating symbols. The master algorithm in their view is inverse deduction, which figures out what knowledge is missing in order to make a deduction go through, and then makes it as general as possible.
- *Connectionists.* Learning is what the brain does. The brain learns by adjusting the strengths of connections between neurons and the crucial problem is figuring out which connections are to blame for which errors and change them accordingly. The master algorithm is back propagation, which compares the predicted output with the desired output and then successively changes the connections in layer after layer of neurons to bring the output closer to what it should be.
- *Evolutionaries.* Learning is natural selection and the learning structure is the key problem to solve. Their master algorithm is genetic programming, which mated and evolved computer programs in the same way that nature mated and evolved organisms.
- *Bayesians.* The focus is on uncertainty and learning is a form of uncertain inference, how to deal with noisy, incomplete, and contradictory information. The master algorithm is Bayes' theorem that will tell us how to incorporate new evidence into human beliefs.
- *Analogizers.* The key to learning is recognizing similarities between situations and thereby inferring other similarities. The key problem is judging how similar two things are. Their master algorithm supports vector machines, which figure out which experiences to remember and how to combine them to make new predictions.

References

Abdelwahed A, Van den Berg P, Brandt T, Collins J, Ketter W (2020) Evaluating and optimizing opportunity fast-charging schedules in transit battery electric bus networks. Transp Sci 54(6):1601–1615

Agarwal A, Hosanagar K, Smith M (2011) Location, location, location: an analysis of profitability of position in online advertising markets. J Market Res 48(6):1057–1073

Agatz N, Campbell A, Fleischmann M, Savelsbergh M (2011) Time slot management in attended home delivery. Transp Sci 45(3):435–449

Akerlof GA (1970) The market for 'lemons': quality uncertainty and the market mechanism. Q J Econ 84(3):488–500

Andrews M, Li T, Balocco F (2018) Increasing mobile search ad spend: cross-device effects. In: Paper presented at the 39th International Conference on Information Systems, San Francisco, pp 13–16 December 2018

Balocco F, Li T (2019) LemonAds: impression quality in programmatic advertising. In: Paper presented at the 40th International Conference on Information Systems, Munich, pp 15–18 December 2019

Bouts S (2016, July 22) Multi-transaction auctioning at Royal FloraHolland: an empirical inquiry into the effect on price. In: Rotterdam School of Management. Erasmus University. https://thesis.eur.nl/pub/35762. Accessed 9 Sep 2020

Davenport T, Kirby J (2016) Only humans need apply: winners and losers in the age of smart machines. Harper Business, New York

Domingos P (2015) The Master Algorithm, how the quest for the ultimate learning machine will remake our world. Penguin Books, London

Erasmus D (1993) The Praise of Folly. Penguin Classics, London

Frick T, Li T (2016) Personalization in social retargeting – a field experiment. In: Paper presented at the 37th International Conference on Information Systems, Dublin, pp 11–14 December 2016

Haag M, Hu W (2019, October 27) 1.5 Million packages a day: the Internet brings chaos to N.Y. Streets. New York Times, https://www.nytimes.com/2019/10/27/nyregion/nyc-amazon-delivery.html

Haring R (2017, July 25) Reinventing the Dutch flower auctions: multi-transaction auctioning in a time frame. In: Rotterdam School of Management. Erasmus University. https://thesis.eur.nl/pub/39863 Accessed 8 Sep 2020

Kane GC, Philipps AN, Copulsky JR, Andrus GR (2019) The technology Fallacy. How people are the real key to digital transformation. The MIT Press, Cambridge

Kendall G (2019, July 2) Your mobile phone vs. Apollo 11's guidance computer. RealClear Science, https://www.realclearscience.com/articles/2019/07/02/your_mobile_phone_vs_apollo_11s_guidance_computer_111026.html

Krohn J, Beyleveld G, Bassens A (2020) Deep learning illustrated. A visual interactive guide to artificial intelligence. Addison-Wesley, Boston, MA

Lu Y, Gupta A, Ketter W, Van Heck E (2016) Exploring bidder heterogeneity in multi-channel sequential B2B auctions. MIS Q 40(3):645–662. https://aisel.aisnet.org/misq/vol40/iss3/8/. Accessed 15 Sep 2020

Lu Y, Gupta A, Ketter W, Van Heck E (2019) Dynamic decision making in sequential business-to-business auctions: a structural econometric approach. Manag Sci 65(8):3853–3876. https://pubsonline.informs.org/doi/10.1287/mnsc.2018.3118. Accessed 15 Sep 2020

Markoff J (2012, June 25). How many computer to identify a cat? 16,000. New York Times. https://www.nytimes.com/2012/06/26/technology/in-a-big-network-of-computers-evidence-of-machine-learning.html. Accessed 8 Sep 2020

Martin M (2019) Designing ethical algorithms. MISQ Executive 18(2)

McAfee A, Brynjolfsson E (2017) Harnessing our digital future: machine, platform, crowd. W.W. Norton & Company, New York

Nguyen QV, Behdani B, Bloemhof J (2020) Data-driven process design: anticipatory shipping in agro-food supply chains. Int J Prod Res 58(5):1302–1318

O'Neil C (2016) Weapons of math destruction: how big data increases inequality and threatens democracy. Crown, New York

Perzanowski A, Schultz J (2016) The end of ownership: personal property in the digital economy. The MIT Press, Cambridge

Prins R (2019, April 30) Human predictions versus algorithmic predictions: improving the supplier's forecasting accuracy in the Dutch Flower Industry. In: Rotterdam School of Management. Erasmus University. https://thesis.eur.nl/pub/47573 Accessed 9 Sep 2020

Provost F, Fawcett T (2013) Data science for business. O'Reilly Media, Sebastopol

Ross JW, Beath CM, Mocker M (2019) Designed for digital: how to architect your business for sustained success. The MIT Press, Cambridge

Shmueli G, Koppius OR (2011) Predictive analytics in information systems research. MIS Q 35(3):553–572

Slutsken H (2019, February 12) Is Boeing or airbus better? We asked an airline pilot. The Points Guy. https://thepointsguy.com/news/is-boeing-or-airbus-better-we-asked-an-airline-pilot/. Accessed 12 Sep 2020

Statista (2020) Worldwide, Digital advertising. https://www.statista.com/outlook/216/100/digital-advertising/worldwide. Accessed 8 Sep 2020

Tsekouras D, Frick T, Li T (2018) Don't take it personally: the effect of explicit targeting in advertising personalization. In: Paper presented at the 37th International Conference on Information Systems, Dublin, pp 11–14 December 2016

Valogianni K, Gupta A, Ketter W, Sen S, Van Heck E (2019) Multiple Vickrey auctions for sustainable electric vehicle charging. In: Paper presented at the 40th International Conference on Information Systems, International Congress Center Munich, Munich, pp 15–18, December 2019

Van Heck E (2014, October 3) Turning data into business. At the RSM Leadership Summit 2014. https://www.rsm.nl/rsm-leadership-summit/previous-summits/2014/eric-van-heck-rsm/. Accessed 8 Sep 2020

Van Heck E (2018) November. Big Data, Disruptie en Bedrijfsmodellen. Digitaliseringsbijeenkomst Sierteelt, Aalsmeer, p 30

Van Heck E, Ketter W, Lu Y, Gupta A (2017, October 18) Selling flowers with analytics. RSM discovery. https://discovery.rsm.nl/articles/311-selling-flowers-with-analytics/. Accessed 8 Sep 2020

Van Heck E, Ketter W, Lu Y, Gupta A, Truong M (2020, March 12) Optimise floriculture and make it more sustainable with AI algorithms. In: RSM discovery. https://discovery.rsm.nl/articles/427-optimise-floriculture-and-make-it-more-sustainable-with-ai-algorithms/. Accessed 8 Sep 2020

Van Zijl R (2016, July 7) Improving the Grower's forecasting accuracy at Dutch Flower auctions by using different models. In: Rotterdam School of Management, Erasmus University. https://thesis.eur.nl/pub/35016. Accessed 12 Sep 2020

Waldrop M (2019) News feature: what are the Limits of deep learning? PNAS 116(4):1074–1077

Wassenaar E (2019) January. What does a day in the life of an auctioneer look like? In, Vlog at Royal FloraHolland, p 8

YouTube (2009, March 29) Hubel and Wiesel Cat Experiment. https://www.youtube.com/watch?v=IOHayh06LJ4. Accessed 8 Sep 2020

7

The Future Is Circular and Digital

7.1 Group Portraits

When you walk over the Damrak toward Amsterdam Centraal Station the view is magnificent. On the right side is the Basilica of Saint Nicholas in the Old Centre district and the departure point for several canal cruises. On the left side is the rental bicycle location (called "OV-fiets"). Here you can rent a bike with the message "happy cycling is safe cycling."[1] Several tram lines depart from here to many different destinations. The central railway station is housed in a medieval castle-like building, combining Gothic and Renaissance styles. It has two turrets and many ornamental details and stone reliefs referring to the capital city's industrial and commercial highlights. Opened in 1889, the station reflects the romantic nationalistic mood of the late nineteenth-century Netherlands, as does the Rijksmuseum. Both monumental buildings were designed by the architect, Pierre Cuypers (1827–1921).[2]

The journey from Amsterdam to Haarlem takes 20 minutes by train along the first railway track in the Netherlands, opened in 1839. Haarlem is a very fine city with several fascinating highlights such as "De Grote Markt," a beautiful square with a seventeenth-century atmosphere, the impressive Church of Saint Bavo, and the visible and working "De Adriaan" windmill. In the 1630s, Haarlem was a city bursting at its seams with 42,000 inhabitants.[3] It hosted around 285 traders who bought and sold flowers. A large number of tulip buyers and sellers owned houses near the Kruisstraat and the Kruispoort, and owned gardens, such as the Rosenprieel district situated outside the Kleine Houtpoort. You can walk from Haarlem Centraal Station to the city center via the Kruisweg. Our destination is the Frans Hals Museum at Groot

© The Author(s), under exclusive license to Springer Nature Switzerland AG 2021
E. van Heck, *Technology Meets Flowers*, https://doi.org/10.1007/978-3-030-69303-9_7

Heiligland, exhibiting very fine individual and group portraits paintings of Frans Hals (1582–1666), the master of "loose brushwork," and others. Every spring the "Museum in Bloom" exhibition takes place here, and the interior of the museum is decorated with stunning flower arrangements. You might wonder if the flower arrangements inspired our visit to the museum, but in fact we have come here to discover one of the key artifacts of Dutch society: the table.

7.2   Cooperation and Concordance

The Frans Hals Museum Hof is situated in what was once the Old Men's Alms House, established in 1609. The Alms House provided single, poor, older men with a regular meal and a clean place to sleep. The residential rooms were situated around a courtyard or *hofje* in Dutch. In Haarlem many *hofjes* were established by wealthy citizens to provide charity for the elderly, the orphans, the poor, or the sick. Hofje van Bakens, Hofje van Loo, and Hofje van Staats, among others, were run by a board of governors, usually five regentesses and/ or regents. Whenever there was a change of board members, a commemorative painting was made.[4] Frans Hals painted many of these group portraits such as the famous "The Regents of St Elisabeth's Hospital" (1641), "The Regentesses of the Old Men's Alms House" (1664), and "The Regents of the Old Men's Alms House" (1664).[5] He captured the diverse characters and emotions of his subjects, yet each of the regentesses and regents have a dignified and serious look about them, and their clothing is sober black. There is another characteristic of these seventeenth-century Dutch group portraits. The women and men are sitting at a table.[6]

The Dutch "table" society and culture of cooperation and concordance was developed over hundreds of years, and the table has become a symbol of the Dutch way of organizing. It is not a throne, or a lectern, nor is it a couch. At the table, the board members discussed their challenges, exchanged ideas, reviewed financial calculations, and made decisions. The influential people each had a seat at the table. Participants at the table were equal to one another, even if they were not similar. The Dutch culture values consensus among different groups and the groups discuss, negotiate, and decide on consensus-based actions at the table. The table continues to hold a prominent place, not only in the Netherlands, but in boardrooms around the world and even in social settings and entertainment.

Consider, for example, the twenty-first-century early evening talk show *De Wereld Draait Door* (The World Keeps on Turning). It is the longest-running show in the history of the Netherlands and the second-most-watched show among Dutch viewers. There were 2428 episodes between 2005 and 2020. The host of the show, Matthijs van Nieuwkerk, and a rotation of guest co-hosts opened the show by inviting people to the table (in Dutch: *Aan tafel*). While seated around a large oval table, the host, co-host, and invited guests had a discussion on a topic of interest. Guests included people involved in interesting projects or organizations conducting charity work, making new discoveries, or working on societal issues, but also artists, scientists, booksellers, musicians, celebrities, or politicians.

Some have observed that meeting the challenges of living below sea level required the people to develop a style of negotiation and cooperation leading to consensus and shared responsibilities. It was only by working together that citizens were able to conquer the rising water levels through well-managed rivers, canals, dikes, and polders. The Dutch word *polder* means the reclaimed land from the sea; thus, the *"polder model"* refers to consensus-based decision making. The involvement of many different groups to come up with an agreed solution for complex societal issues, such as water management, formation of pensions, new laws to regulate complex societal issues like abortion or same-sex marriages, or plans to tackle climate change, continues to be one of the most fascinating strengths of Dutch society.

In Chap. 2, the birth of the Dutch bulb and flower industry is reviewed, initiated by the appointment of Carolus Clusius as professor of Botany at Leiden University in 1593. This appointment strengthened his collaborative actions through a network of correspondents spanning all of Europe. He and his associates exchanged knowledge and ideas, and began to categorize bulbs and flowers in a systematic way. The systematic knowledge discovery led a flourishing community of flower consumers and traders in a society that could afford to spend time and money on flowers and gardens.

We also saw in Chap. 2 that the Netherlands in 1600 was going through a fundamental shift from a feudal society to a bourgeois society. Like a fine woven cloth, the social structure of Dutch society developed with formal and informal networks of connections. It became more egalitarian and very much focused on doing things together for the well-being of society but with a keen eye on doing business and making money, as have been seen in the paintings of Frans Hals.

By the end of the nineteenth century, the collaborative ties among flower consumers and traders were institutionalized in a new form: the cooperative.[7] In the Netherlands, there are nowadays 2531 cooperatives in sectors such as services (consultancy firms, law firms, and credit unions), health (hospitals and healthcare organizations), agriculture (cheese, milk, flowers), real estate (rental corporations), and energy (local electricity cooperatives). These cooperatives accounted for 18% of the yearly gross domestic product (GDP) of the Netherlands. The top 10 countries of the cooperative economy index are New Zealand, France, Switzerland, Finland, Italy, the Netherlands, Germany, Austria, Denmark, and Norway.[8]

The cooperative remains fundamental to the Dutch flower industry, and this institutional form has many advantages. For example, cooperatives pool investments and therefore risks. Cooperatives command a larger and more powerful investment fund when all members chip in. Large investments were needed to introduce new technologies, such as the electronic auctioneer (the "Peace Maker") in 1903, or to transition to a new trading and distribution complex in Naaldwijk when standardized logistical containers were designed and implemented in 1975, or when Tele Flower Auction, the online auction marketplace, was acquired in 2010.

Royal FloraHolland, a cooperative of 5406 growers, is one of the Dutch flower industry's main orchestrators. Growers are family-owned businesses that produce flowers for consumer markets. They compete with each other and at the same time they invest together in one cooperative. The cooperative bundles the production of these different growers and organizes the sales and marketing of the products to wholesalers and retailers. Growers are suppliers of products but also members of the cooperative. Actually, growers—as members—must supply their products via the cooperative to the market, but they also have decision rights with regard to the cooperative strategy and its investments. Therefore, the cooperative has member boards and voting rights for members. In general, this leads to a lot of discussion and consensus-building among members. It takes time to develop a consensus, but once achieved the implementation of the agreed plans can be swift.[9]

7.3   Information Space Theory

As we buy flowers for our family and friends, we take for granted how flowers are produced and where they come from. Indeed, we expect that flowers can be ordered online anytime and anywhere. We assume that flowers will be delivered as fresh as possible even when produced on the other side of the world. The short life of cut flowers is only around five to ten days. The high-speed flower business and its markets take a front-runner position in creating value for customers with advanced, emerging technologies. The complex production and distributional challenges of these very perishable flower products and services were explained in Chap. 5. One crucial success factor for the freshness of flowers is the "freshness" of information and the exploration of the information frontier, i.e., the area where new information will lead to societal value.[10]

To explain the concept of information and the information frontier, the very inspiring work by Max Boisot (1943–2011), a British architect, management consultant, and professor of strategic management, is very helpful.[11] The core of Boisot's work is the Information Space (I-Space) theory about the codification and diffusion of information.[12] It is fascinating both from a theoretical and practical point of view and explains the business world (including the floral business ecosystem) based on two scales of information: codification and diffusion. The codification of information deals with its ability to be coded, i.e., by speaking, writing, or other ways such as the usage of emoji codes or a sign language. The diffusion of information is its ability to be shared with other people (or machines), for example, by digitalization (via Skype, WhatsApp, Facebook, Instagram). Let me explain the core of the theory and its usefulness to guide the development and use of advanced technologies in the flower business and other high-speed businesses. The high versus low level of information codification and the high versus low level of information diffusion can be illustrated by the cyclical information flows through four areas of the business transactional space; see Fig. 7.1.

We begin in the lower left-hand corner and move clockwise through the matrix[13]:

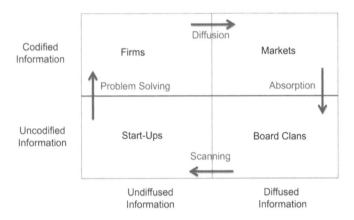

Fig. 7.1 Cyclical information flows through four areas of the business transactional space. Adapted from Max Boisot, *Information & Organizations: The Manager as Anthropologist* (Fontana, London, 1987), Fig. 4.3 and Fig. 5.1, page 80 and 100

- *Startups.* Someone thinks of a new business idea. It could be an idea for a new flower species or the use of drones for insect control in greenhouses. In the very beginning, the business idea developed in someone's brain and the idea is uncodified and undiffused. To explain the idea to anyone (such as other startups, potential collaborators, or investors) one needs to talk about it or write it down, perhaps in an email, and so the idea is codified. Once it has been codified, prototypes are developed, and with field experiments the effectiveness of the business idea is tested and refined.
- *Firms.* A working prototype of the idea has been developed and the idea is highly codified (a new flower variety or a new way of insect control has been developed and all the details of the production process are codified) and it can be produced. The idea was shared among the people who worked on the production and improved it, but it has not yet been diffused in markets.
- *Markets.* The new product or service is launched into the markets. Customers are persuaded to buy and use the new product or service (the expression of the codified information), and it is diffused to the business community or the world.
- *Board clans.* If the new business idea is established and works, it becomes part of what is called "common sense." It is taken for granted and becomes highly diffused—at this stage it is no longer considered to be codified. Examples are business jargon, such as "that's how we do business here" among business participants, usually in a local arrangement, such as among members of a company board or advisory board (sometimes referred to as "clans" or "old boy networks").

As illustrated in Fig. 7.1, a key characteristic of the I-Space theory is the *cyclical* flow of information through four distinct phases, representing the creation and absorption of new knowledge. We begin in the center of the matrix at the bottom:

1. *Scanning.* The creation of knowledge is usually the outcome of a response to a problem. For example, the use of chemicals for insect control had negative effects for greenhouses and workers. The problem in the current way of doing business was identified by the board clans (usually a larger group) and the identified problem inspired a few innovators to search for solutions. The advanced use of drones was not directly developed related to the insect control problem; however, scanning it for a potential application is the vital first step.

2. *Problem solving.* The potential solutions are identified and a choice will be made. Problem solving in itself is a creative process both for humans, via a mental process, and for machines, via a computerized heuristic. During this process, the information will become more codified; thus, problem solving makes information less *heuristic* and more *algorithmic.* Problem-solving procedures and methods will be specified and the outcomes can be guaranteed within certain limits.

3. *Diffusion.* In the third phase, the greater degree of codification makes it desirable and possible to reach new audiences, such as potential customers around the world. However, there is a need to control the diffusion rate. Like flowers, information is perishable. Its value is time sensitive. Companies, but also some governments, exercise the power to control the quality and dissemination of information to control its or to create information asymmetries (think about the "lemons" problem in markets as discussed in Chap. 6, where sellers could sell "lemons," i.e., products with inferior quality, without disclosing the inferior quality information with potential buyers).

4. *Absorption.* The absorption of new, diffused, relevant information into existing knowledge leads to continuous modifying and blending until the information is acknowledged as business as usual. The absorptive capacity of people and machines—human learning versus machine learning—is the ability to blend existing knowledge with new knowledge in a local context.

Having information no one else has, i.e., being at the information frontier, is a crucial source of competitive advantage. Information in the production quadrant (high codification and low diffusion) has the highest potential economic value: information will be utilized and scarce. However, the competitive advantage is very vulnerable: increased diffusion (moving to the markets quadrant) will make information less scarce and therefore less valuable.[14] It is the paradox of the value of "information goods." Information goods are non-rival goods, i.e., the consumption by one consumer will not limit the consumption of other consumers and with the use of digital technologies the information goods can be easily reproduced.

I-Space theory helps companies and business ecosystems to be strategic and value their information and knowledge sources.[15] It also helps to explain the strengths and weaknesses of the Dutch-dominated flower ecosystem and the different factors that make its cycle of knowledge discovery and absorption effective and efficient.

For each of the four quadrants of the matrix Dutch, examples will be provided. These examples have accelerated the cycle of information codification and diffusion and that created new knowledge and ways of blending new knowledge into the floral business. The examples are useful for other sectors and industries, such as media, health, food, energy, water, tourism and travel, transport, and mobility, to determine strength and weaknesses and to speed up the cycle of information exchange and learning.

- *Startup ecosystems.* A collaborative effort among Dutch industry, government, and universities has created several startup centers near various universities, such as Wageningen University & Research, the technical universities of Delft, Twente, and Eindhoven, and the universities of Amsterdam, Rotterdam, Leiden, and Utrecht. These places are incubators for problem solvers and new business developers. For example, since 2011, Wageningen-based StartLife has built, supported, and funded 300+ startups in the domains of food and agriculture.
- *Production by grower networks.* For growers keen on collaboration and sharing information, growers' associations offer attractive opportunities. For example, Decorum Plants & Flowers is an association of 50 growers who bring 4000 products to the market under one label with a reputation for high quality, sustainability, and innovation. A smart business network was created with a clear goal, aligned with certified business partners and information sharing to serve clients in an international and competitive market.
- *Markets' platform design.* Flower markets change from "one size fits all," i.e., the Dutch auction, to multiple markets (spot and future markets) with different price and delivery settings. Platform design is a dominant topic that is discussed with different stakeholders. Other competitors outside the flower industry, such as Alibaba or Amazon, have the digital capabilities to handle such platforms, but they lack the specialized knowledge of the flower industry.
- *Board clans' interlinkages.* Royal FloraHolland has many linkages to thousands of growers and clients worldwide, but also with national and regional governments, other industries, such as seeds or renewable energies, various education institutions, startup centers, and the World Horti Center, located in Naaldwijk at the heart of Glass City.[16] The strong network of interlinkages, both horizontal, among partners in the floriculture chain network, and vertical, between top management and workers (in the relatively egalitarian Dutch society), provides sufficient opportunities and incentives to scan for new opportunities and to absorb new knowledge. For example, the World Horti Center is visited yearly by 25,000 international professionals seeking connections, knowledge, and innovations in horticulture. World Horti Center has an international focus and is a unique collaboration

among education, research, entrepreneurs, and the government. Seven regional Greenports are implemented to stimulate research, innovation, education, and the absorption of new technology and business.

7.4   Circular and Digital Transformations

The "firms" and "markets" quadrants of the I-Space matrix are the most fascinating components of the business transactional space. For the flower business ecosystem, these are the crucial components and the area that is "in transition" at the moment. Let us look forward and focus on the different firm and market models and the way the Dutch would like to stay dominant in the global flower business ecosystem. As we have seen in previous chapters, a mixture of forces will determine the size and focus of the flower business and markets. These forces can be briefly summarized as:

- Spectacular growth of flower consumption in Asia and some growth in Europe and the Americas due to a rising population and income levels.
- A more personalized experience of flower consumption enabled by the modularization of flower products and services.
- A Cambrian-like explosion of flower varieties driven by CRISPR and DL technologies. CRISPR stands for "clustered regularly interspaced short palindromic repeats" and is a powerful tool for editing genomes. DL stands for "deep learning" and is an advanced algorithm for pattern recognition and is applied in flower seed selection, as discussed in Chap. 2 and explained in Chap. 6.
- A transition from a "take, make, and dispose" economy to circular economy with circular activities such as recycling, refurbishing, reuse, and maintenance.[17] The circular economy aims "to keep products, components, and materials at their highest utility and values at all time".[18]
- A redesign of the global economy given the impact of the COVID-19 global pandemic with a transition from global production and global consumption to more regional or local production and consumption.[19] The redesign could be guided by the "Doughnut" compass developed by Kate Raworth, an economist at Oxford University. A radical way of organizing the economy in such a way that the basics of life, such as sufficient food, clean water and decent sanitation, access to energy and clean cooking facilities, access to education and to healthcare, decent housing, minimum income and decent work, and access to networks of information and social support, will be met for all, within the ecological and planetary boundaries.[20]

- Greater demand from end customers to control their own data and market advantages for building up a trusted relationship between customers and firms.
- Greater understanding among business and market makers of the need for certified algorithm accountability and ethics for the algorithms used in the different stages of the flower production and consumption.
- Sustained efforts by startups to provide technology-driven solutions to problems in global and local flower production and consumption.
- Continued market advantages to those who explore the information frontier and create economic value out of "fresh" information.

The flower business ecosystem and most other high-speed business ecosystems will go through two types of transformation: the circular transformation and the digital transformation. The circular transformation deals with the business ecosystem transitioning from a linear form, based on the linear relationship from production to consumption, to a circular form, based on "preserving and enhancing natural capital, optimizing resource yields, and designing out negative externalities." The digital transformation deals with the transitioning from a traditional business design to a digital business design, i.e., "as the holistic organizational configuration of people (roles, accountabilities, structures, skills), processes (workflows, routines, procedures), and technology (infrastructure, applications) to define value propositions and deliver offerings made possible by the capabilities of digital technologies".[21]

The future business ecosystem will have transactional forms with different circular and digital capabilities. These circular and digital capabilities can be visualized in four sub-quadrants as indicated in Fig. 7.2.

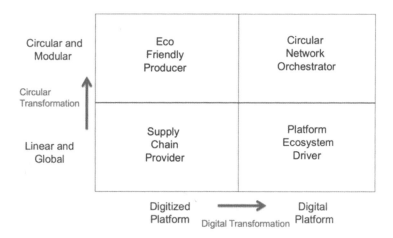

Fig. 7.2 Circular and digital transformations with a matrix of four business models. Author's own figure

We begin in the lower left-hand corner of the matrix:

- *Supply chain provider.* The traditional supply chain providers produce their products for the linear, usually global, supply and demand chains. There is limited transparency among the stakeholders in the supply chain on traceability and environmental impact of products, services, and processes.
- *Eco-friendly producer.* The eco-friendly producer deploys a circular business model with advanced capabilities for the "right" recycling, refurbishing, reuse, and maintenance.[22] They have a traditional information approach to process detailed eco-information from customers and suppliers. They have limited capabilities to develop and use advanced digital technologies, such as the Internet of Things (IoT).[23]
- *Platform ecosystem driver.* The business model of the platform ecosystem driver is connecting the different stakeholders over a digital platform. The two-sided platform between producers on one side and wholesalers/retailers on the other side is linear and trading focused.
- *Circular network orchestrator.* The orchestrator links the different stakeholders with different network positions including supply chain providers, eco-friendly producers, and platform ecosystem drivers. Information sharing among the circular network participants takes place over an advanced digital platform. The circular network is a "smart business network" and therefore modular and data-driven, enabled by the latest digital technologies, such as blockchain and IoT.[24]

One important lesson to be learned, based on the impact of the COVID-19 global pandemic, is that companies, systems, and business ecosystems need to be redesigned to be resilient to extreme shocks.[25] One way to is to use the "agility" concept. An agile company will embrace constant change and be ready to absorb extreme external shocks.[26] The other way is to look at the crucial, systemic elements of the business ecosystem with the use of the "antifragility" concept. Antifragility is a state of a system that gets *better* under stress. There are several principles that can be introduced to develop an antifragile business ecosystem (see the Chapter Notes for more details).[27]

One of the nine top sectors of the economy of the Netherlands is horticulture and starting materials. Under the guidance of the Dutch Top Sector Alliance for Knowledge and Innovation, several innovative projects were initiated that are contributing to the transition to the circular flower business ecosystem.[28] These projects focus on breeding and propagation, greenhouse construction and optimization of growing processes, primary processes, sales, and trade. Some of these fascinating projects are as follows:

- The Beekenkamp Group produces 2 billion young plants annually; some 800 million are cuttings for chrysanthemums, and pot and bedding plants. They produce cuttings in Uganda and Ethiopia and benefit from the local climate and local labor conditions. Their social impact program in those countries includes sustainable production and the provision of higher wages than the minimum wage, medical care, child care, workplace education, healthy food, and water wells and electricity in the surrounding villages.
- Koppert Biological Systems use natural predators that enable a significant reduction in the use of chemicals in horticulture. Controlling pests and diseases in the greenhouse using predatory mites and ichneumon wasps will make plants more resilient. Using fungi in the soil and bumblebees will improve pollination. They share knowledge via the Seed2Feed program with Kenyan farmers. They show Kenyan farmers how to improve their yields by using better varieties and biological control.
- Royal Brinkman, a global specialist in horticulture, developed plant pots using consumer's plastic waste as a raw material. They work to develop products from biodegradable polymers that were tested for 3D printing. Biodegradable twine could be an alternative to the conventional plastic twine. Other innovations are floating solar panels, emissions-free farming, and organic waste that becomes residual power.
- Koppert Cress produces almost 70 different varieties of cress in Glass City. The varieties come from all over the world and the conditions in the glasshouses mimic the different climates in which they grow. The micro-vegetables find their way to some 70,000 restaurants, mostly in Europe. With smart use of geothermal heat, residual heat, harvested heat, pipelines, and aquifers, their glasshouses could become gas-free in the near future. The "Heat Roundabout," a network of pipelines that transport heat from the Port of Rotterdam and industries to greenhouses and the city, will allow industrial heat to be stored all year round for use in glasshouses in Glass City.
- Royal FloraHolland works hard to improve transparency and certification in the flower supply chain with better information about the sustainability and quality of flowers and the suppliers. They signed the Plastic Pact agreement with 75 leading businesses and the Government of the Netherlands, pledging to achieve environmental benchmarks by 2025: single-use packaging must be 100% recyclable, the use of plastic must be reduced by 20%, and plastic products launched on the market must consist of at least 35% recycled plastic.

7.5   Business Ecosystem Transition

The complex transition of business ecosystems is fascinating and challenging. Not only are many stakeholders involved, but during the transition new solutions will be implemented that generate new challenges. In essence there are three types of institutions involved—the so-called triple helix—universities, industries, and government. The triple helix hypothesis is "that systems can be expected to remain in transition." One can expect to have a sequence of "endless" transitions.[29]

Universities are at the core of the helix interactions with both academic research and education. Research in collaboration with industry will create new inventions and innovations and students—educated with the latest knowledge and insights—are the potential inventors.

Fundamental academic research, nowadays the main source of inventions, is carried out by by Wageningen University & Research. It is a powerhouse in world-class research and education with over 6500 employees and 12,000 students. Their down-to-earth engineering approach to life science issues, ranging from food creation for an expanding world population to carbon dioxide reduction in agriculture, is instrumental for the life science sector and society at large.

Industries will develop new business concepts and technologies and will find out how to create sustainable value through a process of trial and error. Governmental organizations are able to help with incentives, regulations, and investment funds. As members of the Business Information Management (BIM) community at Rotterdam School of Management, we work in these intensive "triple helix" configurations with industries and government. For example, the Erasmus Center for Data Analytics (ECDA) is working with the Municipality of Rotterdam on the European "Ruggedised" project on smart energy infrastructure for cities, to encourage the use of electric vehicles in the city center. It also worked with the Dutch Top Sector Horticulture & Starting Materials in the iFlow project on AI applications in the floriculture chain. Actually, several of the BIM students, either before or after graduation, have founded exciting new companies, such as PATS discussed in Chap. 3, a company that develops drones for insect control in glasshouses.

How will innovations be adopted and diffused over time?[30] Some indication is found in the world of agriculture, specifically in research on the adoption of hybrid seed corn in Iowa, in the United States. Bryce Ryan and Neal Gross, two rural sociologists, studied factors that contributed to farmers' rapid adoption of hybrid seed corn in two communities.[31] The increase was phenomenal: "between 1933 and 1939 acreage in hybrid corn increased from 40,000 to 24 million acres (about one fourth of the nation's corn acreage). Between 1936 and 1939 two thirds of the operators in the two communities studied changed to the new seed. Relatively few, however, took over hybrid seed for their entire acreage the first year they tried it. This was true even for operators first using the seed at a relatively late date."

What triggered the rapid adoption of hybrid seed corn and why were differences noticed among farmers that are usually "conservative"? First, there was a difference between the diffusion agencies which informed farmers of the new seed and the sources of influence toward adoption. Commercial channels, especially salesmen, were most important as original sources of knowledge, while neighbors were the most important sources of influence leading to adoption. Although the time pattern of adoption followed a bell-shaped curve, the instance of diffusion could not accurately be described as a normal frequency distribution. Later research identified differences among firms or individuals, labeled as innovators, early adopters, early majority, late majority, and laggards. One size does not fit all. The decision to adopt is complex and has to do with individual or firm strategies, capabilities, and potential costs and revenues.

Adoption of new technologies also has to do with the fact that most individuals or firms do not act in isolation.[32] Firms work in a supply chain or a circular network. Companies that collaborate in a vertical or horizontal way are able to adopt the innovation when others do and vice versa. For example, the adoption of IoT technology and the transformation from a smart tractor to the use of a smart system of systems, based on a farm management system, requires horizontal collaboration.[33] The farm management system may collaborate with a farm equipment system, an irrigation system, a seed optimization system, and a weather data system. These systems have the potential to connect different farmers with different system producers, and therefore the adoption process is complex, decentralized, and fuzzy. Value creation for the producers of these complex systems is risky and will take substantial investments with uncertain profit levels due to fierce technology competition.[34]

Adoption of new technologies is also about power and competition. For example, the traditional coal and oil companies are competing with renewable energy (solar, wind) providers. The transfer of power from incumbent companies to the "new kids on the block" is slow and cumbersome. No single party can set the course of systems innovations, and therefore, it is usually a process of muddling through. Governments are able to stimulate the transition to a carbon neutral economy with the introduction of a carbon tax, for example, on the carbon content of fuels. Nowadays, the most polluted fuels, kerosene-based fuel for aircrafts and diesel-based fuel for shipping, are almost tax free.[35]

7.6   Three Questions and Answers

Technology Meets Flowers focuses on three fascinating questions. Reader, you are almost at the end of the book and you are ready to formulate an answer to this first question: why do the Dutch play a central role in the global production, sales, and distribution of flowers?

Indeed, it is not about the ideal climate or weather, and anyway the climate is changing in the Netherlands, with longer periods of very dry or very wet weather. You have learned that the seed of the bulb flower industry was planted in 1593, when professor Carolus Clusius was appointed at Leiden University. A societal transformation was underway that ultimately led to the birth of the Netherlands as a country. With the benefit of hindsight, the fundamental societal transformation at that time from a feudal society to a bourgeois society was recognized. The bourgeois society had to be invented and the Dutch were eager to do that with the creation of new institutions of commerce such as the multinational enterprises (the East India Company and the West India Company), the stock market, the commodity exchange, the chamber of assurance, the public exchange bank, and the lending bank. These institutions provided trust and attracted capital and mercantile interest from all over Europe to a country that was open to new ideas, tolerant of other religions and worldviews, and with freedom of thought and press. Investment opportunities were used to develop trade routes to the East and the West, to build new types of ships, for drainage projects reclaiming land from the sea, and for luxury objects such as paintings and flowers.

Professor Clusius was appointed at an opportune moment in history because there was enough money at that time to spend on bulbs and flowers. Local markets were organized around new and fast negotiation mechanisms, auctions, and with the abundant usage of promissory notes. The hype of the tulip bulb sales around 1637—called Tulip mania—was not as catastrophic as painted in the popular press. There were hardly any bankruptcies, but there were several court cases and disputes. Knowledge was gained on how to deal with turbulent economic times.

The Dutch society—at that time a society still under construction—evolved to value discussion and communication among different participants. The "table" society was born and remains an essential characteristic of Dutch culture and society. By the end of the nineteenth century new institutions, such as the cooperative, and technological advances in the Dutch auction mechanism ("the Peacemaker"), were invented and applied in such a way that they were improving market efficiency. During the twentieth century numerous mergers and acquisitions led to the establishment of Royal FloraHolland, a grower cooperative with 5406 growers. The local market maker transitioned to a global market maker. There was also sheer luck involved: a natural gas field was discovered right under an area near several main cities, and this was the start of Glass City, further enabling the innovativeness and productivity of Dutch floriculture.

Technology Meets Flowers's second question has to do with the complexity of the flower markets: how are the flower markets able to produce and distribute fresh flowers at such a high speed and global scale?

The chapters of this book have revealed some remarkable "secrets" that led to the optimization of breeding and propagation, growing, sales, and trade. The Dutch bulb industry produces around 8.5 billion flower bulbs every year, of which around 3 billion are tulip bulbs. There are around 1500 bulb growers who specialize in one or more kinds of cultivars. Seed valley—an area in North Holland where most of the plant breeding and seed technology companies are situated—is the hot spot of new seed development. They create "green software", a mix of digital and genetic technology, and they sequenced the DNA of the tulip genome and genomes of other flowers. The DNA patterns linked to desirable characteristics will soon be used in advanced breeding so that these characteristics can be combined into new, improved varieties. With this knowledge, new varieties which are, for example, resistant to common diseases, can be developed faster and in a more targeted way. Once the DNA sequence of the tulip genome is known, one can develop and link genomic selection with phenotype prediction. Automated image analysis with machine learning technology can speed up the selection process dramatically. The combined genetic and digital revolution will create a potential Cambrian-like explosion of new flower types and will create the opportunity to design personalized flowers.

Glasshouses enable full control of the flower life cycle, through the seed planting, germination, growth, reproduction, pollination, and seed spreading stages. Key for life is the photosynthesis process, i.e., the conversion of sunlight, carbon dioxide, and water into sugars. Under controlled conditions of light, temperature, carbon dioxide, humidity, and drought and salinity, the growth and development of flowers is speeded up or slowed down. Automated, robotized, and data-driven glasshouses optimize the production of flowers and are a source of carbon emission consumption.

Sales by growers are traditionally organized by Dutch auction markets. Central to the market design is the Dutch auction mechanism where, under the guidance of the auction clock and auctioneer, the first bidder wins and buys some or all of the lot. The remaining part will be re-auctioned again until the complete lot is sold. The Dutch flower auctions are a fast clearing mechanism with 35 online auction clocks and around 100,000 transactions a day in three hours of trading. Actually, there is one weakness: it is a supply-driven channel in a world where end customers demand flowers through online platforms. More direct channels are used where customer orders are collected by retail web shops, wholesalers, or growers. These bundled orders are processed and distributed to the end customers with the use of AI algorithms and data-driven decision tools.

High-speed flower logistics with its cool chain management is a "secret" of its own. Within two days, flowers are distributed at the right temperature from the grower to local markets around the world. Standardization of trolleys with standardized labels and radio frequency identification (RFID) chips speed up the logistics. Flower bouquets were distributed faster with modular trolleys and buckets. New logistics concepts with the use of big data analytics are explored both at the individual-firm level and at the supply chain level. For example, the predicted inbound volume of cross-docking facilities will be used to forecast the needed workforce. Similarly, predictions of consumer behavior are inputs to anticipatory shipping, i.e., to ship flowers before an order is placed.

In the flower industry there is the direct order flow from consumers to growers and the opposite logistical flow of flower products, from growers to consumers, and the money flow is equally important and also prone to innovation. New digital payments are implemented and the potential of FloraCoin, a digital flower community currency, is explained and discussed.

The new data monetization strategies for Royal FloraHolland are explored, based on my slogan "Selling information about flowers next to selling flowers." These information-based services are provided to growers and sold to clients, such as specific pricing strategies for growers that can be used in the online pre-sales channel. Other offerings include the insights that are already offered at the RFH Floriday Platform.

The key question is: will the production of fresh flowers continue on a global scale? As of April 2020, the global production and distribution of flowers dropped dramatically due to the global COVID-19 pandemic. Uplift capacity at Nairobi's Jomo Kenyatta International Airport for export to

Europe dropped from 5000 tons to 1800 tons per week. In Europe, most physical flower retail shops were closed in March and April 2020, but flowers ordered online continued to be delivered. In May and June 2020, the production and distribution of flowers recovered substantially.

The third question of *Technology Meets Flowers* concerns other sectors and industries: what can they learn from the circular and digital innovations that have taken place or will take place in the high-speed flower markets?

There are several lessons for other higher-speed sectors and industries, such as food, health, energy, water, tourism and travel, transport, and mobility, but also lower-speed industries such as manufacturing or the construction industry. Actually, you can view the flower industry as a living laboratory where new business models and emerging technologies, such as computers, genetics, nanotechnology, robotics, and artificial intelligence, are tested out. There are three lessons.

The first lesson has to do with the current Dutch way of working in the floriculture supply chain networks that produce flowers for the global flower markets and the inventions and innovations there were necessary conditions for success, as reviewed above.

The second lesson deals with the next circular and digital transformation and the shift of the information frontier to circular information about recycling, refurbishing, and reuse, and maintenance of flower products or input resources and the required capabilities for these four circular activities. Four different types of firms will compete in the flower markets. These types will have different business models based on low or high circular capabilities and low or high digital capabilities. These four types are supply chain provider, eco-friendly producer, platform ecosystem driver, and circular network orchestrator.

The third lesson has to do with the complexity and the way to organize and implement successful systems innovations such as the transformation to circular business, with electric transport, and data ownership by citizens. Collaboration among competitors is needed, for example, to adopt sustainability standards to create a level playing field, collaboration among supply chain networks to synchronize adoption of new digital technologies and compensate the unequal distribution of costs and benefits among the network partners, and the leadership of governmental organizations to provide risk-taking investment funds for startups and to scale-up circular and digital activities.

7.7   Epilogue

Well, reader, how did you like it? It took me quite a while to write it. Has it been worth it?[36]

I would like to elaborate on an important element of the story. The business of a non-fiction writer, and also of a professor, is tied to information asymmetry.[37] Actually, it is about codifying information (writing, presenting) and to diffuse the information as far as possible. I know more about the flower markets than you do but if you have read this book carefully, or paid attention in my lectures, you will know almost as much about it as I do. By reading this book and learning from it, the information is symmetrized between you and me. It is up to you to apply the information for your own purposes and to your own situation. You will do that in a subjective way, i.e., based on your personal feelings or beliefs. The possible applications are so vast that it would be challenging for me to predict how you will use the information and what the potential impact will be for you. I can say for sure that the next step is to apply the lessons you have learned to solve problems or challenges around you in your life or work. I hope it is alright to bring this to your attention here, without foofaraw. Prolonged good-byes are not my style, so I will just say a simple farewell by wishing you all the best to apply the lessons learned.

Notes

1. Cycling in Amsterdam is a great way to explore the city but also adventurous. For a first-time biker, please have a look at YouTube (2015, December 5).
2. Pierre Cuypers designed many impressive buildings in the Netherlands, such as Castle De Haar, Nijmegen Railway Bridge, Saint Joseph Cathedral in Groningen, and Saint Lambertus Church in Veghel, where I was baptized.
3. In the 1630s, Haarlem had a population of 42,000 people and was recognized as the center of the trade with "approximately 285 traders who bought and sold flowers." At that time Amsterdam hosted 60 traders with an estimated population in 1635 with 120,000 citizens, and Enkhuizen hosted about 25 traders with an estimated population in 1622 of 22,000. Based on Goldgar (2007).
4. More detailed research on group portraits by Middelkoop (2019) Schutters, gildebroeders, regenten en regentessen: Het Amsterdamse corporatiestuk 1525–1850 (Civic Guardsmen, Governors, and Guild Members: Amsterdam Institutional Group Portraits, 1525–1850), Dissertation, University of Amsterdam

5. For more information and to view the Frans Hals paintings you can visit online the Frans Hals Museum at franshalsmuseum.nl. The three mentioned "table" paintings can be viewed at: https://www.franshalsmuseum.nl/en/art/regents-of-st-elisabeths-hospital/; https://www.franshalsmuseum.nl/en/art/regentesses-of-the-old-mens-alms-house/,: https://www.franshalsmuseum.nl/en/art/regents-of-the-old-mens-alms-house/. Accessed 9 Sept 2020.
6. The role of "the table" in Dutch society and in Dutch group portraits, such as the painting "Regenten en regentessen van het Spinhuis," painted in 1650 by Bartholomeus van der Helst, was inspired by and based on Van Zeil W (2020, January 11).
7. Friedrich Wilhelm Raiffeisen was the founder of the cooperative movement of credit unions and created the first farmers' bank in Germany in 1846. The Raiffeisen bank was merged with other banks into the Cooperative Rabobank headquartered in Utrecht. Nowadays, Rabobank is a global leader in food and agriculture financing and sustainability-oriented banking.
8. Data about cooperatives is from Mgmt. Scope (2020).
   A more detailed discussion of cooperatives is in Van Dijk et al. (2019).
9. A detailed innovation analysis of the Westland area (called Glass City in this book) is provided by De Man and Van Raaij (2008).
10. The academic community of Information Systems is organized by the Associations for Information Systems (AIS), with AIS journals and conferences such as the International Conference on Information Systems (ICIS) and the European Conference on Information Systems (ECIS), the AIS eLibrary, and AIS Communities around the world, see https://aisnet.org/. Accessed 9 Sept 2020.
    Information advantage is a key concept in the field of information systems, see for example the keynote, with a historic overview, by McFarlan (2015).
11. The Information Space Theory is discussed in several books by Boisot (1987, 1995, 1998).
    Boisot et al. (2007).
12. Between 2009 and 2018, I taught the I-Space theory in a lecture on "Information Systems" for 900 Dutch and 400 international bachelor students each year.
13. At the core of the I-Space theory Max Boisot distinguished four different transactional strategies: fiefs, bureaucracies, markets, and clans. Here these four are relabeled as startups, firms, markets, and board clans. In Boisot (1987).
14. Actually, research has seen the positive effect of not distributing information, i.e., the winner identity disclosure in the Dutch flower auctions on auction prices.
    The impact of *not* distributing winner identity information is based on Lu et al. (2019). Research by Yixin Lu (George Washington University), Alok Gupta (University of Minnesota), Wolf Ketter (Erasmus University Rotterdam), and myself will show you the complexity of the research design

and the uncovering of the underlying causal mechanism that will explain the impact on price level and price stability.

When three auctioneers were interviewed about the potential impact of winner identity disclosure on auction prices there were three different opinions. One auctioneer claimed that disclosing winner's identities did not have any impact due to the complexity of the auction markets. The three digits of a buyer's identity, for example, "265," would not have substantial impact. The second auctioneer argued that disclosing winners' identities could lead to buyer collusion and therefore to lower prices. The third view was that disclosing winners' identities could lead to higher prices due to more aggressive bidding in the subsequent rounds by losing bidders.

What could be done to answer the question of the role of winner identity disclosure?

Please think about an experimental design such as the one that was used by Dorothy Cayley, in Chap. 2, with her field experiments to uncover the underlying causality of the breaking in tulips. To discover the cause, Cayley compared two situations that were identical in every respect imaginable, apart from the variable the experiment was designed to test. Similarly, to discover how revealing or concealing information will impact an auction market, we can compare two markets that are nearly identical in every other respect but that differ in what information is available. In fact, a large-scale field experiment was set up at RFH to do precisely that.

The treatment site was chosen randomly among the four major RFH auction sites and the change to hide the winner's identity was implemented at a clock that auctioned chrysanthemums, which were in season at the time of the experiment. The winner's identity would normally be displayed on the auction clock, but this was removed from November 19 to December 7 (the experiment period). None of the bidders except the winner knew who had won in each round, but the researchers could see the winners because that information was registered in the auctioning system and recorded in the logbook.

In addition to data from the experiment period, data were collected before (October 29 to November 16) and after (December 10 to December 21) the experiment period. This allowed the researchers to see if the treatment effect dissipates once the experiment ends. Data were also gathered from a control site where the same types of flowers were auctioned, and the winner's identities were displayed throughout the study period.

With plenty of data for a robust comparison, a difference-in-differences (DID) approach measures the differences between the treatment site and the control site. The DID analysis reveals that, all else being equal, withholding the winner's identity increases the winning price by more than 6%. For chrysanthemums alone, for which the annual turnover was about €300 million, such an increase implies an extra €18 million in expected revenue.

Furthermore, the results indicate greater price stability in sequential rounds, which is good news for both suppliers and buyers.

The next questions are: Why did withholding the winners' identity increase the winning price? What is the causal mechanism?

We evaluated two possibilities. First, it is possible that bidders were engaged in tacit collusion. Withholding the identity of the winner may have prevented bidders from coordinating. Bidder networks at the treatment site were mapped throughout the pre-experiment and experiment period at the treatment site and the control site. The nodes in the networks represent the bidders, and the edges correspond to the dyadic constituents of bid rotation: if two bidders never showed up in the same auction during a given period, they would form a collusive tie represented by an edge.

Bidder 2 never showed up in the same auction with Bidders 1, 4, and 5. For that reason, three edges were generated between Bidder 2 and Bidders 1, 4, and 5. Similarly, Bidders 3 and 4 are connected by an edge as they did not win at the same auction.

Second, we considered that bidders might imitate one another, especially those who won frequently in the same auction. Imitation is possible only if bidders know who they want to imitate. A network analysis was performed to test for imitation throughout the pre-experiment and experiment period at the treatment site and the control site. If one bidder always won after a specific other bidder during the pre-experiment or experiment period, they would form an imitation tie represented by an edge.

Bidder 5 always won after Bidders 1, 3, and 4, and Bidder 4 won after Bidder 1. For that reason, four edges were generated corresponding to these relationships.

Indeed, we have two explanations for the price increase during our experiment period: the disruption of bidder collusion versus the disruption of bidder imitation. Which one caused prices to increase when the winner's identity was hidden?

Our analysis of the data points to the imitation hypothesis! We found compelling evidence that hiding the winner's identity caused prices to increase because it disrupted imitation.

15. Work by the I-Space Institute was published in business-oriented journals such as Ihrig et al. (2011). Ihrig M, MacMillan I (2017, March-April).

16. Information about the World Horti Center in World Horti Center (2020).

A detailed analysis and design of the business-driven campus and its success factors is provided by Van Hemert et al. (2019).

Seven regional so-called Greenports are designed and implemented in the Netherlands: Aalsmeer, Duin en Bollenstreek, Gelderland, Noord-Holland-Noord, Regio Boskoop, Venlo, West-Holland. Greenports Nederland (2020).

17. An excellent overview of the role and impact of logistics management in the circular economy is the farewell address by Bloemhof-Ruwaard (2019) Closing the Loop: A Never Ending Story. https://research.wur.nl/en/publications/closing-the-loop-a-never-ending-story. Accessed 9 Sept 2020.

    Jacqueline Bloemhof-Ruwaard was Professor of Operations Research and Logistics at Wageningen University & Research and very passionate about research and education on circular agribusiness and logistics, a source of inspiration for students and colleagues, and very active in the iFlow project, among other projects. She passed away in June 2020.

18. The definition of the circular economy is from the Ellen MacArthur Foundation (2013). With quotes: "to keep products, components, and materials at their highest utility and values at all time" and "preserving and enhancing natural capital".

19. There is the view that the COVID-19 global pandemic is a warning signal that the current design of the global economy, with too much emphasis on *unlimited* economic growth without accounting for *limited* natural resources, is not sustainable.

20. The Doughnut Economics is explained in Raworth (2017).

21. The digital transformation dimension is based on the digital business design concept of Ross et al. (2019). With the quote: "as the holistic organizational configuration," p. 5.

22. Recycling in itself is not enough. The right recycling is essential, i.e., to design and recycle products in such a way that the recycled components do not harm people and the environment. In: Den Held D (2019, June 13).

23. The circular economy concept and the relationship with the Internet of Things (IoT) technology is based on thesis work of Oliana (2017, August 15).

    In her thesis she explained the working of the circular economy and its business models in detail and analyzed data that can be used with IoT technology to enable the circular business model. She investigated the useful data types for circular activities at IKEA and validated the preliminary results with six companies.

24. The concept of "smart business networks" is based on Van Heck and Vervest (2007).

25. The human population size and density on earth, in total more than 7 billion people with many fast-growing cities worldwide, led to more interaction and virus transmission between bats and humans. Virus infections will lead to a natural restoration of the earth ecosystem's balance. See Volkskrant (2020, June 19).

    And Jabr F (2020, June 17).

26. For a detailed analysis of the agility concept, see Van Oosterhout (2014).

27. For the antifragility concept, see Taleb (2012).

    Research on antifragile software and its development process in Brosch N (2014, August 28).

Nils Brosch explains the Antifragility concept to a wide audience, for example, on LinkedIn, and suggests the following principles: skin in the game, redundancy, optionality, flexibility, falsification, no neomania, and tinkering.

28. The different circular flower business examples are in Top Sector Horticulture and Starting Materials (2020).

Other circular examples in horticulture are the recycling of eco-flower bags for Fresco Flower by Kras Recycling or the reuse of orchids by Orchid grower Koeleman. In the reuse of the orchids business model the customer purchases a circular orchid. After the orchid has bloomed the customer returns the orchid to the retailer. The customer can purchase a new circular orchid with a discount. The original orchid will be sent back to the grower and in a very short time a new orchid is grown out of this original orchid and sent back to the retailer. Kras Recycling (2020).

29. The concept of "triple helix" in Etzkowitz and Leydesdorff (2000). With the quote: "that systems can be expected to remain in transition".

30. The complex process of innovation diffusion is inspired by and based on Leeuwis C (2019, Januari 24).

31. The diffusion of hybrid seed corn is in Ryan and Gross (1943). With the quote: "between 1933 and 1939 acreage in hybrid corn increased".

32. The recent technology adoption and diffusion is based on Gartner's hype cycle concept in Gartner (2019).

33. The example of the connected "system of systems" farmer is in Porter ME, Heppelmann JE (2014, November).

34. Research on producer-side value creations with digitized products in Novales et al. (2019).

35. Carbon tax is a logical next step and some countries have implemented carbon pricing. In Plumer B, Popovich N (2019, April 2).

36. The epilogue, as the end of the book, is inspired by the "Author's Final Note to the Reader" in Hemingway (1926).

37. The word "information" is intriguing and very often used in all kinds of situations, with a range of meanings and objectives. The word is derived from the Latin *informare*, which means to shape, train, instruct, or educate. The concept of information and its subjectivity was inspired by the interview of professor Gert Nielen in YouTube (2010, February 15).

Gert Nielen (1926–2011) received a MSc and PhD degree from Wageningen University. He was a Professor of Information Systems at Tilburg University and established, in 1984, the first bachelor's and master's program of information management in the Netherlands.

The concept of information asymmetry as business model—called the value shop—is in Stabell and Fjeldstad (1998).

References

Bloemhof-Ruwaard J (2019) Closing the loop: a never ending story. https://research.wur.nl/en/publications/closing-the-loop-a-never-ending-story. Accessed 9 Sep 2020.

Boisot M (1987) Information & organizations: the manager as anthropologist. Fontana, London

Boisot M (1995) Information space: a framework for learning in organizations institutions and cultures. Routledge, Oxfordshire

Boisot M (1998) Knowledge assets: securing competitive advantage in the information economy. Oxford University Press, Oxford

Boisot M, MacMillan IC, Han KS (2007) Explorations in information space: knowledge, agents and organization. Oxford University Press, Oxford

Brosch N (2014) Antifragile Software–How an antifragility focused software development process influences Software Quality. MSc. Thesis Business Information Management, Rotterdam School of Management, Erasmus University https://thesis.eur.nl/pub/20513. Accessed 9 Sep 2020.

De Man AP, Van Raaij EM (2008) Making horticulture networks bloom. In: de Man AP (ed) Knowledge management and innovation in networks. Edward Elgar, Cheltenham, pp 122–144

Den Held D (2019) Recycling Won't be enough to save the planet–what we need now is the right recycling. Forbes. https://www.forbes.com/sites/rsmdiscovery/2019/06/13/recycling-wont-be-enough-to-save-the-planet-what-we-need-now-is-the-right-recycling/#d12e4b54ad5b. Accessed 21 Sep 2020.

Ellen MacArthur Foundation (2013) Towards the circular economy: opportunities for the consumer goods. Vol 2:74–76

Etzkowitz H, Leydesdorff L (2000) The dynamics of innovation: from national systems and "mode 2" to a triple helix of university–industry–government relations. Research Policy 29:109–123

Gartner (2019) Hype cycle for emerging technologies. With five trends: sensing and mobility, augmented humans, postclassical computer and communications, digital ecosystems, Advanced AI and Analytics. https://www.gartner.com/smarterwithgartner/5-trends-appear-on-the-gartner-hype-cycle-for-emerging-technologies-2019/. Accessed 9 Sep 2020.

Goldgar A (2007) Tulipmania: money, honor, and knowledge in the Dutch Golden age. The University of Chicago Press, Chicago

Greenports Nederland (2020) Greenports https://www.greenports-nederland.nl/. Accessed 11 Sep 2020.

Hemingway E (1926) The torrents of spring. Arrow Books, London

Ihrig M, Boisot M, MacMillan I (2011) Are you wasting money on useless knowledge management. Harvard Business Review.

Ihrig M, MacMillan I (2017, March–April) How to get ecosystem buy-In. Harvard Business Review.

Jabr F (2020) How humanity unleashed a flood of new diseases, *New York Times,* June. https://www.nytimes.com/2020/06/17/magazine/animal-disease-covid. html. Accessed 9 Sep 2020.

Kras Recycling (2020) Outstanding solutions for waste management. https://www. kras-recycling.com/en/. Accessed 9 Sept 2020.

Leeuwis C (2019) Over opschalen en afschalen in een wereld zonder stuur. Lessen over innovatie uit de landbouwontwikkeling en malariabestrijding. Presentatie voor 'Innovatie in de Stad'. Rotterdam. (in Dutch).

Lu Y, Gupta A, Ketter W, Van Heck E (2019) Information transparency in B2B auction markets: The role of winner identity disclosure. Management Science 65(9):4261–4279. https://doi.org/10.1287/mnsc.2018.3143. Accessed 15 Sept 2020

McFarlan FW (2015) Exploring the Information Frontier–IT Impact and Management: 1960–2020. Paper presented at the International Conference on Information Systems (ICIS), Fort Worth, Texas, 14 December 2015.

Mgmt. Scope (2020) Dossier De Coöperatie, nr. 01, pp. 76–77.

Middelkoop NE (2019) Schutters, gildebroeders, regenten en regentessen: Het Amsterdamse corporatiestuk 1525–1850 (Civic Guardsmen, Governors, and Guild Members: Amsterdam Institutional Group Portraits, 1525–1850), Dissertation, University of Amsterdam.

Novales A, Mocker M, Van Heck E (2019) Producer-side use cases of digitized products: what's best for your company? Paper presented at the 40th International Conference on Information Systems, Munich, 15–18 December 2019.

Oliana R (2017, August 15) The internet of things for circular activities. management of innovation MSc. Thesis, Rotterdam School of Management, Erasmus University https://thesis.eur.nl/pub/39832. Accessed 9 Sep 2020.

Plumer B, Popovich N (2019) These countries have prices on carbon. are they working? *New York Times.* https://www.nytimes.com/interactive/2019/04/02/climate/ pricing-carbon-emissions.html. Accessed 9 Sep 2020.

Porter ME, Heppelmann JE (2014) How smart, connected products are transforming competition. Harvard Business Review: 74–75.

Raworth K (2017) Doughnut economics. Seven ways to think like a 21st-Century economist. Random House Business Books, London

Ross JW, Beath CM, Mocker M (2019) Designed for digital: how to architect your business for sustained success. The MIT Press, Cambridge

Ryan B, Gross N (1943) The diffusion of hybrid seed corn in two Iowa communities. Rural Sociology 8:15–24

Stabell C, Fjeldstad Ø (1998) Configuring value for competitive advantage: on chains, shops, and networks. Strategic Management Journal 19:413–437

Taleb NN (2012) Antifragile: things that gain from disorder. Random House, New York

Top Sector Horticulture & Starting Materials (2020) Top sector horticulture & starting materials and the SDGs: practical examples https://topsectortu.nl/sites/topsectortu.nl/files/files/DEF%20Brochure%20Topsector%20ENG_Topsector%20Horticulture%20and%20Starting%20Materials%20and%20SDG's%3B%20practical%20examples(3).pdf. Accessed 23 Sep 2020.

Van Dijk G, Sergaki P, Baourakis G (2019) The cooperative enterprise. Practical evidence for a theory of cooperative entrepreneurship. Book Series on Cooperative Management, Springer, Heidelberg

Van Heck E, Vervest P (2007) Smart business networks: How the network wins. Communications of the ACM 50(6):28–37

Van Hemert N, Gilissen J, Lie Y, Van den Brink H (2019) Nieuwe tijden, nieuwe concepten: de business-driven campus. Strategy on Demand.

Van Oosterhout M (2014) Business agility and information technology in service organizations. Scholars' Press, Riga

Van Zeil W (2020) Oog voor detail. *Volkskrant Magazine*, p. 64. https://www.volkskrant.nl/cultuur-media/nergens-is-de-symbolische-rol-van-de-tafel-zo-mooi-als-op-deze-van-der-helst-b4b3dca1/. Accessed 7 Sep 2020.

Volkskrant (2020) Viroloog Marion Koopmans: 'Leuk was het niet om op deze manier gelijk te krijgen', *Volkskrant.* https://www.volkskrant.nl/mensen/viroloog-marion-koopmans-leuk-was-het-niet-om-op-deze-manier-gelijk-te-krijgen-bf6e41bd/. Accessed 3 Sep 2020.

World Horti Center (2020) Experience the world horti center Online. https://www.worldhorticenter.nl/en/home. Accessed 9 Sept 2020.

YouTube (2010) TIMAF Interview Professor Nielen. https://www.youtube.com/watch?v=PSNe1LBDQcs. Accessed 9 Sept 2020.

YouTube (2015) The bike instructor's guide to cycling in Amsterdam. https://www.youtube.com/watch?v=sEON08d76oE. Accessed 9 Sep 2020.

Index

Printed in Great Britain
by Amazon

36978259R00142